Internet Security

A Jumpstart for Systems Administrators and IT Managers

D1560909

Tim Speed

Juanita Ellis

Digital Press
An imprint of Elsevier Science
Amsterdam• Boston • London • New York • Oxford • Paris • San Diego
San Francisco • Singapore • Sydney • Tokyo

Library of Congress Cataloging-in-Publication Data

ISBN 1-55558-298-2

British Library Cataloguing-in-Publication Data

A catalogue record for this book is available from the British Library.

The publisher offers special discounts on bulk orders of this book.
For information, please contact:

Manager of Special Sales
Elsevier Science
200 Wheeler Road
Burlington, MA 01803
Tel: 781-313-4700
Fax: 781-313-4882

For information on all Digital Press publications available, contact our World Wide Web home page at: http://www.digitalpress.com or http://www.bh.com/digitalpress

10 9 8 7 6 5 4 3 2 1

Printed in the United States of America

To Linda Speed—my split apart. –T.S.

To my dad, Charles Ellis. –J.E.

Contents

Foreword   ix

Acknowledgments   xi

Introduction   xiii

1   The Internet and Security   1

      1.1   The history of the Internet   2
      1.2   TCP/IP: the nails of the Internet   13

2   The Security Review Process   39

      2.1   Introduction   40
      2.2   Review the state of the business   41
      2.3   Analyze the technology being used   45
      2.4   Risk analysis   49
      2.5   Plans and policies   52
      2.6   Implementation   61

3   Cryptography   67

      3.1   The history   68
      3.2   Key types   71
      3.3   RSA: public and private key   74
      3.4   PKI and business solutions   75

4   Secure Networks   89

   4.1   TCP/IP and OSI   90
   4.2   Denial-of-service attacks   92
   4.3   Virtual private networks   95
   4.4   Secure sockets layer   98

5   Protecting Your Intranet from the Extranet and Internet   107

   5.1   So many choices!   108
   5.2   Firewall product functional summaries   119
   5.3   Firewall buyer's assessment form   124
   5.4   Firewall vendors: Picking the products that are right for you 132
   5.5   SSL network appliance overview   134
   5.6   Secure access—SSL based extranet appliances   138
   5.7   Understanding air gap-based filtering proxies and their
          benefits when used for deploying web applications   141

6   Authentication and Authorization   149

   6.1   The basics   150
   6.2   Authentication   151
   6.3   Authorization   158
   6.4   Smart cards   166

7   E-Commerce: Public Key Infrastructure   169

   7.1   PKI and you   170
   7.2   X.509   172
   7.3   Certificate authority   178
   7.4   Certification practice statement   183
   7.5   Certificate revocation list   187
   7.6   Key recovery   189
   7.7   Lightweight directory access protocol   190
   7.8   Public key cryptography standards   194
   7.9   Public key infrastructure (X.509) standards   195

8   Messaging Security   199

   8.1   Safe communication: Messaging   200
   8.2   Junk mail   207
   8.3   Keep it running   214

9   What Are We Doing Here?   231

9.1	Risk analysis	232
9.2	The threats	234
9.3	Technology security review	237
9.4	Control directory and environment risk table	241
9.5	Competitive asset	243

10 Disaster Recovery   253

10.1	Introduction	254
10.2	Incident handling requirements	256
10.3	Incident handling processes	257
10.4	Incident handling procedures	259
10.5	Incident handling team implementation	262
10.6	Disaster recovery and business continuity	263

Appendix 1	**Security Tools**	**273**
Appendix 2	**The CERT Report**	**283**
Glossary		**313**
References		**321**
Index		**391**

Foreword

Not too long ago it was thought that the only secure network was a network that was completely disconnected, or one that had no power. While that may still be true today, it does not help our local administrator deal with problems he or she never had to deal with in the past. Prior to the World Wide Web, most of our computer networks were islands unto themselves. Organizations may have exchanged e-mail, or hosted bulletin boards, but for the most part Company A's network was completely separate from Company B's network. The biggest problems an information technology professional may have had were someone, stealing floppy disks or hacking the company's telephony switch. With today's Internet, or network of networks, distributors or suppliers can look into their customers' inventory databases, employees can telecommute with broadband connections, students can submit or receive homework without ever leaving home, and thousands of other things are possible that we could not do prior to the advent of http and the World Wide Web. These advances are great for changing the way we all live, work, play and learn; however, it begs the questions: Are my distributors looking past the databases for which they have authority? Is there someone other than my employees accessing my network without my knowledge? Who else is trying to communicate with my child over the Internet?

For the above reasons and many others it becomes apparent that all organizations need to have a plan for securing their assets, both physical and electronic. The corporate, or organizational, security policy is an administrator's strength in applying rules and policies about how the network is to be used. The technology that companies, schools, or other private and public institutions deploy is, by itself, not enough to prevent their networks from being compromised. Once the policy is in place and a plan is set out to secure the network, it becomes apparent that security will never again be point product or niche solution. Instead, network security must become a process, one that is reviewed and updated with each change of the physical, or logical, network that it applies to.

As one starts his or her journey down the path of security, it becomes apparent that network security can no longer be thought of as an after-thought, or a "bolt-on" solution. Security must become a fabric of the network that strikes the balance between security and usability. Policies, architectures, and processes need to be noninvasive to legitimate users, but impenetrable to would-be attackers.

Craig Tiffany
Network Security Consultant
Cisco Systems, Inc.

Craig Tiffany is a security specialist working in the field for Cisco Systems, Inc. for more than four years. Craig earned his CCIE certification for routing and switching in March of 1998. Since then, he has worked with several Fortune 100 companies, and has consulted with hundreds of small to medium businesses, cities, counties, schools, universities, as well as other large enterprises. Prior to working for Cisco Systems, Inc., Craig was a technical marketing engineer for Intel Corporation in the Intel Architecture Labs. Craig also spent several years as a network engineer and technical operations lead at one of Intel Corporation's fabricating sites.

Acknowledgments

Knowledge is based on many different facets—what you know, knowing where information can be found, and who you know. The information in this book is a combination of all these facets. The data sources referenced in this book include references to people, URLs, and other books. But much of the knowledge that is in this book comes from very smart people. The people listed in this "acknowledgment" section did not necessarily participate in the writing of this book, but have influenced and guided me in my life that has culminated in this work. First and foremost I need to thank my wife for helping me with the book and providing some of the editing throughout the various chapters. Next I want to thank Johnny Speed, a great son that not only provided his support but also edited various chapters in this book. I thank my daughter Katherine for tolerating me during the months that I worked on this book. Next I want to thank my mother, Lillian Speed, for teaching me to "think big." Thanks to Ed Speed for the inspiration to keep publishing.

The authors thank CERT, via Sarah Strauss, for allowing us to republish the Cert Reporting Guidelines.

I am very grateful to Juanita Ellis for asking me to participate in writing this book. Special thanks to Julio G. Esperas—Production Editor and to Merrill Peterson and Aaron Downey. Thanks to Theron Shreve for publishing this book. Special thanks to Lotus/IBM (and ISSL), Mark Steinborn, and Jack Shoemaker for allowing me to coauthor this book. Thanks to John Kistler for reading this book before publishing. Many thanks to Katherine Spanbauer, for keeping me in the company security loop.

Thanks to the following content authors:

- Sarah Z. Stanwyck (with Meade Eggleston)—Redline Networks

- Ken Spinner—Neoteris Inc.

- Joseph Steinberg—Whale Communications

A brilliant artist—David DeGrand, provided the cartoons found at the beginning of each chapter.

Now to talk about the really smart people—due to legal issues, the people listed below could not directly contribute to this book, but I have learned a lot from these people via work and their friendship:

Kelly Brooks, Don Nadel, Gregg Smith, Steve Robinson, Brian Baker, Chip Emmet, Chris and Rodger Williams, Robert Nellis, Tony Ollivier, Thomas Hellegers, Will Witten, Rufus and Lisa Woody, Ted Niblett, Sean Murphy, Carol Worthy, Bud Calkins, Jason Erickson, Loren Pusey, Barry Heinz, Bill Kilduff, Kevin Mills, Matthew Henry, Boris Vishnevsky, Brad Schauf, Paul Culpepper, Scott Souder, Baan Al-Shibib, Andrea Waugh-Metzger, Rick Sizemore, Greg Prickril, Chuck Smith, (The brilliant) David Byrd, Glenn Druce, Catherine Yang, Katherine Rutledge, Shawn Scott, Stan Logan, Paul Raymond, Charles Carrington, Aaloak Jaswal, David Little, Ron DiBiase, Ann Marie Darrough, Larry Berthelsen, Ted Smith, Craig Levine, Daniel Suster, Chris Cotton, Mike Faccioli, Mark Harper, Jeff Pinkston, George Poirier, Jordi Riera, David Via, Heidi Wulkow, Dave Erickson, David Bell, Mark Leaser, Gary Wood, David Attardo, Charles J. Lin, John Kistler, C. David Johnson, Jon P. Dodge, Luc Groleau, Mario Figueroa, Mary Joseph, Dee Fleming, Michael Dennehy, Andrew Nolet, Cindy Hopkins, Michael Lamparty, Mike Stover, Mary Laroche, Beth Anne Collopy, Zena Washington, Burk Buechler, Robert Thietje, Elie Winsbacher, Francisco Arroyo, Francois Nasser, Jason Andersen, John Wargo, Kenn Reed, Kim Artlip, Lakshman Srinivasa, Valerie, Kunert, Marlene Botter, Roy Hudson, Mike Dudding, Stephen Cooke, Ciaran DellaFera, Tom Agoston, Vahik Gharibian, Mike Kapfer, Jay Cousineau, Terence Gilbey, Chris Kergaravat, Wanda and Jesse Rodgers, Mike Confoy, Mike Kasher, Carl Baumann, Vadim Gringolts, William Crowell, Dr. Seshagiri Rao, and we cannot forget the very cool—Barbara Robertson.

Finally, sorry if I missed you on this book, I will get you in the next. Sorry, Titus, you don't get an acknowledgment in this book.

Tim Speed

Introduction

On the morning of January 26, 1876, seven men from New York City pulled off what would be, up to that time, the biggest bank robbery in United States history. The gang, who code-named themselves "Rufus," made off with more than $1.6 million in cash and bonds. The robbery was very well planned and several simple techniques were used to rob the bank. Initially, they monitored the bank and its surrounding area for activity and weaknesses. Next, they gathered inside information and secured the help of a safe salesman. Finally, they tunneled into the bank from the building next door. Because they knew everything about the bank, its layout, and its operation, "Rufus" was able to walk away with the $1.6 million. Unfortunately, neither the bank nor the sheriff and his men knew the first thing about "Rufus" until it was too late. Had either of them known what their assailants were up to and how they planned to do it, the $1.6 million might have stayed right where it was.

In September of the same year, a bit west of New York, several men rode their horses into the town of Northfield, Minnesota. Among these men were Frank James and his infamous brother Jesse. Jesse James and his boys had surely come to rob the Northfield bank. However, many of the towns-people, some of them former Civil War soldiers, recognized the look of a "bank robbery" the moment these strangers rode into town. With guns ablaze, the citizens of Northfield took to the street with the intent of one thing: Protect the money in their bank! Jesse James and the Jameses' gang fled Northfield under heavy gunfire without a red cent, leaving two of their own for dead. The notorious James brothers and their robbery scheme had been thwarted.

Things haven't changed much since the days of the Wild West. There are still the good guys and there are still the bad guys; there are still banks and there are still gangs that want to steal from them. But today the men in the black hats can rob the banks without leaving the comfort of their own living rooms. Instead of walking into a bank or any business, the outlaw will just hook on the public Internet, launch a few programs, and then take what they want. The question that needs to be addressed is the outcome: Will the Internet outlaws of today be successful, like the robbery in New York? Or will they fail, due to good planning and watchful monitoring?

Modern-day bank robbers don't rob banks. They rob corporations and companies, and they do so without ever walking into a building or stepping through a door. The Internet enables you to do anything while sitting on your couch, even rob a bank. The modern-day bandits in the black hats sitting on their couches are known as hackers, crackers, phreaks, smurfs, etc.

Today we are going to rob a bank, or in other words, hack into a Lan-based computer site. We ride our horses into town, go into the saloon and we get a drink (I like Dr Pepper). Now we hatch our plan. Do we attack like a hacker (not a lumberjack), or a cracker (not a saltine), or a phreak (not the weird guy at the end of your street), or even smurf (not the little cute blue ones) our way in? Here are a few definitions to help you out:

Hacker: Hackers like to look for internal and external system holes, bugs, and poor system configurations in someone else's system. They may know several programming languages and work extensively with UNIX and NT and they usually have a firm understanding of TCP/IP protocols. In some hacker circles, it is considered unethical to change data aside from the logs that are needed to clean their tracks. Like in our bank robbing scenario, the hacker would try to find an easy way into the bank.

Cracker: These guys break into systems by guessing or "cracking" user and system passwords. The media has a tendency to mistake a hacker for a cracker. A cracker is often not as well educated in the art of breaking into a system as the hacker. If asked about the difference between the two, a hacker might say, "Hackers build things, crackers break them." The cracker would try to open the safe into the bank by guessing the combination.

Phreak: Literally, a phreak is a "phone hacker." However, a phreak can be anyone who messes around with phones or phone lines. The closest comparison to this in the Old West is using the telegraph lines to stop and/or modify a message.

Smurf: The "smurf" attack, named after its exploit program, is one of the most recent in the category of network-level attacks against hosts. A perpetrator sends a large amount of ICMP echo (ping) traffic at IP broadcast addresses, all of it having a spoofed source address of a victim. If the routing device delivering traffic to those broadcast addresses performs the IP broadcast to layer 2 broadcast function noted below, most hosts on that IP network will take the ICMP echo request and reply to it with an echo reply each, multiplying the traffic by the number of hosts responding. On a multiaccess broadcast network, there could potentially be hundreds of machines to reply to each packet. The "smurf" attack's cousin is called "fraggle," which uses UDP echo packets in the same fashion as the ICMP echo packets; it was a simple rewrite of "smurf." There is really no comparison between a smurf attack and an Old West bank robbery.

Now that we are familiar with these definitions, we can simplify all four of them into one broad definition that serves the purpose of this book quite well: "Some dork who keeps screwing up my web site and making it difficult for me to do business." Why do they do it? Lots of reasons: Some are disgruntled ex-employees looking for vengeance; some may be on a crusade against a company with whom they have a moral disagreement; others just like to "push the red button" and see what happens. These events or incidents can cost your system critical time and potential losses of revenue.

Time for the big question: What can these guys do? Most hackers exploit holes in the security of computer operating systems. Most operating system vendors will publish where these weaknesses are and how to fix them. The fixes are typically referred to by terms such as *patches, hot-fixes,* and *maintenance releases.* Just because these fixes exist doesn't mean problems can't surface if administrators are too lazy or busy to keep up with security updates. These holes are what allow hackers to get into systems and access protected data, change content on web pages, and even bring the systems altogether. There have been instances when a hacker has exploited poor programming on a web site and has managed to order an item that costs $100 for $1.

This is what they are capable of and why we recommend the *Computer Crime and Security Survey,* a document released every year by CSI/FBI.[1] It contains the results of many surveys that can really open your eyes to the amount of damage a hacker can do. These are the statistics covered:

---

1.   This document is available at http://www.gocsi.com

1.   Unauthorized use of computer systems in the last twelve months

2.   Number of incidents from the inside

3.   Number of incidents from the outside

4.   Location of attacks—internal systems, remote dial-in, Internet, and so forth

5.   Type of attacks—denial-of-service, sabotage, virus, and so forth

6.   Financial loss

7.   Financial loss by type

8.   Much more

Take the time to browse through this and order it for yourself. You'll find it extremely useful when you start your risk analysis.

Now, let's have a look into the methods these hackers, crackers, phreaks, and smurfs can use:

Denial-of-Service (DoS) Attacks: This is an indirect attack to the site. The hackers are not trying to get into the site itself, however, they *are* trying to keep everyone else from getting *in*. One of the most famous attacks of this type was the "IP Ping of Death" documented as early as January 1998. The "Ping of Death" relied on flaws in the implementation of TCP/IP. Although this method of attack does not threaten the security of systems that are being attacked, it can be used as a lead into more direct attacks on the accounts or data stored on a system. Some older firewall software, for example, can be tricked into letting in unauthorized traffic by overloading legitimate TCP/IP ports.

Distributed Denial-of-Service (DDoS) Attacks: This is an attack directed by several hackers from several locations, thus making it harder to detect and stop. A DDoS is like someone in the Old West today broadcasting, "The bank has free money!" when, in reality, the bank does not. This type of saturation attack would cause so many people to show up at the bank that no one would be able to even enter the doors, including real customers. Hackers can inundate the largest ISPs and consume all of their bandwidth by simply using several smaller network connections.

Trinoo: Trinoo first appeared about the year 2000 in the form of a Trojan Horse program (one with malicious or harmful code in a harmless looking program). All you need to do to activate it is execute the program, usually without even knowing you've done it. It copies an executable to the window\System directory and then will install itself, once executed, in such a way that it will be active all the time. If the Trinoo Trojan Horse program is activated while the user is connected to the Internet, anyone who has the Trinoo Trojan Horse client program can sneak into the user's computer and poke around without the user ever knowing of the invader's existence. As you can guess, this can be a serious problem.

Footprinting: This process involves the hacker obtaining information about your computing environment. They can do this in a number of ways: Internet names and registration sources, business sources and private information. Once the hacker obtains this information, you can be attacked. This information typically includes IP addresses, domain names, SMPT server names and more. Footprinting is essentially what "Rufus" did before they carried out their robbery. They were "casing the joint."

Network Scanning Tools: There are many tools you can use to "scan" a system or web page. They can be downloaded by most anyone and used with little more modification. They will scan, or search, a network or web page for holes and other vulnerabilities, essentially looking for ways into your system. Many Internet scanners specifically seek out and locate files and printer shares whether they are protected by passwords or not. Hackers leave these scanning programs running day and night, collecting IP addresses, then mapping the shares onto their local drive letters to gain total access to others' computer files. The hackers can also use tools that allow "stealth" scanning. Nmap is one such tool. Nmap can precisely learn everything about the files in an attacked system, as opposed to what other scanning programs do, which is essentially groping around in the dark. Other well-known network scanning tools include Port Scanner, Sam Spade, Internet Maniac, and SATAN (Security Administrator's Tool for Analyzing Networks).

Operating System (OS) Attacks: These attacks exploit bugs in specific operating systems, such as Windows 98, Windows 2000, or MacOS. The tools are easy to find: Just check out a software vendor security page on the Web. In most cases, when these problems are identified, the software vendor promptly fixes them. As a first step, always make sure you have the very latest version of your operating system, including all bug fixes. Not everyone installs all of the required patches as the software vendors release them, so this is how these types of attacks can happen. OS attacks are known by various titles, namely Win Nuke or Windows OOB bug.

Remote Access: This is one of the oldest attacks and is also one of the easier ones to do, with the right tools. Many companies are not locking down "analog" lines to keep this attack from being so pervasive. There are two basic tools for conducting a remote access attack: a war dialer and a password hacking tool. The war dialer is a simple database and an automated modem script that dials every phone number in a group designated by the user. Mr. Hacker can then review the database and select a likely target for a hack attempt. The second tool, the password hacking tool, uses a dictionary attack to crack passwords. Requiring the use of passwords that cannot be found in a dictionary, or limiting the number of login attempts before the account is locked out, can thwart password hackers.

Virus Attacks: These are programs that have been put on a PC or workstation without authorization from the user. They are not always harmful but they can cause damage or cause computer systems to overload themselves and stop working. They are often transmitted via attachments on e-mail but can also be transmitted via CD, diskettes, and downloaded files from web sites. The source of the e-mail, downloaded file, or diskette is usually unaware there was a virus. Some viruses take effect as soon as their code is executed; others still lie dormant until certain conditions trigger their code to be executed by the host computer. Recent virus attacks include the media-hyped Love Bug, the Resume Virus, and the NewLove Virus.

Insider Attacks: Contrary to popular belief, hackers and crackers are only half the problem. Assailants from within the corporation or organization attacked can be just as dangerous, if not more so. It can be anything from a case of "Oops" or "What does this button do?" to an administrator exacting vengeance for being fired.

Banks don't get robbed as often as they used to because they made it unprofitable for criminals to rob them; the chances of getting caught are much higher these days than back in 1876. Unfortunately, companies and web sites represent all-too-easy targets when left unprotected, as many are. The purpose of this book is to help you make it unprofitable for hackers, crackers, smurfs, phreaks, insiders, outsiders, jerks, and all other associated idiots to steal or hinder your operations. You know who they are, and how they plan on getting in now. The rest of this book will teach you how to stop them through the creation of an effective and efficient security system.

You will learn to (1) identify what you need to protect; (2) target what you need protection from; (3) analyze the likelihood of threats and risk mitigation; and (4) review the processes for continuous improvements. Now, let's get started.

The Internet and Security

Hacker, on the run—with your data!

1.1   The history of the Internet

1.1.1   The Internet

Back in 1866, the Wild West was "the future utopia" to Americans who were already in what was originally supposed to be "the land of opportunity." Civil War, reconstruction, and corruption in the White House were the current headlines of the day. Thus, eyes turned to the West for opportunity and new beginnings. The Wild West was supposed to be a place where everyone could go for cheap land, free gold, and a good beach (and eventually surfing, if they made it to the coast). The Wild West was often not this ideal, as demonstrated by the word "Wild." Many used it and abused it for the purpose of pillaging, robbing, lawlessness, and bordellos. It is not so different with today's Internet. The Internet is supposed to be a network that links thousands, millions, or even billions of computers together in order to send and receive data in perfect tranquility. First, the Internet is not a single network and, as you may have guessed, it is not always safe. The Internet is changing by the day, by the hour, by the minute, and has changed the face of technology and business both in just under three decades. The Internet is more than 27 years old. The WWW (World Wide Web, e.g., www.lookat-mywebpage.com[1]) is actually less than 10 years old. Before the WWW, there was WORM, the first of which burrowed through the Internet in 1988. As you can see, the Internet has been around for quite some time. Web sites developed more recently. The Internet is not a single agency, a network, or a company. It is a collection of networks and authorities. Following are a few dates (and decades) to tell you how it became as it is today.

In 1858, a telegram of 98 words from Queen Victoria to President James Buchanan of the United States opened a new era in global communication. The queen's message of congratulation took $16^{1}/_{2}$ hours to transmit through the new transatlantic telegraph cable. The president then sent a reply of 143 words back to the queen. Normally, without the cable, a dispatch in one direction would have taken perhaps 12 days by the speediest combination of inland telegraph and fast steamer.

Just a bit more than 100 years later, we see the creation of a new medium of communication, based on the same basic technology of the

---

1.   As of this publishing, this URL was not registered. The authors use many different fake URLs. By the time this book is released, or even during this lifetime of this book, some of these URLs may be registered and used. These sample URLs still stand, as samples only. The person who registers these URLs owns such URLs. We refer to these URLs as any public URL in the Internet.

telegraph, electrons, and wires[2]. Starting in the early 1960s, we see the creation of ARPANET, the beginning of the Vietnam War, and the rise of bell-bottoms and ring pops. A lot happened in the 1960s that has helped develop the Internet into the Ebays, Amazons, AOLs, and hotornots that we know, love, and sometimes hate.

July, 1961:   At MIT, Leonard Kleinrock (i.e., ubernerd) published the first paper on the packet switching theory. Kleinrock convinced his peers that communication using packets, rather than circuits, was not only feasible but also practical. Experiments followed, but only circuit type connections were tested. Thus, the results of these experiments demonstrated the need for packet communications.

August, 1962:   Memos written by J. C. R. Licklider of MIT discussed the possibility and use of networked computers. The concept was titled, "The Galactic Network," by Licklider. Yes, he came up with this term before *Star Trek* was on the air. Licklider envisioned a globally interconnected set of computers through which everyone could access data and programs, no matter where they were physically. He became the first head of the computer research program at DARPA.

Mid-1960s: People began writing all types of papers on the subject of networks. One of the first papers on the ARPANET[3] was published by Lawrence G. Roberts[4]. Also at this time were papers on packet switching. One such paper was written by a good gentleman known as Donald Davies. Donald is the English inventor of packet switching. He theorized at the British National Physical Laboratory (NPL) about building a network of computers to test his packet switching concepts. At about the same time, 1964 (besides the Beatles and James Bond), Paul Baran and others at the RAND group had written a paper on packet switching networks for secure voice in the military. With all of these papers being floated around, it happened that the work at MIT[5] (1961–1967), the work at the RAND corporation (1962–1965) and the work at the NPL (1964–1967) had occurred all at the same time and without any of the researchers knowing about

---

2.   OK, you got us … there is wireless Internet communication also.
3.   ARPANET was the network that became the basis for the Internet. It was funded by the U.S. military and consisted of many different, individual computers connected by leased lines or network.
4.   http://www.landfield.com/rfcs/rfc2235.html
5.   Massachusetts Institute of Technology, "a coeducational, privately endowed research university—is dedicated to advancing knowledge and educating students in science, technology, and other areas of scholarship that will best serve the nation and the world in the 21st century." (http://web.mit.edu/aboutmit.html)

the others' work. The word *packet* was adopted from the work at the NPL. A packet is a unit of data that is routed between a network source and a network destination on any network.

August, 1968:   An RFQ (Request for Quote) was released by DARPA[6] for the development of the key components for the ARPANET. The RFQ included the definition and creation of a device known as the IMP[7]. The IMP's job was to manage the packets and provide an interface to the computer at each site. A group headed by Frank Heart at Bolt Beranek and Newman (BBN) won the job in 1968. The team at BBN worked on the IMP with Bob Kahn, thus playing a major role in the overall ARPANET architectural design. The Network Measurement Center at UCLA was selected to be the first device (or node) on the ARPANET.

1969:   ARPANET was brought to fruition when BBN installed the first IMP[8] at UCLA and the first computer was connected. Another computer at Stanford Research Institute (SRI) provided a second node. One month later, the first host-to-host message was sent across the network. Two more nodes were added at UC Santa Barbara and University of Utah. Finally, by the end of 1969, four host computers were connected together into the initial ARPANET and the future Internet was born. Also, in 1969, a movie was released known as "Colossus: The Forbin Project." An American supercomputer, Colossus, and its Russian counterpart, Guardian, got together to rule the world. This movie was filmed at the Lawrence Hall of Science, Berkeley, California. This great movie, years ahead of its time, showed two computers that became "aware" or "alive" and then decided to connect themselves together—aka a "network." Some concepts you can find in that movie are:

- Computer virus
- Network
- Artificial intelligence
- Voice activation response

Many of the technologies that we have today were alluded to in that science fiction movie.

---

6.   Defense Advanced Research Projects Agency is an independent research branch of the U.S. Department of Defense and launched Sputnik, Russia's first manned satellite.
7.   Interface Message Processors
8.   http://info.internet.isi.edu:80/in-notes/rfc/files/rfc18.txt

Back to the history. At this point, we now have four computers on the ARPANET. A team of engineers/researchers/nerds get together to work on the software that will enable the computers to communicate. At UCLA, Vint Cerf, Steve Crocker, and Jon Postel work with Leonard Kleinrock[9] to create the software. On April 7, Crocker sends around a memo entitled "Request for Comments (RFC)." This is the first of many future RFCs that document the design of the ARPANET and the Internet. The team called itself the "Network Working Group (aka RFC 10)." The team took it upon itself to develop something called a "protocol." This first network protocol was a collection of programs that came to be known as NCP (Network Control Protocol). From 1970 to 1973, several events occurred in our history:

1.   Bob Metcalfe[10] built a network interface between the MIT IMP and a PDP-6 to the ARPANET. Metcalfe asks to build another network interface for Xerox PARC's PDP-10[11].

2.   The Network Working Group[12] completes the Telnet protocol and makes progress on the file transfer protocol (FTP) standard.

3.   Kahn and Cerf design a net-to-net connection protocol. Cerf now leads the International Network Working Group. In September 1973, the two give their first paper on the new Transmission Control Protocol (TCP) at a meeting at the University of Sussex in England.

4.   Ray Tomlinson,[13] a programmer at Bolt Beranek and Newman, invented e-mail in late 1971. Tomlinson created e-mail to send messages over a network to fellow programmers.

The 1970s: Low riders and the Rolling Stones. Ugly pants and Robert Redford.

1973:   We were at a critical juncture. NCP was the dominant protocol but it did not have the ability to address networks (or computers) further down the network than a destination IMP on the ARPANET. NCP needed to be updated or replaced. Here was the problem: If a packet was lost, then the application using the network may crash. For the most part, NCP had

---

9.   Leonard Kleinrock created a doctoral dissertation at MIT on queuing theory in communication networks.
10.   Bob Metcalfe later creates Ethternet.
11.   PDP 10—from Digital Equipment—now, HP/Compaq.
12.   http://info.internet.isi.edu:80/in-notes/rfc/files/rfc85.txt
13.   http://info.internet.isi.edu:80/in-notes/rfc/files/rfc561.txt

no end-end host error control and since the ARPANET was to be the only network around, it would need to be so reliable that no error control would be required. As a result, Cerf (pronounced "serf") and Kahn developed a new protocol. This protocol would eventually be called the Transmission Control Protocol/Internet Protocol (TCP/IP). The TCP/IP protocol was the glue that the future Internet needed. This single protocol was able to solve many different issues and problems:

1.   TCP/IP was able to stand on its own within each distinct network. As a result, no internal changes were required to "connect" the network together.

2.   Communications within the network would be on a best effort basis. If a packet didn't make it to the final destination, it would shortly be retransmitted from the source.

3.   Special boxes would be used to connect these disparate networks; these would later be called gateways and routers.

4.   There would be no global control at the operations level.

5.   Defined Gateway functions would forward packets as needed to the correct network.

6.   Checksums were used and packets could be "fragmented"[14] or sent out of order and, at the destination, be put back into the correct order.

It is amazing how scalable the original TCP/IP protocol was. Today we call the protocol IP(v4), or version 4 of the IP protocol. The original model that Cerf and Kahn put together was designed to accommodate the requirement of the ARPANET. The idea of thousands of networks was not really on their mind. The IP protocol uses a 32-bit base. If you take off of these bits and factor out the numbers available you have about 4 billion possible addresses (2^{32}) bits. The original idea was to use a 32-bit IP address and cut it into chunks. The network used the first 8 bits and the remainder (24) was to be used by the hosts (or computers). Take a look at 2^8 bits, you have 256 possible combinations that you could use for networks. In the 1970s, that was plenty, but today we are out of network numbers (We will discuss TCP/IP addressing in a later chapter, and a bit on IP(v6). We will not discuss UDP, ever. Well all correct, maybe a bit later on). In the 1970s, the addressing scheme was genius. I don't know if Cerf and Kahn were lucky or brilliant,

---

14.   http://info.internet.isi.edu:80/in-notes/rfc/files/rfc815.txt

but in any case, we benefited from their design. Thanks, Mr. Cerf and Mr. Kahn!

The early implementations of TCP were done for large time-sharing[15] systems such as Tenex and TOPS 20. Good old TOPS 20 was software that ran on a system known as the KL-10 from Digital Equipment. The KL-10 was a 36-bit "mainframe" from DEC. When desktop computers first appeared, it was thought by some that TCP was too big to run on a personal computer. This dude named David Clark (as far as I know he was not part of the Dave Clark 5) and a research group from MIT set out to show that a compact and simple implementation of TCP was possible. The first implementation was for the Xerox Alto and the IBM PC.

From 1974 to 1980, several events occurred in the history of the Internet:

- By 1974, daily traffic on the ARPANET exceeds 3 million packets and the Ethernet was demonstrated at Xerox PARC's center.

- In 1975, the ARPANET geographical map shows 61 nodes.

- In 1976, the packet satellite project went into use. SATNET, Atlantic packet Satellite network, was born. This network linked the United States with Europe.

- In 1977, Steve Wozniak and Steve Jobs announce the Apple II computer. Also introduced is the Tandy TRS-80. These off-the-shelf machines create the consumer and small business markets for computers.

- In 1978, Continuing work on TCP/IP, Vint Cerf at DARPA expands the vision of the Internet, forming an International Cooperation Board chaired by Peter Kirstein of University College London.

- In 1979, Newsgroups are created, aka USENET.

The 1980s: This decade saw a string of important developments in ARPANET's journey to becoming the all-seeing, all-knowing, all-selling, and all-buying Internet. The decade also had something to do with disco, but who cares about that. It died anyway.

1980: TCP/IP was adopted as a defense standard. This enabled the defense complex to begin sharing in the DARPA Internet technology base. By 1983, ARPANET was being used by a significant number of defense research and development and operational organizations. As of January 1, 1983, the ARPANET moved over to a single protocol, TCP/IP. All hosts

15.   http://www.landfield.com/rfcs/rfc2235.html

converted simultaneously. Over several years, the transition was carefully planned[16] within the community before it actually took place. The year 1983 saw another critical point for the Internet: DNS was invented. Here is the issue. Every computer had an address, for example, 192.9.200.123. We could keep track of these numbers if we had about 30 to 40 computers. But what if we had thousands of computers, how would we (humans) keep track of all those numbers? Numbering the Internet hosts and keeping tabs on the host names simply failed to scale with the growth of the Internet. In November 1983, Jon Postel and Paul Mockapetris of USC/ISI and Craig Partridge of BBN developed the Domain Name System (DNS). The DNS system provided an on-line mechanism to track the names of computers in relation to their IP address. Previously, each computer needed to maintain its own list. So if you added a computer to the network, you would need to edit each list on each computer. In the case of DNS, all you need to do is edit the list at one place.

1984:   The DNS system was introduced across the Internet with domain suffixes. You have seen these before: .gov, .mil, .edu, .org, .net, and .com. The Internet was starting to mature. By 1985, the Internet was already well established as a technology supporting a broad community of researchers and developers and was beginning to be used by other communities for daily computer communications. Electronic mail (via SMTP[17]) was being used broadly across several communities, often with different systems, but interconnection between different mail systems was demonstrating the utility of broad based electronic communications between people.

1985:   By the end of this year, the number of hosts on the Internet (TCP/IP interconnected networks) had reached about 2,000. Also, at this time there were several RFCs created that described a concept known as subneting. This process involved a mask number being placed along with an IP address. This, in effect, would divide an IP network into several networks[18]. Between the beginning of 1986 and the end of 1987, the number of networks grew from 2,000 to nearly 30,000. TCP/IP[19] was now available on workstations and PCs such as the Compaq portable computer. Ethernet[20] was starting to grow and become available across college campuses. In 1986, the U.S. National Science

16.   http://info.internet.isi.edu:80/in-notes/rfc/files/rfc801.txt

17.   http://info.internet.isi.edu:80/in-notes/rfc/files/rfc821.txt

18.   http://info.internet.isi.edu:80/in-notes/rfc/files/rfc932.txt and http://info.internet.isi.edu:80/in-notes/rfc/files/rfc936.txt and
        http://info.internet.isi.edu:80/in-notes/rfc/files/rfc940.txt

19.   http://info.internet.isi.edu:80/in-notes/rfc/files/rfc983.txt

20.   http://info.internet.isi.edu:80/in-notes/rfc/files/rfc826.txt and http://info.internet.isi.edu:80/in-notes/rfc/files/rfc894.txt

Foundation (NSF) initiated the development of the NSFNET, which provided a major backbone communication service for the Internet.

As we look into the 1980s, the question comes up about … not Boy George and Duran Duran, but something more comical: Al Gore and the Internet. There is no explanation better than the one from Cerf and Kahn:

> *As a Senator in the 1980s, Gore urged government agencies to consolidate what at the time were several dozen different and unconnected networks into an "Interagency Network." Working in a bi-partisan manner with officials in Ronald Reagan and George Bush's administrations, Gore secured the passage of the High Performance Computing and Communications Act in 1991. This "Gore Act" supported the National Research and Education Network (NREN) initiative that became one of the major vehicles for the spread of the Internet beyond the field of computer science. http://www.isoc.org/internet-history/gore.shtml*

A great deal of support for the Internet community has come from the U.S. federal government, since the Internet was originally part of a federally funded research program and, subsequently, has become a major part of the U.S. research infrastructure. Throughout its history, the Internet has provided a platform for collaboration and communication. The Internet Activities Board (IAB) was created in 1983 to guide the evolution of the TCP/IP Protocol Suite and to provide research advice to the Internet community. During its short existence, the IAB has reorganized many times and now has two primary components: the Internet Engineering Task Force (IETF) and the Internet Research Task Force. The IETF[21] has responsibility for further evolution of the TCP/IP protocol suite and its standardization.

As we continue down the road of history we find The Morris WORM. In 1988, this worm burrowed into the Internet and into 6,000 of the 60,000 hosts now on the network at this time. This is the first worm experience and DARPA forms the Computer Emergency Response Team (CERT[22]) to deal with future such incidents[23].

1989:   The number of hosts has increased to 160,000. Also, we see the advent of commercial e-mail relays. Network speeds are up to 45Mbps and 100Mbps is on the horizon based on FDDI. Now we hear the first rumblings of the "Web." In Switzerland, at CERN[24], Tim Berners-Lee addresses the issue of the constant change in the currency of information and the

---

21.   http://info.internet.isi.edu:80/in-notes/rfc/files/rfc1539.txt
22.   http://www.cert.org/
23.   http://www.apcatalog.com/cgi-bin/AP?ISBN=0122374711&LOCATION=US&FORM=FORM2
24.   http://cern.web.cern.ch/CERN/

turnover of people on projects. Mr. Berners-Lee[25] proposed something called "Hypertext" which is a system that will run across distributed systems on different operating systems.

The 1990s: The Internet, as we know it, is born. Millions of web sites appear and try to sell you everything you ever wanted, including the things you wouldn't have bought unless they had appeared right there on your monitor in your living room while you were drinking coffee and listening to the news. Oh, and Clinton gets elected. Twice.

1990 to 1992:   We see a number of changes and enhancements to the Internet:

- The number of networks exceeds 7,500 and the number of computers connected grows beyond million.

- Over 100 countries are now connected with over 600,000 computers.

- The Web is born. SLAC, the Stanford Linear Accelerator Center in California, becomes the first web server in the United States. It serves the contents of an existing, large database of abstracts of physics papers.

In 1993:   We saw some of these events:

- The U.S. White House comes on-line (http://www.whitehouse.gov/).

- RFC 1437: The Extension of MIME Content-Types to a new medium.

- RFC 1438: IETF Statements of Boredom (SOBs).

- Marc Andreesen and NCSA and the University of Illinois develop a graphical user interface to the WWW, called "Mosaic for X."

No major changes were made to the physical network in 1994, except for its significant growth. Other events from this year include:

- Pizza Hut offers pizza ordering on its web page.

- Shopping malls arrive on the Internet.

- Internet traffic passes 10 trillion bytes/month.

- RFC 1607: A View from the 21st Century (this is another great RFC … check it out at http://info.internet.isi.edu:80/in-notes/rfc/files/rfc1607.txt).

---

25.   http://www.w3.org/People/Berners-Lee/ShortHistory.html

- First Virtual, the first cyberpunk, opens.

- The URI is defined—http://info.internet.isi.edu:80/in-notes/rfc/files/rfc1630.txt.

- The URL is defined—http://info.internet.isi.edu:80/in-notes/rfc/files/rfc1738.txt.

On October 24, 1995, the Federal Networking Council (FNC) unanimously passed a resolution defining the term "Internet." A resolution was drafted that stated the following:

The term "Internet" refers to the global information system that:

(i)   is logically linked together by a globally unique address space based on the Internet Protocol (IP) or its subsequent extensions/follow-ons;

(ii)   is able to support communications using the Transmission Control Protocol/Internet Protocol (TCP/IP) suite or its subsequent extensions/follow-ons, and/or other IP-compatible protocols; and

(iii)   provides, uses or makes accessible, either publicly or privately, high level services layered on the communications and related infrastructure described herein.

1995:   We also saw these events:

- The National Science Foundation announced that as of April 30, 1995 it would no longer allow direct access to the NSF backbone. The National Science Foundation contracted with four companies that would be providers of access to the NSF backbone (Merit). These companies would then sell connections to groups, organizations, and companies.

- A $50 annual fee is imposed on domains excluding .edu and .gov domains, which are still funded by the National Science Foundation.

- WWW surpasses ftp-data in March as the service with greatest traffic.

- RFC 1825, Security Architecture for the Internet Protocol, http://info.internet.isi.edu:80/in-notes/rfc/files/rfc1825.txt

- RFC 1882—you need to see this one. http://info.internet.isi.edu:80/in-notes/rfc/files/rfc1882.txt

The Internet has changed much since it came into existence. This ubiquitous network was designed before LANs were even thought of and yet, today it can accommodate a massive amount of traffic. From 1996 to 2001, the Internet continued to grow. New applications and features were developed and implemented. The hot topic became security. In fact, from 1996 to today we have seen these events:

- U.S. Communications Decency Act (CDA) becomes law in order to prohibit distribution of indecent materials.

- Various ISPs suffer extended service outages, bringing into question whether they will be able to handle the growing number of users.

- A malicious program is released on USENET, wiping out more than 25,000 messages.

- Human error at Network Solutions causes the DNS table for .com and .net domains to become corrupted.

- Viruses such as Melissa, ExploreZip, and Love Letter.

- Stolen identities, denial of service attacks, child pornography, and the famous dot-com crash of 2001. And the very sad death of the sock puppet. Why? Because pets can't buy (or use a credit card for that matter). The fact that pets can't drive is a moot point.

1.1.2   The Ethernet

Why pick on the Ethernet for its own section and history? Because many of the examples we will be discussing are on the Ethernet. The Ethernet is a system for connecting computers within a building (or your house) using dedicated hardware and software running from machine to machine.

Xerox's Palo Alto Research Center (PARC) is where some of the first personal computers were created. Robert Metcalfe was a member of the research staff and was asked to build a networking system for PARC's computers. The motivation for the computer network was that Xerox was also building the world's first laser printer and wanted all of the PARC's computers to be able to print with this printer. Mr. Metcalfe had two challenges:

1.   The network had to be fast enough to drive the new laser printer.

2.   The network needed to connect hundreds of computers within the same building.

There are several disputing stories about when the Ethernet was really invented. For us it really does not matter. If you want a date, use the date from Robert Metcalfe. He said, "gradually over a period of several years."

In about 1979, Metcalfe left Xerox to evangelize the use of personal computers and local area networks. Metcalfe was able to sell Digital Equipment, Intel, and Xerox Corporations on this concept and get them to work together to promote Ethernet as a standard. In fact, one of the original connectors used was called a DIX connector. Get it? **D**igital, **I**ntel, **X**erox.

1.2   TCP/IP: the nails of the Internet

History has evolved into a present as wild as the West of old. There aren't any wagons, but there are quite a few cowboys, some lawmakers and some lawbreakers, and some posses (though most aren't half as cool as Jesse and the gang, I'll admit), and there are even some screaming villagers to muck things up in the middle of a showdown.

How does this work? If Jesse James wanted to break into a house, he would just walk up to it and shoot the lock. Today things really aren't all that different, if you only take into account the workings and layout of TCP/IP (Transfer Control Protocol/Internet Protocol). These protocols allow computers to "talk" to each other and to send one another a variety of happy and sometimes not so happy "gifts." Here's how it works.

The Internet is held together like a cabin is held together with nails and a certain amount of ingenuity. Each nail connects one board to another and each board connects to another board to form the entire house. The nails are called TCP/IP. In order to understand how to set up a home network, you will need to understand a bit about TCP/IP. So let's start off with an analogy. There is a street in your neighborhood, a nice, clean street. On this street there are two houses. One house will be the sender house and the other house will be the receiver house. We want to send a piece of mail from one house to the other. Now we are talking about postal mail, or "snail" mail. In reality, the postal person will pick up the mail, take it to the post office, and then return it back to the same street. We will suspend reality for a moment and believe that the postal person will pick up the mail and deliver it directly to the destination house. What components are required for this postal mail to be picked up and then delivered?

1.   A postal person

2.   A source house (with a source address)

3.   A destination house (with a target address)

4.   A letter or a package

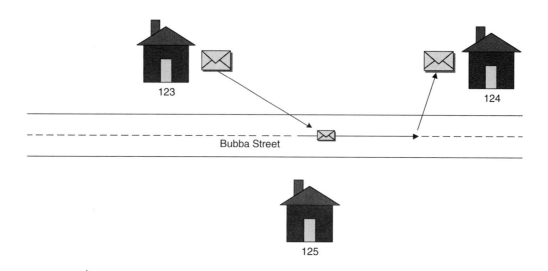

Figure 1.1

5.   Some type of address information on the letter or package

6.   A street (with a list of addresses and a street name)

Figure 1.1 shows the process.

You are at 123 Bubba Street. You want to send a message to 124 Bubba Street. You create a message and place it into an envelope, address the envelope, and send it to 124 Bubba Street. OK, not bad, this works.

Let's see how the computer does it. In Figure 1.2, the source computer, Computer 123, sends a packet of data on a network. This network is called Network A. The data packet travels over the network looking for Computer 124. Once found, it delivers the packet to the computer.

TCP/IP address works much like the postal mail analogy. Every computer has a source address, and if you want to send data to another computer, you need to know its "target" address.

The Transmission Control Protocol/Internet Protocol provides connectivity between equipment from many vendors over a variety of networking technologies. The Transmission Control Protocol (TCP) is intended for use as a highly reliable host-to-host protocol between hosts in packet-switched computer communication networks.

The Internet Protocol (IP) is specifically limited in scope to provide the functions necessary to deliver an envelope of data from one computer system

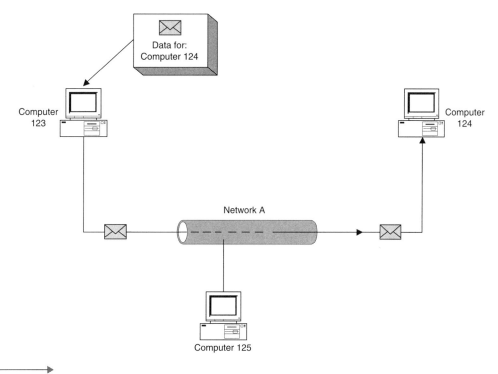

Figure 1.2

to another. Actually, we are not limited to PCs. This can be any network-connected device, a computer, a printer, a cell phone (see WAP in the glossary). Each computer or device on a network will have some type of address that denotes where it is on the network. Every device will have one of these addresses, assigned via a permanent mechanism or a temporary addressing scheme. You will notice that we are referencing a network; IP and TCP are used on the Internet but also can be used on any network. Many networks use TCP/IP as their primary protocol.

When data is sent via a network (e-mail note or a web page), the data (or message) is carved into little chunks called packets. The packets contain the information required to determine who sent the message as well as the reception of the message.

An Ethernet LAN typically uses some type of cable or special grades of twisted pair wires. Basically, the computer is connected to the cable via a card (or NIC, Network Interface Card) and that NIC card puts the data onto

6 Bytes	6 Bytes	2 Bytes	46–1500 Bytes	4 Bytes
Target Address	Source Address	Protocol Type	Data	CRC

Figure 1.3

the cable. In our examples for your home network we will be discussing the Ethernet LAN. This is a complex system, known as Carrier Sense Multiple Access with Collision Detection (CSMA/CD), that keeps data from running into each other. Every NIC card will have some type of address. This address is known as a MAC address and is typically a 48-bit address that is unique for every card. All Ethernet data is crafted into packets with each packet having the information needed to find its target computer and knowing where it came from. Figure 1.3 shows an example of an Ethernet Packet:

As you can see, there is a "target address" and a "source address." Each byte shown is an 8-bit byte, so we end up with 48 bits for each address. See the IEEE 802.3 for a description of the address assignments (http://www.ieee.org/). The protocol type tells the computer that is receiving the data what the packet is, e.g., 0800 = IP4 or Internet packet, 0806 = ARP packet (APR used by TCP to determine what other computers are on the network). The 1500 bytes of data is where TCP/IP live. The CRC is a checksum to make sure the packet did not get corrupted in transmission.

We have just described the first layer in the TCP/IP model. This is similar to the OSI (Open Systems Interconnection) model. OSI is a standard reference mode for how network data is transmitted between any two points in a computer network. TCP/IP supports the Defense Advanced Research Projects Agency (DARPA) model of internetworking and its network defined layers: Network Interface, Internet, Hosts-to-Host, and Process/Application. This model was developed in the early 1970s; it preceded the Open Systems Interconnection reference model (OSI). Much like the DARPA model, the OSI was designed to connect dissimilar computer network systems. The OSI reference model defines seven layers of functions that take place at each end of a network communication. OSI divides the communication into seven layers:

Table 1.1 *OSI*

Application	**Application layer:** This is the layer at which programs are identified, user authentication and privacy are implemented.
Presentation	**Presentation layer:** This is a layer, usually part of an operating system, that converts incoming and outgoing data from one presentation format to another.
Session	**Session layer:** This layer sets up, coordinates, and ends conversations, exchanges, and dialogs between the applications at each end of the dialog.
Transport	**Transport layer:** This layer manages the end-to-end control and error-checking.
Network	**Network layer:** This layer handles the routing of the data. The network layer does routing and forwarding.
Data Link	**Data link layer:** This layer provides error control and synchronization for the physical level.
Physical	**Physical layer:** This layer transmits the bit stream through the network at the electrical and mechanical level. Cables, Cards,...

TCP/IP also has a much simpler protocol model:

Table 1.2

Process Layer	**Process Layer:** This is the layer where each process is defined and communicates. FTP, Telent,...
Host-to-Host Layer	**Host-to-Host:** This is where TCP lives. This is the mechanism that actually ports the data to the correct application. TCP ports are defined here.
Internet Layer	**Internet Layer:** IP address are used to direct the packet to the correct destination. Routing protocols live here along with ARP and ICMP.
Network Interface Layer	**Network Interface Layer:** This is the physical connection to the network. Ethernet, Token Ring, etc. The packets are placed onto the network at this point. Also, the CRC is done here.

There is no direct correlation between the TCP protocol model and the OSI model, but they are roughly equivalent in the services provided. The following diagram shows a comparison between the models:

Table 1.3   *Protocol Implementation*

DARPA Layer				OSI
Process/ Application	FTP	TFTP		Application
	SMTP	NFS		Presentation
	TELNET	SNMP		Session
	RFC 959,821,854	RFC 783,1094		
Transport	Transmission Control Protocol (TCP) RFC 793	User Datagram Protocol (UDP) RFC 768		Transport
Internet	(ARP) Address Resolution RFC 826,903	(IP) Internet Protocol RFC 791	Internet Control Message Protocol RFC 792	Network
Network Interface	Network Interface Cards: Ethernet, Token Ring RFC 894 RFC 1042			Data Link
	Transmission Media: Twisted Pair, Coax, Fiber, Wireless, etc.			Physical

The first layer of the DARPA model is the Network Interface Layer; it links the local host to the local network hardware. This loosely maps to the Physical and Data Link layers of the OSI reference model. The Network Interface Layer makes the physical connection to the network cable, be it Ethernet or Token Ring. In each case, a frame is generated with data from the upper layers. The Internet Layer transfers the packets from a host to a host. Each packet will contain address information relating to the source and destination of the packet. The third level of the Internet software is called the Transport Layer. It is responsible for providing communication between applications residing on different hosts. This can also be called the host-to-host layer. Depending on the application, the Transport Layer will provide a reliable service (TCP) or an unreliable service (UDP). In a reliable service, the receiving station acknowledges the receipt of a datagram. The top layer of the DARPA model is the Application Layer. This is where actual applications like TFTP and Telnet reside.

So we have seen the Ethernet Packet and where it lives in the TCP/IP model. Next, let's look at the IP packet. The IP packet is how the TCP packet finds which computer it is destined for. The Internet Protocol is defined in RFC 791[26]. IP provides the most basic level of service in the Internet. It is

---

26.   http://info.internet.isi.edu:80/in-notes/rfc/files/rfc791.txt

the basis upon which the other protocols stand. IP provides the protocol above it with a basic service model and is really similar to the postal service. Using its address scheme, a packet is routed from a source to a destination much like a letter having a street address. Overall, IP does not promise the best service, hence it is known as a "Best Effort Service." If you send a postal message from your house, you rely on "best effort" that the message will arrive to its destination. Without special handling you will not know if the letter (i.e., message) has been delivered to its destination. IP routing is outside the scope of this document; see this URL for a basic overview http://www.sangoma.com/fguide.htm.

Figure 1.4 shows the Ethernet Packet carrying TCP/IP. Notice that IP is first, then TCP.

Figure 1.5 shows how it looks in each section.

6 Bytes	6 Bytes	2 Bytes	46–1500 Bytes			4 Bytes
Target Address	Source Address	Protocol Type	IP	TCP	Data	CRC

Figure 1.4

6 Bytes	6 Bytes	2 Bytes	46–1500 Bytes			4 Bytes
Target Address	Source Address	Protocol Type	IP	TCP	Data	CRC

4 Bits	4 Bits	3 Bits	5 Bits	2 Bytes	2 Bytes	2 Bytes	1 Byte	1 Byte	2 Bytes	4 Bytes	4 Bytes
IP Version	IP Header	Precedence	Type of Service	Total IP Length	ID#	Fragment	TTL	Protocol	Check Sum	Source IP Address	Target IP Address

Figure 1.5

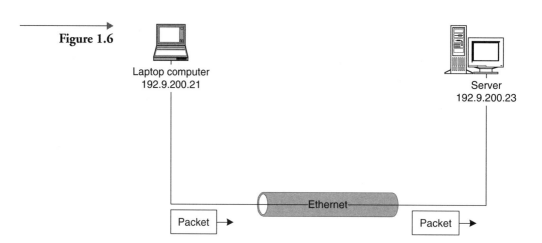

Figure 1.6

This is how an address is accomplished on the Internet. As we mentioned before, all network-connected devices will have an address. Keep in mind that every NIC card has a 48-bit address, but this is how the packet finds its way to a specific NIC card. Addressing between applications happens using the IP address.

Figure 1.6 is an example.

The laptop computer is sending an IP packet to the server. The source address is 192.9.200.21 and the target address is 192.9.200.23. Using this nomenclature, the server now knows how to respond back to the laptop computer, assuming the application needs to do that. This address scheme is how computers talk to each other on the Internet or any IP network. Returning to the postal analogy: The IP address is much like the address on the letter, or the address on your house. The letter (packet) is dropped into the postal box and it is sent via a network of postal employees, with one finally dropping the letter at your house or mailbox.

Part of the IP architecture is the address methodology. Out of the 32 bits of which it is composed, there are approximately 4 billion possible addresses. The addresses are categorized into five different classes of addresses: A, B, C, D, and E. IP addresses are broken down into octets. Each octet represents a part of the address. Example: "192.168.0.1." This address, as with all IP addresses, contains 4 octets. Each portion of the address is separated with a dot (.). This is known as Dotted-Decimal IP addressing. The address range for any octet is 0–255. Also each address, via octet, can be displayed in binary:

Binary	Dotted-Decimal IP Address

11000000 10101000   00000000   00000001   192.168.0.1

Each octet is 8 bits with a maximum decimal value of 255.

An important part of TCP/IP is subnetting. This is so important that we will not be covering it in this book. Now you are really confused. A subnet is a network that is created by using, or borrowing, bits from the host portion of an IP address. This is needed to split out the address from the various classes. Why is this so important? Subnetting can be utilized to get full use of an assigned address from an ISP.

1.2.1 IP address classes

Class A addresses are used with large networks with many hosts. The leading bit in the address is 0 (Bit 0 = 0). Mathematically, 128 networks are available, but the architecture reserves address 0 and 127. Bits 8–31 will make 16 million (16,777,214) addresses available to assign as hosts.

Figure 1.7

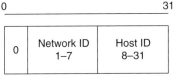

Class A Address

Class A

Networks:126

Hosts: 16 Million

Leading Bit = 0

Address 0 and 127 as reserved.

Octet range: 1–126.x.y.z

Host component of address: x.y.z

Default subnet Mask: 255.0.0.0

Class B addresses are used with medium sized networks with many hosts. The leading bit in the address is 1 (Bits 0,1 = 10). Mathematically, 16,384 networks are available from bits 2–15. Bits 16–31 will make 65,000 (65,534) address available to assign as hosts.

Figure 1.8

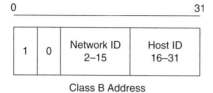

Class B Address

Class B

Networks:16,384

Hosts: 65,000

Leading Bits = 10

Octet range: 128–191.x.y.z

Host component of address: y.z

Default subnet Mask: 255.255.0.0

Class C addresses are used with small networks with few hosts. The leading bit in the address is 1 (Bits 0,1,2 = 110). Mathematically, 2 million (2,097,152) networks are available from bits 3–24. Bits 25–31 will make 254 addresses available to assign as hosts.

Figure 1.9

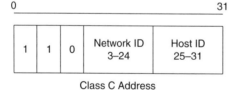

Class C Address

Class C

Networks: 2,097,152

Hosts: 254

Leading Bits = 110

Octet range: 192–223.x.y.z

Host component of address: .z

Default subnet Mask: 255.255.255.0

Classes D and E are not used for addressing. Class D, leading bits 1110, is used for multicasting and Class E, leading bits 1111, is reserved.

Example and uses of the addressing classes:

Class A   By definition, a class address of 9.2.3.4 is on a different network than an address of 11.2.3.4. The reason is by definition of the class. If computer A is on 9.2.3.4 and computer B is on 9.3.4.5, then they are considered to be on the same network. If that is the case, then they can communicate without the need of a gateway (router).

Class B   By definition, a class address of 130.2.3.4 is on a different network than an address of 131.2.3.4. Again, if computer A is on 130.2.3.4 and computer B is on 130.2.4.5, then they are considered to be on the same network. But 130.2.3.4 is on a different network than 130.3.4.5. See the difference? Look at the host component of the address to understand the address of an IP address in the table below.

Class C   By definition, a class address of 193.2.3.4 is on a different network than an address of 194.2.3.4. Again, if computer A is on 193.2.3.4 and computer B is on 193.2.3.5, then they are considered to be on the same network. But 193.2.3.4 is on a different network than 193.2.4.5. See the difference? Look at the host component of the address to understand the address of an IP address in the table below.

Address Components, based on the following format—w.x.y.z—with each letter representing an octet.

Table 1.4

Address Class	IP Address Range	Network Component	Host Component	Example Network. Host
Class A	0–126	w	.x.y.z	**9.2.3.4**
Class B	128–191	w.x	.y.z	**131.2.3.4**
Class C	192.223	w.x.y	.z	**193.2.3.4**

So far in our review of TCP/IP, we have discussed Ethernet and IP. Our new stop down the network trail is Transmission Control Protocol. TCP is a connection-oriented, end-to-end reliable protocol designed to work within a hierarchy of protocols that support networked applications. The TCP provides for reliable communication between pairs of processes (applications) in host computers attached to separate but interconnected computer networks. TCP is designed for error-free bulk data movement and provides error detection and recovery. This can make up for IP's "best effort" delivery service. TCP will setup a connection between two hosts before the actual data transmission begins. It will break the data into chunks, add some sequencing information, and then place these chunks into IP packets. IP then will actually route the data through the Internet to its destination.

6 Bytes	6 Bytes	2 Bytes	46–1500 Bytes			4 Bytes
Target Address	Source Address	Protocol Type	IP	TCP	Data	CRC

Figure 1.10

TCP rides in the Ethernet packet after the IP packet. The TCP packet contains information about the application. Although IP routes packets through the Internet using the destination address, more information is needed to identify which application on the destination host should receive the data once it arrives. This is accomplished via ports. Both sending and receiving applications are assigned port numbers to send and receive data. Coupled with the source and destination IP address, the source and destination port number, a small integer number, identifies which application is associated with any given data transfer. As mentioned before, the IP address is like the addressing scheme of the postal service. Once the postal service delivers the letter to your house, further addressing on the letter determines who actually gets the letter. This is where TCP helps out.

2 Bytes	2 Bytes	4 Bytes	4 Bytes	4 Bits	4 Bits	1 Byte	2 Bytes	2 Bytes	2 Bytes
TCP Source Port	TCP Target Port	Seq Number	ACK Seq Number	TCP Header Length	Res	Flags	Win Size	Check Sum	Urgent Data Size

Figure 1.11

The TCP port addresses, source and target, provide a mechanism to direct data to a specific application. Once the IP packet arrives at the host then the port determines which application receives the data. With two bytes of data you can have up to 65,000 different addresses. These addresses are defined by RFC 1700, http://info.internet.isi.edu:80/in-notes/rfc/files/rfc1700.txt. In this RFC, the ports are categorized. The TCP/IP port numbers below 1024 are special in that normal users are not allowed to run servers on them. These ports are called "well known ports." There are a number of commonly used "well known ports" that include: the SMTP mail service (25), the network news (NNTP, port 119), Telnet (23) and the FTP service (21). The normal port number for web access and server is port 80.

The sequence number and ACK sequence number are used as part of the TCP handshake process. The header length is used to tell the target computer the size of the current TCP header in 32 bit words. The session flags are used to control the various data elements sent to the target computer. For example: Urgent points, Valid Ack, Push Request, and Sync sequent number. The Window size is the number of bytes that the sending computer will accept from the target computer without requirement or acknowledgement. The checksum is an error check for the TCP header fields. The urgent data size can be used if the target computer is congested and it will clear the buffer space as needed to receive and process the data.

So far, so good. Now, how can I access a web site? Let's say you want to go to a site. You will need an address. Let's use 207.69.200.100. Easy to use and remember, but what about remembering numbers for 20 or 30 sites. A process known as DNS solves this problem. Today we access web sites via domain names. Domain names are a method of looking up addresses without having to remember some long number. Remembering a 32-bit number (that really maps to a 48-bit number) can be difficult. Thankfully, the Domain Name System was created. The following extract describes how domains work.

1.2.2   Domains

Getting where you want to go can often be one of the more difficult aspects of using networks. The variety of ways that places are named will probably leave a blank stare on your face at first. Don't fret; there is a method to this apparent madness.

If someone were to ask for a home address, they would probably expect a street, apartment, city, state, and zip code. That's all the information the post office needs to deliver mail in a reasonably speedy fashion. Likewise, computer addresses have a structure to them. The general form is:

a person's email address on a computer: user@somewhere.domain

a computer's name: somewhere.domain

The user portion is usually the person's account name on the system, though it doesn't have to be. For example, somewhere.domain tells you the name of a system or location, and what kind of organization it is. The trailing domain is often one of the following:

com   Usually a company or other commercial institution or organization, like Convex Computers (convex.com).

edu   An educational institution, e.g., New York University, named "nyu.edu."

gov   A government site; NASA is "nasa.gov."

mil   A military site; the Air Force is "af.mil."

net   Gateways and other administrative hosts for a network (it does not mean all of the hosts in a network). One such gateway is "near.net."

org   This is a domain reserved for private organizations that don't comfortably fit in the other classes of domains. One example is the Electronic Frontier Foundation named "eff.org."

Each country also has its own top-level domain. For example, the U.S. domain includes each of the fifty states. Other countries represented with domains include:

au   Australia

ca   Canada

fr   France

uk   The United Kingdom. These also have sub-domains of things, like "ac.uk" for academic sites and "co.uk" for commercial ones.

The proper terminology for a site's domain name (somewhere.domain above) is its Fully Qualified Domain Name (FQDN). It is usually selected to give a clear indication of the site's organization or sponsoring agent. For example, the Massachusetts Institute of Technology's FQDN is "mit.edu"; similarly, Apple Computer's domain name is "apple.com." While such obvious names are usually the norm, there are the occasional exceptions that are ambiguous enough to mislead, like "vt.edu," which, on first impulse, one might surmise is an educational institution of some sort in Vermont; not so.

It's actually the domain name for Virginia Tech. In most cases, it's relatively easy to glean the meaning of a domain name. Such confusion is far from the norm.[27]

The DNS is a distributed database of name-to-IP address mappings. Give the DNS the name of a computer and it returns the address, e.g., www.lotus.com is 198.114.68.10. To look up a name, the computer sends a request to a remote domain server. This server will answer the query and return an actual 32-bit IP address. This address is then used by the application to access the resource and return the data.

1.2.3   ARP and routing

ARP stands for Address Resolution Protocol. This is the mechanism that IP uses to get the Ethernet address for a packet. ARP resolves IP addresses to hardware addresses also known as a MAC address. Each network adapter has a unique hardware address that it uses for identification on the network. When there is a need to locate a computer/peripheral on the TCP/IP network, ARP first checks its local cache to see if it contains the hardware address for the computer/peripheral it is trying to connect to. If the address is not in the ARP cache, ARP broadcasts a message to the known IP address for its hardware address. The computer it's trying to locate will receive the broadcast and send a reply with its IP and hardware addresses. Once the hardware address has been attained, ARP stores the resolved IP and hardware addresses in cache, then proceeds with communication. But this is only part of the story. IP really only communicates on its own network. Remember, we talk about the various classes of networks, A, B, and C. Figure 1.12 shows some examples for a Class C Network:

Computer	Address
Computer A	192.9.200.2
Computer B	192.9.200.3
Computer C	192.9.201.5

Computer A and Computer B are in the same IP network. Computer C is on a different IP Network. Also, in our example, all computers are connected to the same physical network. So from an IP perspective, Computer A and Computer B can communicate. Computer C cannot communicate

27.   From Request for Comments 1591, http://info.internet.isi.edu:80/in-notes/rfc/files/rfc1591.txt.

Figure 1.12

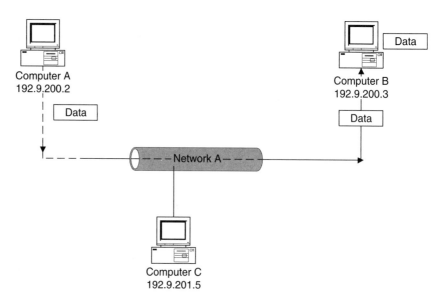

with Computer A or Computer B. Why? The answer is routing. Routing in IP is based entirely upon the network number of the destination address. Each computer has a table of IP network numbers. If these IP numbers show that the destination computer is in the same network, then the computers can establish a point-to-point communication. If the computers are not in the same network, then a "gateway" will be needed. A gateway is an IP communication facilitator.

In Figure 1.13, we have two IP networks, 192.9.200.x and 192.9.201.x. How can Computer A (192.9.200.2) establish a connection with Computer D (192.9.201.5)?

Let's follow the steps:

1.   When a computer wants to send a packet of data, it first checks to see if the destination address is on the system's own local network.

2.   If yes, then the data is sent point-to-point.

3.   Our example has computers that are not in the same IP network so the data will be sent to a gateway that is on the source network.

In our example, the gateway (aka the "default gateway") is at IP address 192.9.200.5. So if the target computer is not on the local network, then all "unknown" traffic will be sent to the gateway. All traffic for 192.9.201.x will be sent to 192.9.200.5. Then the computer will route the data (traffic) to

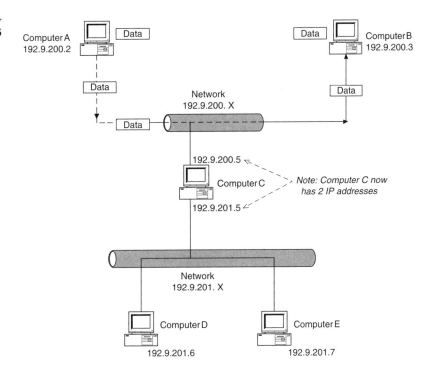

Figure 1.13

Note: Computer C now has 2 IP addresses

192.9.201.x network. This concept is very important. If you are going to set up your own private network, you will be using these simple routing concepts.

Now, at this point, you may be thinking this routing stuff is easy. It is easy as long as you have a small network. There are books, courses, and companies that are dedicated to routing implementation, software, and hardware. IP routing can get very complicated very quickly. Remember, this book is trying to give you the concepts to set up and protect your home network. If you need to set up a business, then you need a different book or a consulting service.

1.2.4   Ports

At this point we need to return to our postal analogy. Remember that when you want to send a message from one house to another you will use an addressing scheme. You have a source address and a target address. In the IP world, this is managed by the IP address. In our example you sent that message to your friend at the end of the block. But in our analogy the address was not complete. You put the house address on the message but you did not put "who" the message was going to. The "who" part of the message is very similar to a concept known as "ports." The port in TCP/IP (actually just the TCP part) tells the computer what application needs this data (or message).

Table 1.5   *Protocol Implementation*

DARPA Layer				OSI	
Process/ Application	FTP	TFTP		Application	
	SMTP	NFS		Presenta- tion	
	TELNET	SNMP		Session	
	RFC 959,821,854	RFC 783,1094			
Transport	Transmission Control Protocol (TCP) RFC 793	User Datagram Protocol (UDP) RFC 768		Transport	Who (App)
Internet	(ARP)Address Resolution RFC 826,903	(IP) Internet Protocol RFC 791	Internet Control Message Protocol RFC 792	Network	Street Address (IP Addr.)
Network Interface	Network Interface Cards: Ethernet, Token Ring RFC 894 RFC 1042			Data Link	Street Name (NIC Card)
	Transmission Media: Twisted Pair, Coax, Fiber, Wireless, etc.			Physical	The Street (Cable)

In our analogy we can compare each feature to the OSI reference mode.

1. At the physical layer, which is the cables, wires, etc., the street is how the message gets from house to house.

2. The data link layer would be the same as the street name, e.g., the MAC address lives here.

3. The street address of the house would be the same as the IP address at the network layer.

4.   The transport layer would have the person's name on the letter (or the message). At the TCP layer, the port would point to the application receiving the message.

TCP port numbers are divided into three basic ranges: the well known ports, the registered ports, and the dynamic private ports. The well known ports are those from 0 through 1023. The registered ports are those from 1024 through 49151. The dynamic private ports are those from 49152 through 65535. The well known ports are controlled and assigned by the IANA and on most systems can only be used by predefined system processes or by programs executed by privileged users. The registered ports are not controlled by the IANA and on most systems can be used by any program or processes.

Following are examples of well known ports:

- ftp-data 20/tcp File Transfer [Default Data]
- ftp 21/tcp File Transfer [Control]
- telnet 23/tcp Telnet
- smtp 25/tcp Simple Mail Transfer
- http 80/tcp World Wide Web HTTP
- www-http 80/tcp World Wide Web HTTP
- pop3 110/tcp Post Office Protocol—Version 3
- nntp 119/tcp Network News Transfer Protocol
- imap2 143/tcp Interactive Mail Access Protocol v2
- https 443/tcp https

So why all this fuss about ports? Hacking into computers can include port scanning or surfing. The essence of port surfing is to pick out a target computer and explore it to see what ports are open and what a hacker can do with them. If you understand ports then you can understand what hackers can do to you and/or your systems.

Scanning, as a method for discovering exploitable communication channels, has been around for ages. Over time, a number of techniques have been developed for surveying the protocols and ports on which a target machine is listening. They all offer different benefits and problems. TCP port scanning is used to find any TCP ports that are "listening." If the port is listening then the scan will succeed; otherwise, the port isn't reachable. Later you will learn how to block ports from the modern-day Jesse James.

1.2.5 DHCP

DHCP (Dynamic Host Configuration Protocol) is a network protocol that enables a DHCP server to automatically assign an IP address to an individual computer. This process is controlled by a server but initiated by a client computer. The DHCP server assigns a number dynamically from a predefined range of numbers. In DHCP terms, this is called a "scope." If the DHCP is configured properly, then the IP address and DNS address can be assigned at the same time.

Following is the transaction that a server and client will implement:

1. The client is started.

2. The client computer sends a broadcast request out on the network looking for a DHCP server to answer its request.

3. A DHCP server returns a DHCP OFFER packet.

4. The DHCP client sends a DHCP REQUEST packet back to the server.

5. The client then sends out a DHCP ACK packet.

6. The DHCP server then assigns an IP number according to the scope range defined in its DHCP configuration.

7. As part of the process the DHCP server may also send the DNS information.

Figure 1.14 shows the configuration for a DHCP client on Windows 98. Open the control panel in Windows 98 and select Network.

Once in the Network configuration (see Figure 1.15), select the Configuration tab. Select TCP/IP. If you do not see TCP/IP listed then you will need to add it to the list. A big assumption is that you have a network card (NIC) in your system at this time.

Select the TCP/IP binding, as shown in Figure 1.16, and select the Properties button.

The next screen shows the TCP/IP Properties dialog box. Select IP Address, then select "Obtain an IP Address automatically." Press "OK" and reboot your system.

When your system restarts, you should have an address that was assigned to you. But what if you wanted to check out the IP address that

Figure 1.14

was assigned to you? Again, if you are using Windows 98, here are the steps:

At the Start button select "Run" and type "Winipcfg."[28]

The Winipcfg utility allows a user to view the current IP address and other useful information about his or her network configuration. The user can reset one or more IP addresses. The "Release" or "Renew" buttons can release or renew the assigned IP address. The user can also release or renew all IP addresses by just clicking "Release All" or "Renew All."

---

28.   On NT and Win2000 use IPConfig. Commands: IPCONFIG/Release and IPCONFIG/Renew

Figure 1.15

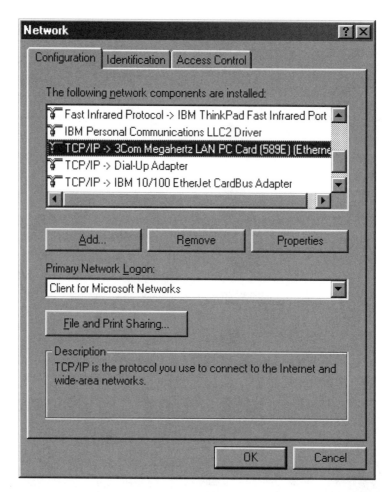

Once you press "OK" on the "Run" dialog box, you will see the dialog box shown in Figure 1.18.

Select your network card in the drop-down list as shown in Figure 1.19. This card will display the following:

- Adapter Address: This address is the address of the card, in this case the MAC address.

- IP Address: The IP address is one of the addresses in the "scope" of available addresses

- Subnet Mask: This is the mask used for subnetting (not covered in this book).

- Default Gateway: The gateway address to other networks.

Figure 1.16

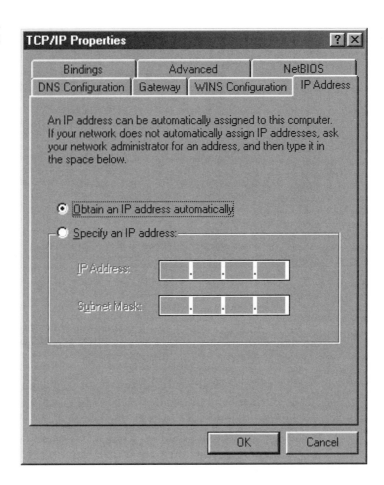

Figure 1.17

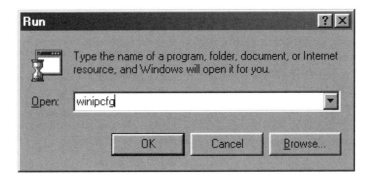

Figure 1.18

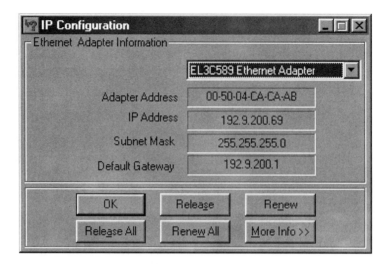

Select "More Info >>". This will display more detailed information about the address that was assigned and any DNS names and addresses that have been assigned to your computer.

Why all this talk about IP addresses? As we mentioned, every computer on the Internet has an IP address. Of the 32 bits of an IP address, there are just a limited number of addresses (the potential is 4 billion, but true registered addresses are much less than that). If you want more information about the registration process then check out http://www.arin.net/regserv.html. At this point, we are running out of what is known as IP4 addresses. How can we deal with this issue? One answer is known as IPV6. This is a new IP addressing scheme that will have 128 addressable bits. As we say in Texas, that is a truckload of addresses. But for now IPV6 is not as widespread as IPV4. One method is to use a system known as 10-net[29]. RFC 1918 discusses the 10-net address allocation. The Internet Assigned Numbers Authority (IANA) has reserved the following three blocks of the IP address space for private Internets:

10.0.0.0   10.255.255.255
172.16.0.0   172.31.255.255
192.168.0.0   192.168.255.255

---

29.   http://info.internet.isi.edu/in-notes/rfc/files/rfc1918.txt

Figure 1.19

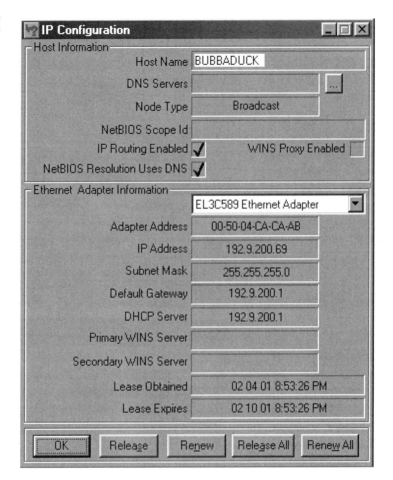

These addresses are not registered and cannot be allocated to anyone on the Internet. But we can use these address for our internal networks. So how do we communicate with addresses that cannot be registered? The answer is NAT. Network Address Translation is the technique that we will discuss in Chapter 4.

The Security Review Process

"I was caught breaking into a DMZ with a loaded URL—What are you in for?"

2.1   Introduction

It is 1860, and you are the bank manager. Your number-one goal is to keep the money safe. What steps will you take to keep the money from the men in the black hats? Some of these steps may be to understand how the bank will be robbed:

- Will the robbers enter by the front door?

- Will they enter by the back door?

- Will they try to use explosives on the safe?

- Will they use "social engineering" to get the money? "Joe sent me down to get his money. Give it to me and I will give it to him in the bar."

- Will they try to use someone on the inside to help get the money?

Next, the manager will determine what steps are needed to keep the bad guys out:

- Use a safe with a combination lock.

- Put bars on the door.

- Get a security guard—Hire a gun slinger.

- Keep a gun and use it if needed.

- Train employees how to keep the money safe.

- And, most important, make sure that the bank manager knows the sheriff.

You will need to take similar action as the owner and/or manager of your network infrastructure. Using the following five steps will get you started with your security review:

1.   Start by reviewing the current state of the business.

2.   Analyze the technology currently being used.

3.   Start a risk analysis process.

4.   Create the plans.

5.   Begin your security implementation process.

Each step will link into a succeeding step. This approach should be used for each process or department within the business, as well as for the holistic enterprise.

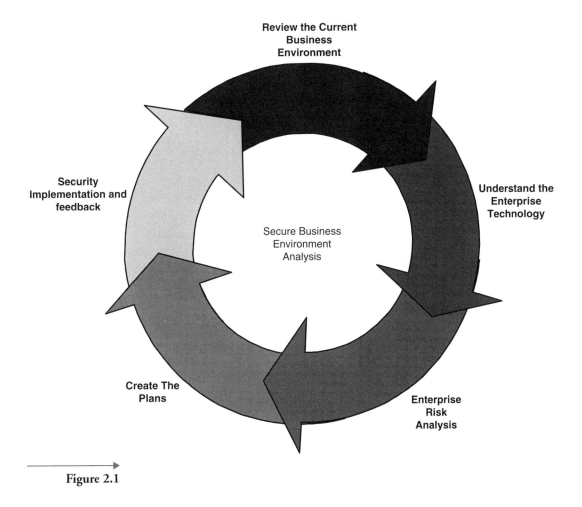

Figure 2.1

2.2   Review the state of the business

In most companies some type of systemic security is already in place; it is unlikely that you will need to start your security analysis from scratch. An evaluation must be performed to allow you to review the security already in place relevant to current security requirements.

The following steps will help you identify the security requirements for your Internet interfacing enterprise:

1.   Identify the core business.

2.   Identify the stakeholders.

3.   Compile customer demographics.

4.   Identify the vendors and business partners.

5.   Identify the competition.

6.   Identify industry trends and standards.

2.2.1   Identify the core business

Unless you are a business consulting company and/or a security software vendor, security is likely not a core competency of your business. One of the biggest mistakes companies make is that they start with security first and look at the business after the fact. When asked, "Why did you install a firewall?" the answer is commonly, "Well, because we needed one!" The next question, "What policies did you use to determine that you needed a firewall and what procedures did you use to effectuate that decision?" may elicit the response, "Well, because we thought we needed a firewall." Following are the questions a business should start with:

1.   "What are we protecting against?"

2.   "What segments of the business do we need to protect?"

3.   "How can we conduct business securely[1] and safely?"

4.   "How can we use a secure infrastructure as a competitive advantage?"

To answer these questions we need to understand what the core business is and why it needs an interface to the Internet or any network. As part of any analysis, you will need to document your findings. In each step, write a short summary of the results of your analysis.

Example: The Company is a publicly traded enterprise that provides the automotive industry with Widgets. The core business is to manufacture Widgets and market and sell the Widgets to automotive parts distributors and to individual customers. The Company currently sells most of its products via a dedicated sales force, mail order catalogs, and an 800 number advertised in trade publications. The Company wants to expand its Internet presence quickly and, at the same time, securely.

This example provides a quick start on what your business needs are and where you will need to start putting your time and resources.

---

1.   Business continuity and disaster recovery plans should be included with this analysis.

2.2.2   Identify the stakeholders

The stakeholders can be the company owners and stockholders. The CxOs are the owners of the applications. In many enterprise companies, there will be several applications or processes that will need to be secured. Each application and/or process will have an owner who makes the decisions about the application or process and is responsible in the event that the application or process does not function. The stakeholder can also be anyone who has any type of ownership in security.

2.2.3   Compile customer demographics

Understand the company from both an internal and external perspective. Identify the number of employees, the customer base, and the volume of sales.

Example: The Company has been in business for 15 years and has 800 employees. The Company has 500 parts distributors to which it sells Widgets. The Company has 15 vendors that supply raw materials. The Company has few direct sales customers. Selling directly to the parts distributors generates the most sales for the Company. Once you have this data, you can begin compiling the types of access rights each group has and will need.

2.2.4   Identify the vendors and business partners

It is important to understand the vendors with which you do business. In many cases, you may have the vendors connected directly to your data processing systems. This is a great advantage but it can also be a point of entry for unauthorized access.

Example: All but three of the Company's vendors connect directly into the data process systems. This allows for the vendors to automatically process orders for the JIT (Just in Time) Widget manufacturing process.

The business partners are not necessarily the same as a vendor. In many cases, the business partners will work with the business to extend products or services rendered.

Example: The Company has five business partners that take raw Widgets and create "extended Widgets." The business partners need to share encrypted e-mail and will need to access secure web pages for product updates.

Be sure to map out in detail the business partners' access levels, account names, and what trusted networks they have access to.

2.2.5   Identify the competition

Yes, the competition will keep track of what you are doing. In fact, they may even be using these steps to create a profile on what your business is doing. So you are well advised to complete the profile before they do. (Beware if you see one of your competitors with a copy of this book!) Begin by compiling a list of your competitors and what information or resources they would be interested in obtaining. For example, you may have a secret formula or some specialized personnel that you would not want to lose. In today's changing economy, it is hard to keep first-rate personnel. Your competition also faces this problem, and they may find that your company web site is a great place to acquire potential candidates' names.

Example: The Company's main competitor is Bubba Inc. Bubba Inc. creates Sprockets, which can be used in place of Widgets. Bubba Inc. has a strong web presence and has many of the same customers, business partners, and vendors as the Company. Bubba Inc. could hurt the Company if it could access the Company's internal price list and sales commission rates. Also, the Company could lose valuable people to Bubba Inc. if Bubba Inc. could access the Company's corporate personnel directory. In the September 2, 2002 issue of *Business Week*[2] an article on page 78 reviews a case in which a series of passwords may have been stolen and used by a competitor. According to the article, industrial espionage was used via web sites to download data about a set of new products. The advice here is to know your competition and also try to monitor if any previous employees have moved to a competitor company.

2.   A McGraw-Hill Company magazine.

2.2.6   **Identify industry trends and standards**

This step can identify a common trend that businesses in all sectors are currently undergoing. Your business may be moving data via the Internet. Supply chain integration may use virtual private networks (VPN) to communicate with the vendors, including on-line ordering and JIT (Just in Time) raw material order and delivery management.

Example: Both companies that create Widgets and Sprockets share the same parts distributors (customers), vendors, and business partners. All the major players in this market communicate with their suppliers via a VPN over the Internet. Also, the parts houses are requesting the ability to generate JIT orders and on-the-fly orders via the Internet.

2.3   **Analyze the technology being used**

Next, you need to review your current use of technology. This review will include your "trusted network." A trusted network is the network that a company uses to conduct internal business. In many cases, the trusted network is by default defined in the organization as "secure." The trusted network typically supports the backend systems, internal-only-based web pages, data processing, messaging, and, in some cases, internal instant messaging. In many companies, the trusted network allows direct interaction between systems without encryption. Also, various protocols will exist within the trusted network without any type of filtering or even virus scanning.

The problem with this definition is that many assumptions are being made at these companies. A trusted network is not always a secure network. In fact, in many cases the trusted network cannot be trusted, because an internal network is composed of many different networks. These include new acquisitions, old acquisitions, international access points, and even several access point to the outside world.

A common practice is to define the trusted network as the network that internal employees use when at the office or via a secure, controlled dial-in mechanism. A single access point is established to the outside world via a mechanism called the DMZ (demilitarized zone). A DMZ is an isolated network placed as a buffer area between a company's trusted network and the nontrusted network. The DMZ prevents outside users from gaining

Figure 2.2

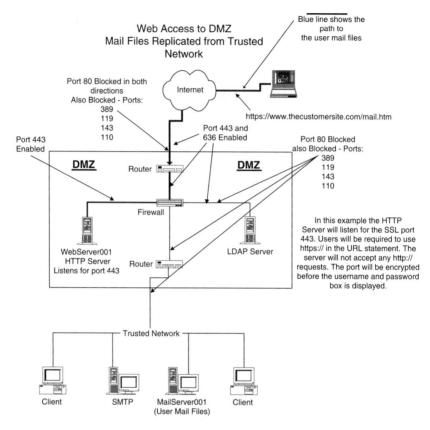

Web Access
HTTP

direct access to the Trusted Network. There are several methods to set up/ configure a DMZ.[3]

For most of our discussion in this book, we will use the following example.

Example: Our DMZ will have flanking routers on either side of a firewall to shield us from unwanted traffic. The firewall's job is to work within the DMZ to filter all network packets to determine whether to forward them to another server or to a computer workstation.

Firewalls will be covered in detail in a later chapter. Let's focus on the DMZ for now, as seen in Figure 2.2.

3.   Access this URL at Cisco for several examples. http://www.cisco.com/warp/public/cc/cisco/mkt/security/iosfw/tech/
        firew_wp.htm

A DMZ is similar to a set of steel bars set up between the bank tellers and the bank customers. That way a person cannot just reach in, grab some money, and run off. The "bad dudes" will need to jump over the steel bars to get to the money. In the same way, DMZs are configured to keep someone from directly accessing the trusted network. Sets of DMZ rules are enabled in the DMZ. These rules are controlled by the policies and implemented via the procedures for your organization. One of the most common rules is that a single protocol cannot transverse the DMZ. So if you are entering into the DMZ via http on port 80, you cannot continue into the trusted network on the same port and protocol. This is what the DMZ does: It keeps "untrusted" traffic from entering the trusted network. It is the job of the DMZ to filter the traffic and limit access to the trusted network via filtering and authentication and even to completely block traffic as needed.

What can a DMZ do for inbound traffic?

- Filter and manage Denial-of-Service attacks

- Scan e-mail messages for virus, content, and size

- Provide passive eavesdropping/packet sniffing

- Prevent application-layer attack

- Provide port scans

- Limit access to the trusted network via a single protocol

- Provide IP address spoofing

The following example is used for discussion only. We cannot make a recommendation on DMZ configurations for all cases.

Example: Some companies will make a partial copy of the data that is in the trusted network and then place it (or replicate it) onto servers in the DMZ. This is a good idea, unless the company has stated, "No business data is to be placed into the DMZ." Okay, now what do we do? A complex application needs to be created to intercept requests, possibly authenticate the users, and then forward the requests into servers in the trusted network. As you can see, one size does *not* fit all.

So far, we have discussed using the DMZ to control inbound traffic, but the DMZ is also used to control outbound traffic. It is also used to hide (mask) the design and configuration of the trusted network. The DMZ can be designed to limit access to the Internet via proxy servers and filter servers. These servers, as regulated by the limits set in the policy documents, can do the following.

- Control e-mail messages based on destination
- Control e-mail messages based on size and even content
- Scan for viruses going out of the DMZ
- Limit access to unauthorized access sites
- Monitor access to unauthorized web sites

Why should we care about messages that might have a virus going out of the company? This will be covered in detail in a later chapter, but for now, imagine these headlines: "Dimwitted User at the Company Sends Out Virus to Their Competitor Via a Résumé!" We are all responsible for controlling viruses. You can do your part by checking for viruses before you send out a message.

Make a list of your network configuration. Identify the access points to the Internet. Determine if you are using a trusted network. In the process, you will determine if you have any unauthorized access points.

Example: Someone uses a PC connection product to check his or her work e-mail by dialing into his or her computer from home. This is a common technique and may be authorized by your company. But without proper controls and procedures, this can be an access point for a hacker to access your trusted network.

Mergers and acquisitions are the norm of the business world, but with each merger there is some of type of change to a network. Many businesses will merge the trusted networks between the companies. This may seem like good business, but it may not be good security sense. If you have a "new" network that has been created by combining previous networks, review the following.

1. Access points to the Internet

2. The number of DMZs each company involved has in the merger. Why?

3. The protocols being used on each network

4. Directories being used to authenticate users

5.   Is there an authoritative directory?

6.   The type of remote access available to the new combined network

Now for the opposite scenario. Your corporation has just sold a company or division. Review the same points in reverse. You may need to completely isolate the networks.

1.   What access points to the Internet are/were in common?

2.   How many DMZs does each company created from the split have?

3.   What protocols are being used on each network?

4.   What directories are being used to authenticate users?

5.   Was there an authoritative directory?

6.   What type of remote access is available to the new network?

So far in the discussion we have talked about a trusted network as a single entity in a company. This is not always true. In a large enterprise or multinational company, there can be many trusted networks, and each network does not necessarily trust each other. Due to individual country laws and requirements you may need to isolate your trusted network, and you may even separate your networks via mini-DMZs. The common term for this is "zones and perimeters." Security zones define the areas that need to be protected. Each zone may have different security requirements. The zones may be within a perimeter area that protects all zones or specific zones.

Now you may be saying, "I don't have a DMZ or a trusted network." No problem—all that means is that we have a lot of work ahead of us. So let's move on to the next phase: initial risk analysis and the determination of whether you need a DMZ or a trusted network.

2.4   Risk analysis

We have reviewed the business and the network. At this stage in the process we will combine the information we have collected, which will give us a high-level snapshot of our organization and our network.

Look at each business statement that you created from the "Identify the Core Business" section. Identify each point where security could be an issue or a concern.

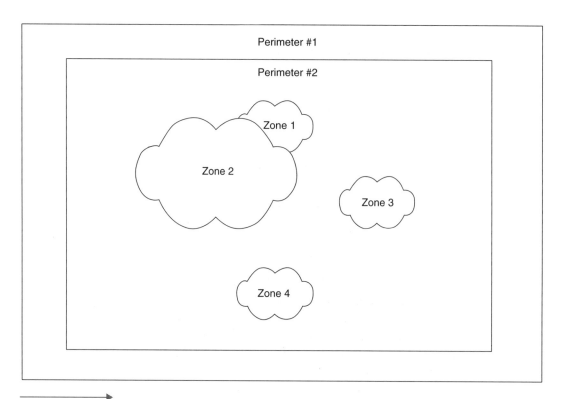

Figure 2.3

Example: The Company has been in business for 12 years and has 7000 employees. It has 600 parts distributors to which it sells Widgets. The Company also has 22 vendors that supply raw materials. The Company has few direct sales customers. Selling directly to the part distributors generates the most sales for the Company.

In this example we have several areas of concern.

- 7000 employees—security training awareness. What are the definitions of trust with each group of employees?

- 22 vendors—what is the trust level of these vendors? Do the vendors need to have direct access to the systems on the trusted network?

- Parts distributors—how does the company communicate with the parts distributors? Is encrypted mail used? Are secure web pages established?

Remember at all times what your goals are. Ask yourself, "Does this business need a web presence?" The answers can drive you to the solutions that you need. Security is not set up simply for the exercise of setting up security. It is set up to give you a competitive asset in driving your business. With that said, look at the security requirements from a business delivery model.

1. How can the business security enable the employees to drive the business in a cost-effective method?

2. How can the business save money by giving the vendors limited access to business data?

3. How can the business improve service by assisting the parts distributors with order and billing systems?

Next, combine your network analysis with your business needs. Your network may not have the necessary features that you would like it to have. No problem—list what features are needed to support your requirements.

1. The network will have a DMZ that will isolate traffic between the trusted network and the Nontrusted Network.

2. The network will provide support to the employees by giving them access to all authorized business systems.

3. The network will allow limited access to extension of systems in the DMZ for the parts distributors.

4. The network will allow for encrypted messages to be exchanged between employees and the parts distributors.

A detailed risk analysis will be covered in later chapters. This step is "priming the pump." You need to understand what your business requirements are before building the security. Some sites have such strong security requirements in place that the business just bypasses the security. For example, in one company, the security departments set up a file that prevented files greater than two megabytes from being sent. One department could not send its drafting files (four to six megabytes each), so they set up their own access point to the Internet via dialing into a private ISP (Internet Service Provider) and then sending the files. This creative solution caused several problems.

■ The files sent were not encrypted and thus could not be controlled or monitored for viruses, inbound or outbound.

■ An access point was made to the trusted network that was not controlled or monitored by a central security point.

The next step is to compile a list of high-level threats to the organization. Here are a few examples.

- Management does not encourage or support security measures. (Management must be involved in security from day one.)
- There are no security policies or procedures, or the policies and procedures have not been updated for months or years.
- There are no formal user training procedures.
- The trusted network is not defined.
- There is no DMZ (although not required in all cases).
- There is a direct connection to the Internet and no filters or firewalls.
- There are no monitoring systems in place. (This can be deadly for public utility companies.)
- No physical security is in place for the server room; anyone can just walk in.

2.5   Plans and policies

This is an area where many companies fall short of the mark. Check your environment to see if you have any existing security plans, policies, and/or procedures. These can include physical security, LAN security, Internet access, and even disaster recovery. At this point, you have decided which threats pose an unacceptable risk to your computing environment and what level of action you are willing to take to defend against them. Studying the security plans that your company has and their implementation may help you decide which security measures are most important for your environment. One of the most important parts of this review is the identification of policy compliance. Policies are only good if they are implemented; a thorough implementation plan is required. Part of your security implementation plan should be a review of any existing policies that concern security.

- Policy goals and objectives
- Scope
- Responsibilities
- Physical security
- Network security

- Data classification (data categorization)

- Access control

- Password change and enforcement policies and procedures

- Incident handling procedures

- Acceptable use policies

- Change control

- Training

- Compliance

2.5.1   Policy goals and objectives

Define what you are trying to accomplish with your policies. The objective defines your approach to Internet security. These approaches could include the use of tools, systems, and employee/user training.

2.5.2   Scope

The scope specifies the assets that will be protected by security policy. The scope could define a specific policy or a body of policies. The scope should include who is impacted by the policy: end-users, employees, customers, vendors, and so on.

2.5.3   Responsibilities

The responsibilities section of the policy document describes how the individuals defined in the scope section will be responsible for the security of your environment. Detail the security responsibilities as needed by region, department, or groups. Depending on the company size, responsibility may be assigned to the following personnel.

Executives

The top directors—the CxOs—are responsible for high-level security strategy and must make the necessary resources available to combat security threats to the business.

Security manager

The security manager is responsible for the entire enterprise security. The security manager defines the enterprise security policies and procedures and works with the business managers to implement the initial risk analyses as well as the individual process risk analysis. The security manager implements each facet of security, such as:

- Secure network

- Security applications

- Auditing

- Incident handling

- Facilitation of legal reviews of the various security issues

Process owner

The process owner is directly responsible for a particular business process and can be a department manager, a lead engineer, a specification custodian, or any employee tasked with accountability for a business system. The process owner will work with the security manager to analyze risks and recommend the countermeasures for each process. The process owner may not have extensive experience with security, so the recommendation may be at a business level only. For example, the process owner will say, "We need to limit access to this application to a single group." The security manager hears, "Access control will need to be set up and implemented for applicable personnel in the process group via the corporate policies and procedures."

Legal

The legal department needs to be involved with the design of the security policies and procedures from day one. Make sure the following issues/items are covered within each policy.

- Guidelines for acceptable use

- Ethics, for users and administrators

- Access by customers, including liability and damages, performance, and compliance

- Risk and exposures in the event that business data is compromised

- Analysis of communications sent to customers in the event of a security event (e.g., hackers, data compromised)

- Auditing and use of logs for evidence

- Copyright issues

- Use of electronic signatures and encryption

- Management of unauthorized access

- Review of any agreements with Extranet vendors, customers, and ISPs

- Interpretation of the Uniform Commercial code in relation to business use of the Web for your particular business (http://gopher.law.cornell.edu).

Developers

The developers define the responsibilities of the application developers. Security needs to be built into the application from day one of the development cycle.

Users

The users are responsible for security in the enterprise as much as the CxOs. Every user needs to be trained on the company security policy, data categorization, and system procedures as well as understand what the consequences of their actions are and how to act accordingly.

Auditors

The auditors should be familiar with but independent of the activities performed by the organization or group being audited. They will perform audits specific to requirements in the security policies and procedures.

2.5.4   Physical security

Physical security measures must provide for the protection and access to the physical assets of the business (e.g., servers and applications). The physical security document should describe how the various assets are to be protected (such as locked server rooms, card readers with limited access, or logging systems to track who has access to each type of server).

2.5.5   Network security

The network security document describes how you will protect assets stored on the network. This document could include security steps on the following.

- Network access

- Use of sniffers

- Access to Internet services

- Methods of DOS attacks

2.5.6   Data classification (data categorization)

Every business possesses data that is owned by someone. The value of this data can vary from one application to another, from one business to another, and even from one competitor to another. Business data should be classified based on the security requirements of that data. A data classification policy document should describe the requirements to classify the data. Do not confuse the classification of data and the service level of that data. You can have data that is open to the public, but if the public cannot read the data due to a DoS attack, then that data is useless no matter what your classification is.

Following are examples of data classifications.

Public

This data/information is available to the public. Access to this data by competitors is acceptable and does not represent a threat to the business.

Vendor restricted

This data is available only to approved vendors and/or business partners. Access to this data by competitors can pose a risk to the business. Access to this data must be logged and restricted.

Internal information (proprietary)

External access to this data is restricted. Access to this data by competitors or the general public could put the business at risk or cause embarrassment. Access to data is restricted to internal employees only and access will be logged.

Confidential information (limited)

This data is confidential within the company and protected from external access. Access to this data can give competitors an advantage in the marketplace. Access will be limited to select employees and groups. All access will be logged. Backup tapes will be controlled.

Secret information

This data will not be placed onto any networked systems. Access will be limited to very select individuals and all access will be logged and monitored. If this data is compromised, the business can be at risk.

2.5.7   Access control

Depending on the application and the data, users may need to be authorized. Define your requirements in this section of the document. Define the access to the authoritative directory for this authentication, and include the following access control features as needed.

- Users should be prevented from deleting other users' files in shared directories.

- Users should be able to manage the privileges of data elements that they own.

- Access control should be linked into data classifications.

Note: Not all authentications will necessarily be from an authoritative directory.

2.5.8   Password change and enforcement policies and procedures

Be careful with this section of the document. Not all applications or operating systems have the same password management systems or rules. You may need several documents to cover each type of password management. Also, consider using a single sign-on system, which can help manage passwords and the password rules. Consider the following examples when setting up your policy document.

Set up password rules to prevent "crackable" passwords

- Require a combination of numbers, upper- and lowercase letters, and punctuation.

- Use a password that you can remember without having to write it down.

- Use short passwords.

Create some guidelines for users on how to manage their passwords

- Do not share or give your passwords to others. Do not allow others to tailgate into applications using your password.

- Do not write down the password or send it to someone via e-mail.

- Do not create a single administration user name and password that will be shared between several administrators (this compromises the ability to audit).

- If possible, set up an administration account and password separate from the administrator's personal account. For example, your messaging administrator, Joe Smith, will be assigned two accounts: Joe Smith and Joe SmithAdmin, each with its own password. Additionally, the privileges will not be the same. The Joe Smith account will have the standard user access privileges that a typical user will have. The administrator will send all e-mail via this account, and will access any applications from this account. If the administrator needs to make any changes to the environment, he would then use the Joe SmithAdmin account. This account will provide the needed level of access to administer the environment. Joe will not use the Joe SmithAdmin account to send e-mail or to use any applications.

- Educate users about the dangers of password hacking/cracking.

- Encrypt passwords within the directory.

- Define the age expiration limit of the passwords and management and tracking of password history.

- Define the encryption strength.

- Define the mechanism and systems to track and stop directory attacks.

- Define the use of smart cards, tokens, and biometrics.

2.5.9   Incident handling procedures

An incident is an unplanned, unexpected event that requires immediate action to prevent a loss of business, assets, or public confidence. All policies must have an incident handling component plus a feedback component. The feedback loop is the mechanism that will keep the policies current and updated. An incident handling process is critical to permit continuity of important business processes in the event of an incident and allow the business to function. Service levels will be needed to determine what level of handling is needed based on each incident type. An incident where the web site is down and the business cannot conduct electronic transactions will generate a different response than a situation where a user may have lost an e-mail message.

The response team should include representation from these individuals.

- Management
- Technical personnel
- Legal counsel
- Team coordinators
- Communication specialists

Be sure to define the basic procedures for handling an incident. In case of an incident, each of the following points should be implemented.

1.   Preparation. The team should have a charter.

2.   Incident detection. The processes and tools to detect an incident should be in place.

3.   Immediate action. This needs to be prioritized based on a scale of importance (more in Chapter 11).

4.   Communications. This is critical to handling an incident.

5.   Detailed situation analysis. Observe and report what happened.

6.   Recovery. Get the business running again.

7.   Feedback. How can we keep this from happening again?

Following are some general guidelines to help you set up and manage your incident response team.

- Take a look at http://www.cert.org/nav/recovering.htm.
- Create a hard-copy list of contact names, telephone numbers, and e-mail addresses.
- Test the processing on a regular basis.
- Test your backups.
- Test your communication process.

2.5.10   Acceptable use policies

The acceptable use policy section states how users will be allowed to use network resources. There should be several policies created.

- Acceptable use for e-mail
- Acceptable use for network access
- Acceptable use for data disclosures

2.5.11   Change control

Some people may argue that change control is not a security concern, but without adequate change control, a site can crash without warning. Hence, our future discussions will address change control as a security concern. Just a simple change can impact the infrastructure and/or application. A concrete check for this is, "Does the site have a change control system and/or policy in place?"

2.5.12   Training

End-user training if very important. A successful security program will include various training methods. These can include:

- Classroom training

- Frequently Asked Questions (FAQs) documentation

- An Internal Web page (Intranet) shows
    - Current Bugs
    - Virus information
    - Corporate Security policies
    - FAQs

An educated user is an important weapon in keeping your environment secure.

2.5.13   Compliance

The Compliance section of your security policy will show how you maintain your security. Compliance can include:

- Audit procedures

- User training schedules

- Vendor use, via audits, of corporate resources.

Most companies also include an employee compliance application. This application is used to track when employee read and agree to the corporate security policies. Most companies required employees 'certify' themselves every year.

2.6   Implementation

We started by reviewing the business, looking for the methods to securely conduct business both internally and externally. From this analysis we determined the core business requirements and identified the stakeholders, customer requirements, and our business partners. We also identified our competition as well as industry trends and standards. As a result, we know what we are trying to protect and from whom to protect it. We also saw that security can be a competitive asset.

Our next step was to review our network and determine what was needed to set up a secure network. We then examined the risks involved and saw how to expand business influence by mitigating the various identified risks.

The policies were defined to protect and educate the various parts of the business. Now we are ready to create our first plan. This first cut will drive us throughout the rest of the security implementation process. Create a plan (the "security project") that will detail the steps required to secure your business environment.

Your project should address the design, structure, and configuration of an evolving secure business infrastructure. The technical infrastructure will ensure that a business security environment is in place to support the user community and keep the business running.

The security project should include the following:

1.   Definitions of the goals and objectives of what is needed based on the analysis obtained so far. This will include designing, building, and configuring the technical infrastructure environment.

2.   Definitions of the scope of what is needed to secure your environment. This will include implementing performance and tripwire monitoring of the new security environment.

3.   The plans for roll-out of the new infrastructure that you designed. Be sure to include a pilot run(s) to test your assumptions about what you have designed.

4.   Finally, the roll-out of the new infrastructure. Indicate the communications systems needed to support the implementation, including training requirements and end-user support.

2.6.1   Goals and objectives

Following are the overall goals of the security project.

1.   Deliver a steady-state platform to support the business's security "vision." This includes design, implementation of a comprehensive common security infrastructure, effective support organization, and technology management processes needed to support the use of security by all business professional and support staff.

2.   Define and facilitate enterprise strategies for secure network evolution and remote connectivity.

2.6.2   The scope

The scope should describe key elements of the project, including the following.

- Designing, building, and configuring secure business networks.

- Creating the budget to implement the security. Each process in the organization should drive the budget. Every process has a security component.

- Procuring the equipment and/or tools, including secure facilities, equipment, and tools.

- Configuring and testing the secure environment, including equipment and internal and external connectivity.

- Reviewing any recommendations for short-term and long-term modifications to the network environment as necessary.

- Establishing an interim strategy until any identified network traffic issues can be resolved. Understand the network traffic volume and network SLAs (Service Level Agreements).

- Designing the security for servers and workstations (e.g., physical and logical topology, replication schedules, remote access, external connectivity, etc.).

- Defining the migration strategy for existing security plans, procedures, tools, systems.

- Establishing a security infrastructure implementation plan.

2.6.3 **Infrastructure**

The network(s) will need to be set up and configured. One mechanism to help determine the appropriate level of security is to monitor the existing networks before and after the security changes. The performance monitoring of the traffic on the various networks (trusted and nontrusted) will drive a better understanding of the actual usage of security within the business. Performance indicators should be defined in the following areas.

1.   End-user applications—from both the end-user workstation and the server

2.   Server-to-server traffic

3.   Overall network traffic utilization

4.   Remote communications

The performance indicators should be derived from the business requirements. These service levels will need to be tied in to the security requirements. The performance indicators will show both the SLA performance and the security performance. If the security implemented is impacting the business service, then that particular security tool/service will need to be reevaluated. The performance monitors will generate information that, when analyzed, will show the historical system performance trends. It is expected that the type of user and the applications used will affect the performance of the network. The roll-out plan will need to include all the various aspects of the security project. Be sure to include the following items:

1.   End-user training

2.   OS security

3.   DMZ design

4.   Incident handling procedures

5.   Disaster recovery

6.   Pilot (test the systems before going on-line)

7.   Change control systems

8.   Schedule for: pilot, training, network changes, and OS changes

Once the implementation recommendations have been generated, they need to be piloted or tested before the deployment begins for the following reasons:

1.   Prove the processes

2.   Check assumptions

3.   Determine potential failure points before production

4.   Assess individual systems and risks

A pilot will identify critical path issues, risks, and potential roadblocks. It is most interesting that the biggest detractor of a new technology solution will magically appear during a pilot. You will get all types of responses such as, "Why did you choose that tool?" and, "I know a better one." Yet this is an opportunity to refine your implementation plan and revise your tool or system selections. Just make sure you are selecting the process or tools based on security and business requirements and not the ad hoc political environment. Thus, the message here is to pilot your assumptions before going into production.

2.6.4   Pilots

Create a pilot plan. This should include the goals of the pilot, the scope, the user groups to be included, specific applications, and the evaluation criteria. The following items should be included in your pilot:

1.   Definitions of pilot goals

2.   Pilot scope

3.   Pilot evaluation criteria—what will make the pilot a success?

4.   Pilot participants—select a known group of users.

5.   Definitions of the pilot application and systems

6.   Training schedule—yes, you need to pilot the training!

7.   Pilot schedule—Who, when, and where

2.6.5   Training and execution

This is it. It's time to implement what you have been building: the client/server hardware and software to the end-user community. This includes network connectivity, operating systems, user accounts, and definition of security access levels. This should also cover the administration and support requirements, server network configurations, and maintenance procedures. This step must involve pushing the technology to the end-user community and should focus on end-user acceptance as well as evaluation of the administrative impact of end users. The following items should be considered in the final roll-out:

1.   Training—"train the trainer" and user training

2.   Installation and/or upgrading of hardware

3.   Setting up and configuring servers and network

4.   Assigning security/privileges

5.   Installing client and server software

6.   Setting up user/server accounts

7.   Evaluating and refining system and maintenance procedures

8.   A published schedule

9.   Use of ethical hackers to "confirm" the security of the environment

10.   Communications documents and memos

3

Cryptography

"I have two RC2s, and a MD5."

3.1   The history

20 8 9 19 9 19 1 19 5 3 18 5 20 (A coded message)

Picture some good ol' boys sitting around a poker table, smoking cigars, and drinking at the local saloon. Pistol Jack says, "I have an RC2, but I will raise you with a DES." Caught off guard, Tex Hunter says, "Well, if that is how you want to play, I will spike you with a triple-DES and match your RC2 with an MD5."

This all sounds like some high-stakes poker game, but what about those peculiar acronyms? In this game, our cowboys from west Texas were betting various encryption types. Now, they had no idea what they had or even what they were saying. Your job, if you choose to accept it, is to gain an understanding of what the acronyms mean and the impact this can have on how you do business on the Internet. So let's start with a bit of history. Once upon a time someone had a secret. . . .

Both Pistol Jack's and Tex Hunter's family histories trace back to a group of early pioneers known as the Securites. Pistol Jack's and Tex Hunter's ancestors had enemies known as the "Hacker Dudes." These bandits would listen in on the conversations that the Securites were having around the campfire about the next day's hunt. The Hacker Dudes would get the location of the next buffalo hunt and then go and scare off all the buffalo before the Securites could get their kill for the day. The conversation would go like this: Texasawa would say, "I saw buffalo out beyond the Crooked Sky. Let's go and get some, and afterwards we can have a feast." Then Jackawa would say, "Yup." But, thanks to the Hacker Dudes, our friends would trek to the plains only to find no buffalo. Well, Texasawa and Jackawa figured out what was going on, so they created a complex code that would keep the bandits from finding out where the buffalo were. The code went like this: Texasawa would say, "I saw some buffalo out beyond the Crooked Sky today"—wink, wink. Jackawa would say, "Yup." The translation of this was "The buffalo are really out beyond the Raging River." So the bandits would go off to the wrong place, and Jackawa and Texasawa could kill their buffalo!

Cryptography is one of the oldest systems of protecting data. Historians have found evidence of this dating back at least 4,000 years. Cryptography is believed by many to have been created around 2000 B.C., in Egypt. The ancient Chinese also used codes to hide the meaning of their works. Over the years, various systems have been used, from a simple substitution of letters or numbers to complex mathematical theorems. One of the simplest forms of cryptography is a substitution of letters for numbers. This idea was a popular prize in cereal boxes many years ago.

Table 3.1

A	B	C	D	E	F	G	H	I	J	K	L	M
1	2	3	4	5	6	7	8	9	10	11	12	13
N	O	P	Q	R	S	T	U	V	W	X	Y	Z
14	15	16	17	18	19	20	21	22	23	24	25	26

Granted, the Hacker Dudes may have been able to figure this one out, but most codes are not this simple. Cryptology is the process of changing text into some type of code or text, called ciphertext, that is not readable to the general reader. Ciphertext is the result of using a key (sometimes secret) and creating a body of text that needs to be deciphered. A key is typically some quantity or mechanism to encrypt or decrypt text or ciphertext.

Now that we know what a key is and what ciphertext is, we can encrypt and decrypt data. Using this chart, here is an example. Start out with "HELLO." Encrypting it with our code, we have "8 5 12 12 15." The formula follows:

```
Text ⇒ Encryption System ⇒ ciphertext

HELLO ⇒ Table Look-Up ⇒ 8 5 12 12 15
```

Now using the same key, we will decrypt the ciphertext.

```
Ciphertext ⇒ Encryption System ⇒ Text

8 5 12 12 15 ⇒ Table Look-Up ⇒ HELLO
```

Throughout history, all governments have used some type of encryption. During the Middle Ages, encryption was used quite heavily. Many of the early European governments used cryptography to communicate with government ambassadors.

Over time, encryption was enhanced by the use of various tools. One was a Cipher Wheel invented by Thomas Jefferson. This tool consisted of a set of wheels, each with a random order of the letters of the alphabet. The key to the system is the order of the wheels. Each wheel was placed on an axle. The message was encoded by aligning the letters along the axis of the axle such that the message was created. Any other row of aligned letters could then be used as the ciphertext. The decryption required the person who received the message to configure the letters of the ciphertext along the axis and find a set of the letters that was readable. The recipient then had a readable message.

Go to your favorite search engine and do a search for "Cryptography and Shakespeare." There are many listings for URLs and books on the use of code in Shakespearean works. Many scholars believe that either Francis Bacon, Christopher Marlowe, or Edward de Vere actually wrote the various plays and sonnets and that the clues are encoded in the writings. It may be that if you somehow decoded the plays, you could perhaps find that Romeo actually loved a girl named Ethel!

As you can see, encryption and cryptography are not new and are not a technology created for the Internet. They are as old as language itself and have been used for many different purposes, mostly to keep secrets from an adversary. If you study any war throughout history, you will find the use of some type of encryption. During the U.S. Civil War, both the Northern and Southern armies used ciphers. During World War II, the Americans broke a Japanese code known as "Purple." The ability to decrypt the information contained in the code assisted the Americans in battles with Japan. The "Purple" team was led by William F. Friedman, who, during his spare time at Cornell University, worked with cryptologists in trying to prove that Francis Bacon, through his encrypted signature in plays, actually wrote works credited to Shakespeare! Also in World War II, the Navajo Native American language was used by American military forces to transmit messages by telephone and radio. Its syntax and tonal qualities, not to mention dialects, make it unintelligible to anyone without extensive exposure and training. It has no alphabet or symbols and is spoken only on the Navajo lands of the American Southwest. One estimate indicates that fewer than 30 non-Navajos could understand the language at the outbreak of World War II. Check out *Windtalkers* (MGM-2002). This movie, based on actual events during World War II, explains how U.S. troops utilized Navajo Indians and their complex language to communicate without the Japanese intercepting messages. Nicolas Cage and Christian Slater play Marines assigned to act as bodyguards to protect the Navajo soldiers. URL http://www.mgm.com/windtalkers/.

Also during World War II, German codes were predominantly based on the "Enigma" machine. On an old farm outside of London, known as Bletchley Park, Alan Turing, a leading mathematician, developed an electromechanical machine that would crack the code of the Enigma keys. With this system and the capture of Enigma machines from U-boats, the Allies were able to learn of the planned activities of the U-boat, panzer, and bombing raids. For a picture of the Enigma machine see http://www.turing.org.uk/turing/pi1/emac.gif or http://www.turing.org.uk/turing/bio/part4.html. A great Enigma emulator in the form of an applet can be found at http://www.ugrad.cs.jhu.edu/~russell/classes/enigma/.

Here is some code to make with this applet. See if you can crack an Enigma code from World War II.

    NMQXIOWFPB

E-mail the results to Tim-Speed@charter.net. Sorry, no prizes for this!

3.2   Key types

So how does all this wonderful history impact our businesses and us? We need to get to present-day technology. Let us take one more look at the keys and how they are used in encryption.

There are basically two types of key-based algorithms: symmetric (secret-key) and asymmetric (public-key). The difference between these is that the symmetric keys use the same algorithms for encryption and decryption. The asymmetric algorithm uses a different key for encoding, another for creating the ciphertext, and another for decoding, or translating, the ciphertext into readable text. You may have heard of the term "public-private key." This is the technique that current encryption systems use within today's Internet environment.

Figure 3.1 shows how a public-private encryption system works. The system will generate a key pair for an assigned user. One public key and one private key are generated. These keys are mathematically related so that the

Figure 3.1

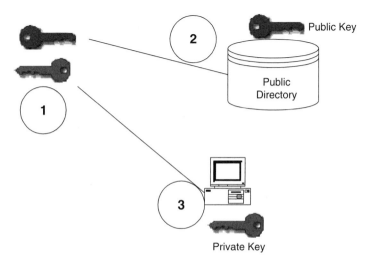

private key can decrypt any messages that are encrypted by the public key. Here is an example of encrypting a message.

1. The public-private key pair is created.

2. The public key is placed into a public directory. A directory is a storage facility that can house user names and information about the users (e.g., e-mail address, phone numbers, and the public key).

3. The private key is stored in an area that only the designated user can access, such as his or her local PC or laptop. Note: This example does not address roaming users and the management of keys.

4. You can now send an encrypted message. From the directory you select the intended recipient's user name (this is managed via a software program).

5. The message is encrypted using the targeted user's public key (see Figure 3.2).

6. The data is now transferred between systems, applications, or e-mail as ciphertext. You now have an encrypted message that is difficult for a third party to read (see Figure 3.3). But how can we read the message? This is where the private key is used.

Figure 3.2

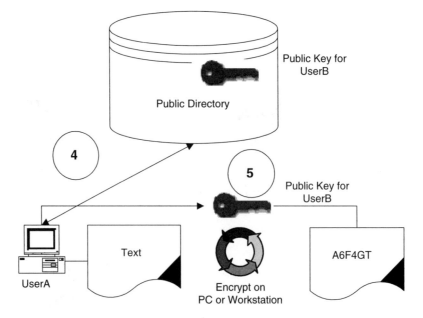

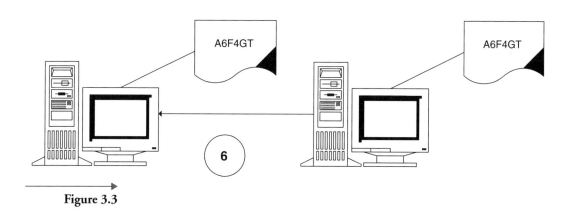

Figure 3.3

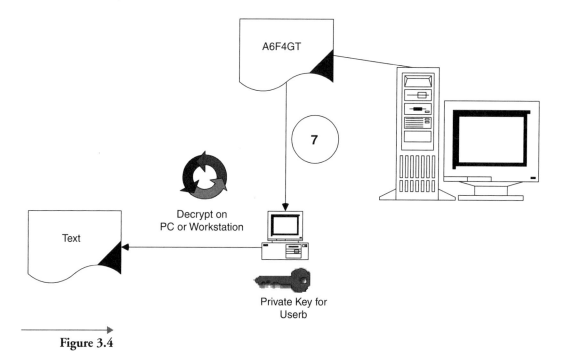

Figure 3.4

7.   The user then retrieves the message and decrypts it with his or her private key. The private key may be locked with a password that only the user knows. The message is now readable by the targeted user (see Figure 3.4).

3.3   RSA: public and private key

We now have a better idea about how the public-private system works. It is based on a technique patented by Diffie-Hellman in 1974 and formatted into architecture by Rivest, Shamir, and Adelman (RSA Data Security, Inc.). You can find more information at http://www.rsa.com and http://www.verisign.com.

One example of the RSA implementation is PGP (Pretty Good Privacy). Philip Zimmermann originally created PGP. Zimmermann was the first person to make military-grade cryptography available to the general public. PGP can be used to send encrypted messages via most any e-mail system. All that is needed is software available from http://www.pgp.com and the public key of the party to whom you want to send an encrypted message.

There are several methods to encrypt messages. One standard is S/MIME. There are also secret key systems and other systems to encrypt data as it travels from one location to another.

One process that can be used from a byproduct of public-private keys is "digital signatures." Digital signatures can be used to authenticate messages and prevent forgeries and/or tampering.

Following are encryption techniques that you will need to be familiar with:

- DES—the U.S. government's data encryption standard, a cipher that operates on 64-bit blocks of data using a 56-bit key. IBM developed DES under contract to NIST (National Institute of Standards and Technology).

- Triple DES—a cipher like DES that operates on 64-bit data blocks. The difference is that Triple DES uses the basic DES cipher three times.

- RC2—a variable-key-size symmetric block cipher that can serve as a replacement for DES.

- RC4—a variable-key-size symmetric stream cipher known for being faster than DES.

- PEM—the Internet privacy-enhanced mail standard. PEM includes encryption authentication and key management. The details of PEM can be found in Internet RFCs (Requests for Comments) 1421 through 1424.

- S/MIME (Secure/Multipurpose Internet Mail Extensions)—provides a method to send and receive secure MIME messages. S/MIME is included in the latest versions of various web browsers from Netscape and Microsoft. S/MIME is based on the RSA public-key cryptography systems. See RFCs 2311 and 2312 for more information on S/MIME.

- MD2, MD4, and MD5 (MD stands for Message Digest)—A digest is a computed value known as a hash. A hash creates a fixed-length string from a block of data. The hash is created based on the content of the message. Using a hash or message digest, a user will digitally sign a message. This process will identify the person who sent and/or created the message. MD2, MD4, and MD5 are hash functions created by Ron Rivest of RSA, Inc. Each one will create a 128-bit digest. MD2 is the slowest, MD4 the fastest. At the time of this writing, the MD5 algorithm is the de facto hashing standard for digests. See Internet RFCs 1319, 1320, and 1321 for more information.

- SHA-1 (secure hashing algorithm)—an NIST-sponsored hashing system that has been adopted by the U.S. government. SHA-1 produces a 160-bit hash, which is larger than the 128-bit hash and is slower than MD5. One fact about all computed digests is that they are very difficult to duplicate. Example: If you change one bit in message for an existing MD5 digest, then up to half of the digest will change.

At this point you may be thinking, "My head hurts! MD2, RC2, RFCs! 160-bit hash! I'll never use all these things!" So before we delve any further into this topic, let us take a break and address a few business concerns. We will take a side trip—a three-hour tour, if you will.

3.4   PKI and business solutions

What will all this security do for your business and how will it keep it secure? Let's look at several business scenarios.

- You are sending important messages to sales reps via the Internet to different parts of the world. These sales reps travel extensively and carry a laptop with them. How can you protect these messages from unauthorized access?

- Vendors place orders into an Extranet. This Extranet will take the orders and trigger an immediate shipment to the vendor. "But wait," the vendor says. "I did not order 10,000 horseshoes." How can you prove the vendor actually ordered the horseshoes?

- Your business also sells horseshoes to customers who pay by credit card. How can you keep the credit card information safe and secure during transmission between the customer's browser and your web server (i.e., prevent the bandits from getting the card and expiration data)?

- Your business has 1,000 users worldwide. You know who these users are, and these users provide at least 80 percent of your sales via the Internet. You have heard from your techie smart people that user names and passwords are not secure without SSL. But these users also need to send encrypted e-mail. Wow! How do you solve this problem?

Before we start to review each scenario, we need to add a disclaimer. These scenarios are here to facilitate a discussion for real-life examples. There are several methods to solve these problems, and the method presented may not necessarily be the right one for your business. As you read in Chapters 1 and 2, you must balance the solutions with your business requirements. These examples are presented here to demonstrate technical solutions. With that said, here they are.

3.4.1   Scenario one

Example: You are sending important messages to sales reps via the Internet to different parts of the world. These sales reps travel extensively and carry a laptop with them. How can you protect these messages from unauthorized access?

S/MIME is the solution for this problem. S/MIME has nothing to do with Marcel Marceau. The problem here is that you need to send important messages via the Internet, a potentially dangerous place where someone unscrupulous can easily intercept your messages and decipher them unless you encrypt the message via a method such as S/MIME. Other methods such as PGP may be better, but first a point will be made here and then we will talk more about PGP.

As we said before, S/MIME provides a method to send and receive secure MIME messages. So what exactly is a MIME message? MIME is described in the IETF standard RFC 1521 and explains how an electronic message is formatted. MIME (Multipurpose Internet Mail Extensions) is a set of specifications that describes a method to offer text via various character sets and multimedia. In order to fully understand S/MIME we also need to cover a topic called "certificates." Chapter 7 will take you through a detailed certificate discussion.

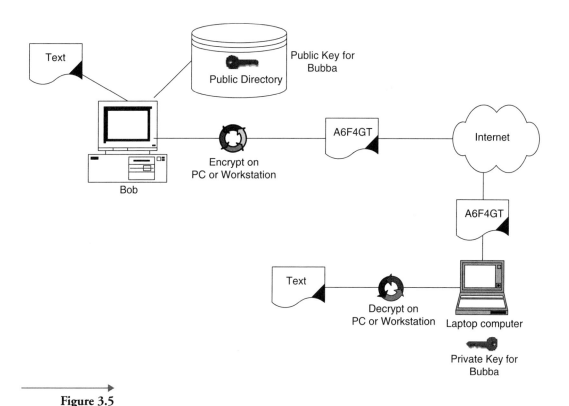

Figure 3.5

Figure 3.5 is an example of a certificate, a digital identity that is linked to a specific user or person. In our example, a certificate will be placed into each user's e-mail system, another is placed into the public directory (the public key), and another is placed into the e-mail client (the private key).

In our example, Pistol Jack sends a message to Tex Hunter. Jack finds Tex's public key in the directory and sends him a message. Jack's workstation software encrypts the message and it is then sent via the Internet (SMTP) to Tex's workstation (via a service provider and a POP account). When Tex opens the message, it is automatically decrypted. Now Tex can reverse the process. If he has Jack's public key or access to the directory where Jack's key is stored, then Tex can send an encrypted message back to Jack. This process is accomplished by the S/MIME protocol. See these RFCs for more information.

- S/MIME Version 2 Message Specification (RFC 2311)
- S/MIME Version 2 Certificate Handling (RFC 2312)

The solution for our first problem is to implement a mechanism to send S/MIME messages between the home office and the person in the field.

3.4.2   Scenario two

Example: Vendors place orders into an Extranet. This Extranet will take the orders and trigger an immediate shipment to the vendor. "But wait," the vendor says. "I did not order 10,000 horseshoes." How can you prove the vendor actually ordered the horseshoes?

In this example, the vendor said they did not place the order that you received into your on-line order system. From the Internet perspective, it can be difficult to say exactly who "someone" is. It is easy to impersonate another person, unless a digital certificate is being used.

The same digital certificate that is used for reading encrypted mail can also be used to digitally sign documents. When the document is signed, you can then tell who actually sent the document. With messages sent on the Internet, it is easy to modify the "from" field and spoof the identity of the sender. No problem there. We will require that the sender digitally signs all orders so we can prove that the messages really originated from the vendor. There are many issues to this problem, and we will stick with our case in point, digital signatures. (The assumption is made that the order did arrive and our order processing department did not make an error.) This process of proving who actually sent the message is called "nonrepudiation." This service provides virtually unforgeable evidence that a specific action occurred or, in our case, a transaction was fulfilled. This is all possible via a certificate. (Another assumption made is that the vendor has not lost control of the certificate—stay with us on that.) Nonrepudiation can be used by both the sender of the order and the recipient—that is, the business receiving the order—to prove to a third party (such as a judge) that the sender did indeed send the transaction and also that the recipient received the same transaction that was sent. Remember the MD2 and MD5 message digests? If any one character of a message were changed, then up to half of the message digest would change. It is very difficult to modify a message and keep the message digest the same (for most of the world's population, it is impossible).

In our example (see Figure 3.6), Jack has digitally signed a message and it is sent to Tex. The software that Tex has will automatically attempt to verify

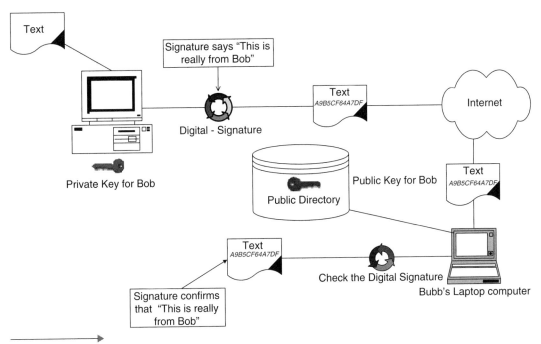

Text

Signature says "This is really from Bob"

Digital - Signature

Text
A9B5CF64A7DF

Internet

Private Key for Bob

Public Directory

Public Key for Bob

Text
A9B5CF64A7DF

Text
A9B5CF64A7DF

Check the Digital Signature

Bubb's Laptop computer

Signature confirms that "This is really from Bob"

Figure 3.6

that the signature is from Jack via the public directory. Now back to the scenario: If the vendor says that they did not send the order or that the order was for 1,000 horseshoes instead of 10,000, then you have proof that the order was sent for 10,000 horseshoes, thanks to the digital signature that they sent you (and that you required before filling the order).

3.4.3 Scenario three

Example: Your business also sells horseshoes to customers who pay by credit card. How can you keep the credit card information safe and secure during transmission between the customer's browser and your web server (i.e., prevent the bandits from getting the card and expiration data)?

Data is transmitted between your browser and the web server via some type of network and protocol. The network could be your network at the office or a dial-in system from your house. There are also networks that connect to the cable in your house. The protocol that is used in most cases by the Internet is TCP/IP, which we will discuss in a later chapter. Using a packet sniffer, the bandits can hook on to your network or at your ISP and capture your network packets. There are many places on the Internet where someone can "steal" your packets. A network packet, for this discussion, is an envelope of data. Much like you would send a letter in an envelope to a friend via the post office, you would send e-mail via packets of data via a network. This is all done for you with software and protocols. TCP/IP is the underlying protocol of the Internet. So with a packet sniffer, these packets can be captured and read. It is possible to extract all types of information such as the following:

- Where the packet is going

- Where the packet is from

- If the data in the packet is encrypted

- Any user name in the packet

- Any password in the packet

- Any data contained in the packet, such as a message or a part of a message, such as your credit card number

- Much more

In our discussion of TCP/IP to come, we will see the OSI reference model, which helps us understand the technical aspect of where we should encrypt data. In this chapter we will discuss why we encrypt the data: to establish customer trust and customer confidence. We can enable a feature on our servers called SSL (Secure Sockets Layer). SSL uses encryption technology developed by RSA Data Security, Inc. The encryption is implemented at the network layer so that anyone trying to capture a packet will receive a packet with encrypted data, which would be very difficult to decode or crack. In order to start a secure session between the client and server you need to have set up certificates on both the server and the client.

Today, most browsers used will have some type of "root certificate." This root certificate is a mechanism that identifies what company issues the certificate. There are companies known as (actually, that act as) certificate authorities (CA). These CAs will act as an authority that certifies that the server you are accessing is really the server you want. Say, for example, when you go to www.amazon.com and purchase something, you want to be sure that you are actually putting your credit card information at amazon.com and not at www.fakeyououtwithafalseaddress.com. The CA will certify that you are talking with the server to which you want to be connected. There are mechanisms that can route you to the wrong server. So, using a CA such as Verisign, you can be sure that you have connected to the correct server. You may ask, "How will I know this?" Here is how it works.

You have a business and you want to set up a secure server that will accept credit cards. Following are the steps to follow:

1.   Install the hardware.

2.   Install the software.

3.   Install the web server (called the "HTTP stack" or "HTTP server").

4.   Set up the application to process the credit card information.

5.   Set up the DNS.

6.   Create a key ring file request for your HTTP server.

7.   Send the key file request to a CA (with payment and some identification on your company).

8.   The CA will certify the request.

9.   The CA will send the request back to you.

10.   You will merge the request into your key ring file.

11.   Now you are ready to turn on SSL.

Now your question is probably, "What is the process to turn on SSL?" The answer for the most part is simple.

1.   Turn on the port (more on that later) and the port number you want to use for SSL. The default port is 443, so turn this setting "on" in your server.

2.   At the URL, enter "https" (note the "s"). Example: https://www.thisismywebpageanditissecure.com.

There are several methods to enable SSL. You can turn off the main port on a server that will accept HTTP requests: For example, Port 80. You can redirect http requests to SSL. See your server Help file to determine if your server supports these functions. Also, you can force a redirect to SSL in your application.

So how does all this information solve our business problem?

■   It enables SSL, using a known CA to certify your server key ring file.

■   It forces the credit card application to only accept https (or SSL) to send the credit card data. This will encrypt the data at the port level (more to follow on this) and keep the data safe. Safe in this case is defined as "very difficult to break."

- It tells the customer that you are using some type of encryption to keep their credit card information safe. This is the customer confidence part of the business transaction—very important.

- It monitors your server and your systems to break-ins and hacking attempts.

Figure 3.7 shows a browser accessing a server with SSL enabled. The user will use, or be forced to use, https:// in the URL name. The transmission will not be encrypted using SSL.

Stay with us, and you will see that SSL will keep the transaction safe. You may point out that the credit card information may still not be safe.

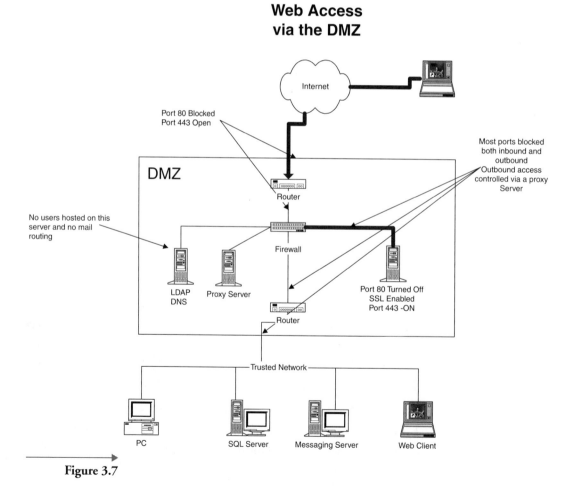

Figure 3.7

True—there have been some break-ins where credit card data was stolen. In that case, SSL could have been used and the data still be ripped off. How is that possible? Easy; the transaction was safe, but someone broke into another part of the system and ran off with the credit card data. Security must cover many facets—it's not much good if you lock only the front door and have no locks on the back door.

3.4.4   Scenario four

Example: Your business has 1,000 users worldwide. You know who these users are, and these users provide at least 80 percent of your sales via the Internet. You have heard from your techie smart people that user names and passwords are not secure without SSL. But these users also need to send encrypted e-mail. Wow! How do you solve this problem?

At some point you have likely received from your browser a pop-up window like the one in Figure 3.8. This is what is known as a "Basic Authentication" dialog box. Typically, the user name is one that a program has assigned to you or that you have assigned to yourself. The Web is full of places that require a user name. The user name is a mechanism that identifies who you are in relation to the program or data you are trying to access. The password is the key that allows you in under that user name. This is a simple and effective mechanism to access "controlled" data, but it is not very secure. In Basic HTTP Authentication, the password is passed over the network neither encrypted nor as plaintext but is "unencoded." Anyone

Figure 3.8

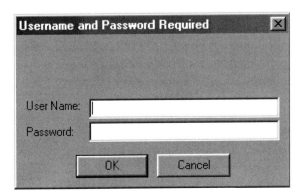

watching packet traffic on the network will not see the password, but it can be easily decoded by anyone who happens to catch the right network packet. Using a packet sniffer, you would monitor the traffic on a network and extract the password, then use a simple decoder to extract the password. You can see an on-line extract of RFC 2617 that explains more of the problem.[1]

The most serious flaw in Basic Authentication is that it results in the essentially cleartext transmission of the user's password over the physical network. It is this problem that "Digest Authentication" attempts to address.

Because Basic Authentication involves the cleartext transmission of passwords, it *should not* be used (without enhancements) to protect sensitive or valuable information.

A common use of Basic Authentication is for identification purposes, requiring the user to provide a user name and password as a means of identification, for example, for purposes of gathering accurate usage statistics on a server. When used in this way, it is tempting to think that there is no danger in its use if illicit access to the protected documents is not a major concern. This is only correct if the server issues both user name and password to the users and in particular does not allow the user to choose his or her own password. The danger arises because naive users frequently reuse a single password to avoid the task of maintaining multiple passwords.

If a server permits users to select their own passwords, then the threat is not only unauthorized access to documents on the server but also unauthorized access to any other resources on other systems that the user protects with the same password. Furthermore, in the server's password database, many of the passwords may also be users' passwords for other sites. The owner or administrator of such a system could therefore expose all users of the system to the risk of unauthorized access to all those sites if this information is not maintained in a secure fashion.

Basic Authentication is also vulnerable to spoofing by counterfeit servers. If a user can be led to believe that he is connecting to a host containing information protected by Basic Authentication when, in fact, he is connecting to a hostile server or gateway, then the attacker can request a password, store it for later use, and feign an error. This type of attack is not possible with Digest Authentication. Server implementers *should* guard against the possibility of this sort of counterfeiting by gateways or CGI scripts. In particular it is very dangerous for a server to simply turn over a connection to a gateway. That gateway can then use the persistent connection mechanism to engage in multiple transactions with the client while impersonating the original server in a way that is not detectable by the client.

If you want to send the user name and password, then use SSL. This method will encrypt the data at the network level so someone with a sniffer cannot easily decode (decrypt) the data or your passwords.

There is another method that you can use. Remember the S/MIME discussion with Scenario One? We can use the same certificate to provide authentication on the web server. There may be reasons to use both user name and password certificates but not in this discussion. So how can we do this? Following are the high-level steps:

1.   Design a certificate infrastructure.

2.   Create a certification management system. Many web servers and many vendors offer this type of service. Entrust and Verisign are two examples.

3.   Next, get the certificates to the browsers and a directory. Again, this should be part of the certificate management system.

4.   Train the users on the technology! This is critical and will be repeated again and again.

5.   Set up a support system to help the end users and administrators with any problems.

6.   Enable the application to use the certificates.

When the user accesses the web page that is enabled for https, he or she will get a prompt like the one in Figure 3.9. The user will be able to select a certificate. You may have several. Now with the selected certificate, the user can authenticate with the server. The authentication process will occur via a directory source that is internal or external to the web server. Figure 3.10 shows an example of a web server with a directory that is integrated with the web server.

In Figure 3.11, the authentication takes place at the LDAP server. The LDAP server offers several services, including directory assistance for e-mail address and authentication. The LDAP server will have the user information along with his or her public key. This key is matched (authenticated) with the authentication credentials that are sent in from the web server to which the user is attempting to get access. An LDAP-formatted query is sent to the LDAP server from the web server. This is called a bind operation. If the

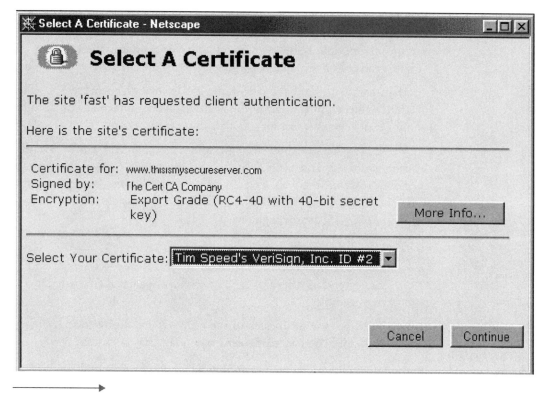

Figure 3.9

authentication is successful, a "Distinguished Name" (DN) is returned back to the web server. This name can then be used for access control to the applications. Note: You can also use the LDAP directory as a source to store passwords for basic authentication if your web server supports it.

There are several software vendors that will allow you to integrate the Web features and e-mail features under a single package. This package will allow you to share the user certificate between the mailer and the web browser. Thus, this is the solution for your business problem. The users will have access to a directory (again LDAP) for user names and public keys. When they need to send an encrypted message, they only need to select the user name and then tell the mailer to encrypt the message. Now with the same package, the user can then authenticate with the web site that is on the Internet. There is no need for any user name or passwords.

Following is an extra complication that could be a part of this or any of the above business scenarios.

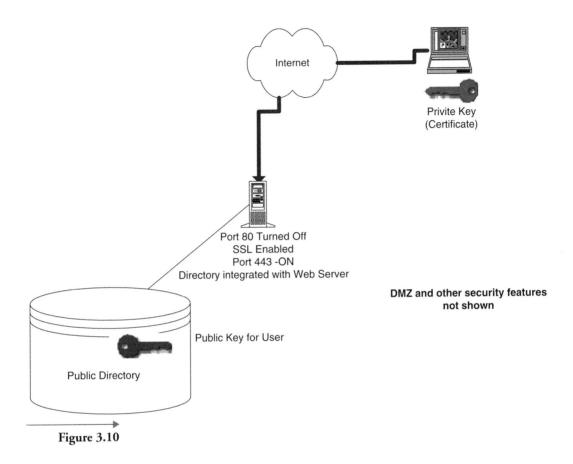

Figure 3.10

Example: The users will need to occasionally send encrypted messages to a small percentage of vendors. Each user may only have one or two vendors to whom he or she needs to send encrypted mail.

As with all these scenarios, several methods exist to solve this problem. Here is a solution: Train the users in the methods to add a new user to their personal address book in their mailer program. Many programs will allow you to add new users. Following are the steps (in this example, a vendor is a single user, not an organization with a single certificate):

1. The user will tell vendor A to send him or her a digitally signed message.

2. The user will receive the message and then add the vendor A name to the address, using an action dialog box, button, and/or script.

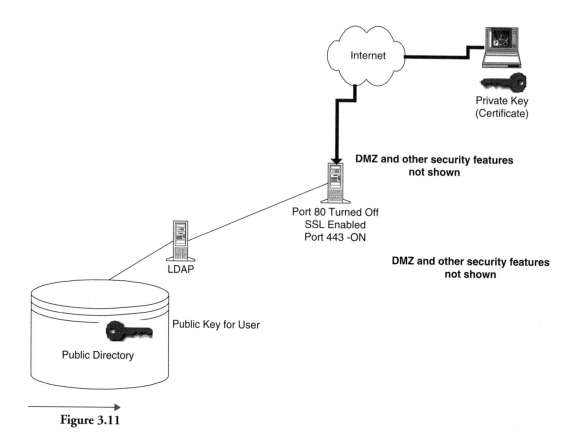

Figure 3.11

3.   This script will add vendor A's name, e-mail address, and public key to the user's personal mail directory.

4.   Now the user can send an encrypted message to that particular user (vendor).

5.   Repeat the process for each additional vendor.

6.   The user sends a digitally signed message to vendor A, and vendor A follow the same steps. (Note: There are other options available for large lists of users. This example is for managing single certificates on an exception basis.)

4

Secure Networks

Hello, I am here to hack into your network!

4.1   TCP/IP and OSI

Imagine if you will, a classroom filled with entry-level web technology students. We have some questions from the audience: "What makes up the Internet?" "What is it?" One answer is TCP/IP. "Oh that tells me a lot! It sounds like some kind of drug!" The next question is, "Where should we start and what level of detail should we go into?" The useful answers to these questions will be answered in this chapter.

TCP/IP is a very complex protocol. There are entire books dedicated to the subject. We need to discuss TCP/IP at some length in order to understand the security issues with the protocol. Throughout this chapter, we will list some books and URLs that provide further information on TCP/IP. Most major operating system vendors offer some type of course on TCP/IP. As part of the MCSE program from Microsoft (MCSE © 2000 Microsoft Corporation), there is a test that is specifically dedicated to TCP/IP. Please see the references or take a course for a full coverage of TCP/IP. We will start with a high-level overview of TCP and its components and then cover a few security-related issues.

In 1973, Vinton Cerf, a UCLA graduate student who is also known as the "father of the Internet," and Robert Kahn, an MIT math professor, developed a set of software "protocols" to enable different types of computers to exchange data. These protocols are now known as TCP/IP. The base part of the protocol is called IP, or "Internet Protocol." It is the IP part of the protocol that actually transports the packets of data between the various computer systems on the Internet. The part of the protocol that actually ports data to the applications is called "TCP." TCP is the mechanism that allows the WWW (World Wide Web) to communicate. Programs are built on top of this medium that allow communication between server and client.

There is an old story about Vinton Cerf. He was at a computer convention and was trying to make a point about the protocol, which he did by removing his overcoat to display this message on his T-shirt: IP on Everything.

We have no idea if this story is true, but it is a good one anyway.

The Transmission Control Protocol (TCP) is intended for use as a highly reliable host-to-host protocol between hosts in packet-switched computer communication networks. Hacking into computers can include port scanning, or surfing.

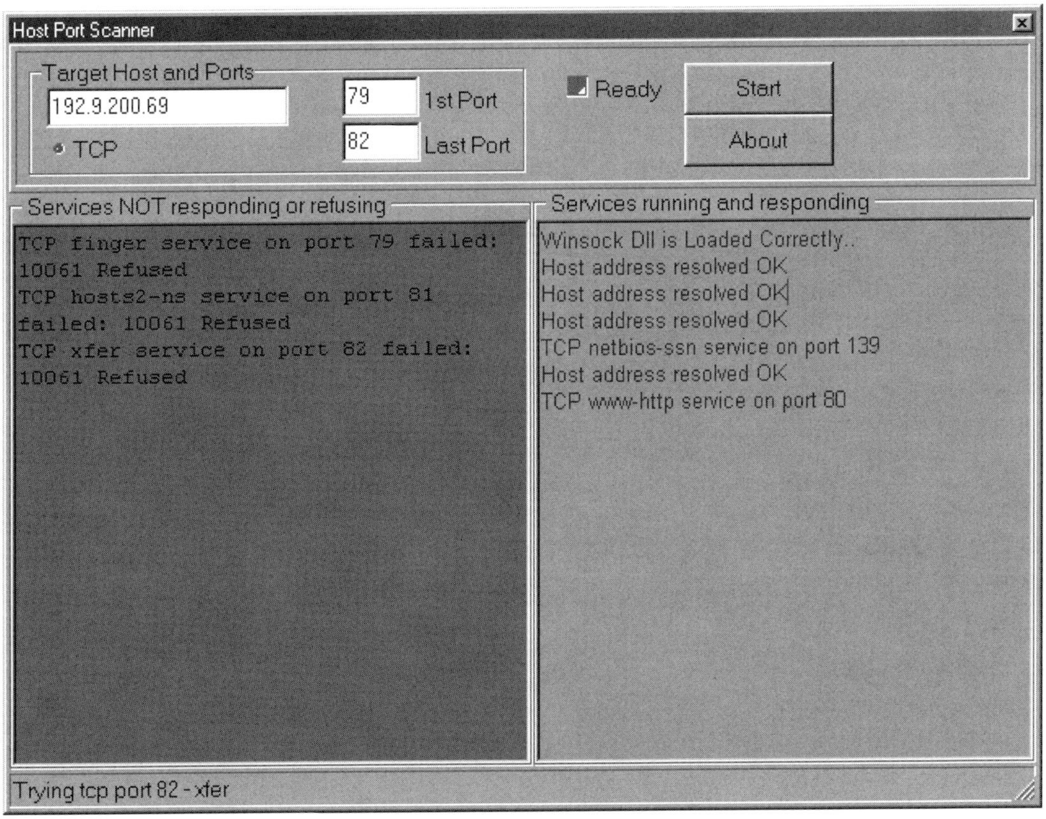

Figure 4.1

Figure 4.1 shows a port scanner run on the program on a private address on a home network, 192.9.200.69. The results showed that ports 80 and 139 were open. Looking at this, we can see that we could access those ports with some type of application. We could possibly even flood those ports with requests from several sources. Also, we could test other addresses to see if other services were available, such as Telnet, FTP, and TFTP. Then, using that information, we could attack those IP addresses and attempt to access the sites or block access to the sites with a denial-of-service attack.

Figure 4.2 shows an example from the Savant Software Program—HostScan Version 1.5.

Figure 4.2

4.2   **Denial-of-service attacks**

We have seen numerous news articles about the attacks on major web sites such as Yahoo and eBay. These premeditated attacks show the various weaknesses in the armor that surrounds many of the leading web sites on the Internet today. We see hackers taking down huge corporate web sites much like David took down Goliath. Yet, these DoS (denial-of-service) attacks are certainly not a new phenomenon. It is easy to overload a corporate switchboard, for example. Protestors will dial the target site's 800 phone number repeatedly and prevent the company from receiving legitimate business calls. The DoS can do the same thing. Actually, these incidents are but one form of a DoS attack. According to CERT, "A denial-of-service attack is characterized by an explicit attempt by attackers to prevent legitimate users of a service from using that service."[1]

One example of these DoS attacks includes flooding a network with bogus traffic. These attacks will prevent legitimate users from accessing the server. One simple but effective DoS attack was called the "Ping of Death." The Ping of Death was able to exploit a simple maintenance tool that is used to test IP networks. Using this tool, hackers would flood a network with large packet requests, causing a system to crash. Subsequently, the service would not be available. Following are some other examples of DoS attacks:

---

1.   (http://www.cert.org)

Tribe flood network

The Tribe Flood Network distributed a denial-of-service attack tool. http://www.securityfocus.com/templates/archive.pike?list=

   1&date=1999-12-01&msg=Pine.GUL.4.20.9912071044490.9470-100000@red7.cac.washington.edu

WinArp/Poink

The WinArp/Poink denial-of-service attack involves the attacker sending very large amounts of ARP packets to the target machine. http://www.indy.net/~sabronet/dos/winarp.html

TCP SYN flooding and IP

This attack can overload TCP with its own handshake protocol. http://www.ciac.org/ciac/bulletins/g-48.shtml

Spoofing attack domain name system (DNS) query

This attack may allow remote denial-of-service attacks against target hosts whose IP addresses are spoofed in the DNS query. http://www.ciac.org/ciac/bulletins/j-063.shtml

WINDOWS NUKE (newk) OOB attack on port 139

Taking advantage of the Out of Bound (OOB) security hole on port 139. Also known as "Nuke aka Newk." The bug in both Win95 and NT makes almost any Windows OS running machine an easy target. http://www.cert.org

The ping of death (ICMP attack)

The attacker will send a string of oversized packets to try to lock the target systems. Normally a ping packet's size is about 32 to 64 bytes. The "Ping of Death" is when you send a very large ping. Example: "ping -l 65510 host.ip.address"

Spamming/flaming (E-mail bombing)

This is actually very easy. Just send someone 10,000 messages each of 10 meg or more. This can screw up many different systems:

- The inbound gateways
- The ISP
- The corporate network

It can also overload the mail server and fill up the disks.

As you can see, hackers can take advantage of the systems and processes built into the TCP/IP architecture. Denial-of-service attacks are TCP/IP attacks (although not limited to just TCP/IP) designed to tie up your servers (or workstations) by sending a series of bogus requests. A well-directed denial-of-service attack is likely to have some impact on your computing business infrastructure, because at some point along your Internet defense, there will be a weakness that will accept these bogus requests.

So how do you keep the "bad dudes" from performing a DoS on your systems? First the bad news: There will always be new methods that hackers will find to attack your systems, so there is no one solution. There are some basic steps you can take to minimize disruptions from a DoS attack:

1.   Monitor the server's system performance metrics and determine normal operating activity for disk, CPU, and network traffic. Have a baseline of daily, monthly, and yearly activities levels. Also, implement real-time monitoring to detect any deviation from the defined baseline.

2.   Monitor the disk space limits and amount of messages that travel through your network or gateways (more on messaging security in a later chapter).

3.   Review the various advisories, including CERT and your software vendors. This review should include keeping up with the maintenance releases from your O/S vendors and/or other software vendors.

4.   There are several products on the market that can analyze network traffic and determine if a DoS is occurring. See your router hardware vendor for this type of software/hardware.

5.   Work with your ISP and see if they have any tools or processes that can detect or deter the DoS attacks.

6.   Log and report the DoS attacks, including the DoS attacks as part of your incident handling processes. Record the following information:

     1. The time of the attack

     2. Your own IP address at the time of attack

     3. The attacker's IP address if possible

     4. What domain the attacker's IP address is from

7.   Contact your SP for help and have them advise you of your rights in this matter.[2]

4.3   Virtual private networks

Here is the scenario: You are the network manager of a large company. You know that you must have secure access to five sites around the world. Each site will need to have 20 to 30 computers with a bandwidth of an equivalent of T1 (1.544 Mbps) to each site. One answer to this problem would be to set up direct connect circuits to each site—in essence, set up a private network. This actually can be the "right" answer. But for our discussion, this is not a good answer. Why? Cost and availability are just two issues. In some countries, this could be very expensive and may not even be available. So what can you do? You can use the Internet. Now you may have the same problem with availability, but more and more countries are providing T1 access speeds to local businesses. Using the Internet, you can see that your data is not secure, and options like SSL and e-mail encryption are not viable options. A solution in this case is a "virtual private network" (VPN). A VPN is a collection of technologies that creates secure connections via the Internet. In simplest terms, a VPN is a secure connection between two or more locations over some type of a public network. Let's look at four different protocols for creating VPNs over the Internet:

1.   PPTP—point-to-point tunneling protocol

2.   L2F—layer 2 forwarding

3.   L2TP—layer 2 tunneling protocol

4.   IPSec—IP security protocol

PPTP, L2F, and L2TP are largely targeted at remote access, like dial-up. LAN-to-LAN solutions would use IPSec.

4.3.1   Point-to-point tunneling protocol (PPTP)

PPTP has been deployed for remote users since Microsoft included support for it in RAS (remote access server) for Windows NT Server 4. PPTP builds on the functionality of PPP to provide remote access that can be tunneled through the Internet to a destination site or computer. PPTP encapsulates PPP packets using generic routing encapsulation (GRE) protocol, which

---

2.   See http://www.cert.org/tech_tips/denial_of_service.html#3A2 for more information.

gives PPTP the flexibility of handling protocols other than IP. PPTP is designed to run at open systems interconnection (OSI) Layer 2 and IPSec operates at layer 3.

4.3.2   Layer 2 forwarding (L2F)

L2F is another protocol, developed by Cisco Systems. It is similar to PPTP in that L2F is a layer 2 tunneling protocol.[3]

4.3.3   Layer 2 tunneling protocol (L2TP)

L2TP is a combination of Microsoft's PPTP and the Cisco L2F. L2TP is a network protocol and it can send encapsulated PPP packets over IP, X.25, Frame Relay, or Asynchronous Transfer Mode (ATM) networks.[4]

For example, say each city has its own network but all of the networks are connected via a VPN as in Figure 4.3. The VPN is secured by using a technology known as IPSec. IPSec is a simple version of an emerging Internet IP security protocol. (Review the series of IETF standards for IPSec, which have been published as Request for Comments 1825 to 1829.) A virtual private network is a network that is not in actuality private but is as safe as a private network. If a company has its main office in Dallas and a branch office in London, the traditional solution for connecting the networks would be to lease a line for each site.

4.3.4   IP security protocol (IPSec)

The VPN technology using IPSec will encrypt all outgoing data and decrypt all incoming data so that you can use a public network, like the Internet, as transportation media. IPSec can support two encryption modes: transport and tunnel. Transport mode encrypts the data portion of each packet but leaves the header unencrypted. The more secure tunnel mode encrypts both the header and the data. At the receiving side, an IPSec-compliant device decrypts each packet. For IPsec to work, the sending and receiving devices must share a key. Remember the public-private key system? This system uses a public key to encrypt the data. This is accomplished through a protocol known as Internet Security Association and Key Management Protocol/Oakley (ISAKMP/Oakley), which allows the receiver to obtain a public key and authenticate the sender using digital

---

3.   For more information regarding L2F, check out http://www.ietf.org/rfc/rfc2341.txt.
4.   See http://msdn.microsoft.com/library/backgrnd/html/msdn_vpn.htm for more information.

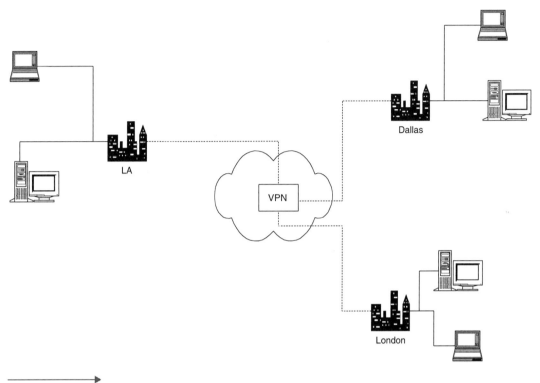

Figure 4.3

certificates. Key-based cryptography requires a method of exchanging a key, or one key of a pair, between the sender and the recipient. This mutually agreed-upon information forms a security association. In the IPSec architecture, this security information is exchanged as part of the key management session, which precedes any exchange of sensitive data. ISAKMP/ Oakley supports more negotiation and has been selected as the basis for the IPSec's mandatory key management protocol for IPv6. ISAKMP/Oakley uses the Diffie-Hellman combination algorithm. It continues with detailed descriptions of how to install and use VPN technologies that are available for Windows NT and UNIX, such as PPTP and L2TP, Altavista Tunnel, Cisco PIX, and the secure shell (SSH).

Following are some VPN product examples you can check out.

- http://www.ibm.com
- http://www.cisco.com
- http://www.microsoft.com
- http://www.baltimore.com/products/unicert/

4.4   Secure sockets layer

In Chapter 3, we introduced you to the term SSL. SSL (Secure Sockets Layer) is a protocol designed by Netscape Communications. SSL provides for the encryption of a session or authentication of a server. It is a network protocol layer, located directly under the application layer with responsibility for the management of a secure, encrypted, communication channel between a server and client. SSL is implemented in major web browsers such as Netscape and Internet Explorer. The address keyword https:// is used to designate a secure, or SSL enabled, connection.

One of the most basic functions of SSL is message privacy. SSL can encrypt a session between a client and a server so that applications can exchange and authenticate user names and passwords without exposing them to eavesdroppers. Hackers can use IP sniffers and scanners to capture copies of all packets that pass between a client and server during a session. This information is then available in an unencrypted, cleartext format. One example could be a basic authentication between a browser and a server. The browser attempts to access a page that requires authentication, a user name, and a password. The server will return a status code back to the browser (for example, 401). This status code tells the browser to generate a prompt for the user name and password. The user then enters the user name and password, and this data is sent back to the server. In this example of basic HTTP authentication, the password is passed over the network, not encrypted, but not as plaintext either; it is "unencoded." Anyone watching packet traffic on the network will not see the password in the clear, but the password will be easily decoded by anyone who happens to catch the right network packet, and this is very easy to do. With SSL, however, all transmissions following the initial handshake are encrypted to prevent transmissions from being captured. The client and server prove their identities by exchanging certificates. All traffic between the SSL server and the SSL client is encrypted using a key and an encryption algorithm negotiated during the SSL handshake, which occurs at session initialization. Next, the SSL protocol ensures that messages between the sender system and receiving system have not been tampered with during the transmission. This ensures a secure channel between the client and server. SSL uses a combination of mathematical functions known as hash functions. (Hashing was discussed in Chapter 3.) Also, a shared secret is used to encrypt the data with a strong cipher. If, during a session, a packet is damaged or indecipherable, we must assume that tampering has occurred. An ongoing process of verifying and checking the packets will preserve the integrity of the messages. In SSL v3.0, initiation of the handshake can even be carried out by the client or in the middle of an open session, thus allowing the systems to change the algorithms and keys used whenever they want. Included in this process is server authentication (with X.509v3, clients can also be authenticated). This is the process of determining the server identity via the exchange of X.509 certificates. A server's identity is coded into a public-key certificate that is exchanged during the SSL handshake.

SSL was designed to make its security and services transparent to the end user. Normally a user would follow a URL (see RFC 1738) to a page that connects to an SSL-enabled server. The SSL-enabled server would accept connect requests on 443 (default). The default port for non-SSL access is port 80. When it connects to port 443, the handshake process will establish the SSL session. Now, all traffic between the server and client will be encrypted. The handshake is composed of three basic steps:

1.   The client and server (or server and server) exchange X.509 certificates to prove their identity. As part of the process, the certificates are checked against expiration dates and for evidence of tampering.

2.   Next, the client generates a set of keys to be used for encrypting the data. The client encrypts a cipher key with the public key that it received from the server. The client then sends the encrypted key to the server. The server now decrypts that key with its private key.

3.   Finally, the client and server select the hash function and the message encryption cipher algorithm. The server will ask the browser to provide a list of all possible ciphers that it holds. The server then selects a cipher to encrypt the data, using the strongest allowable cipher that it holds in common with the client.

Figures 4.4 and 4.5 show examples of the ciphers that can be used with other servers, in these cases SSL v2 and SSL v3.

You will notice in Figure 4.5 that there are many different key strengths. Servers use these key strengths and browsers to determine the strength of the encryption that should be used. But, alas, all is not well in "encryption land." The issues are complex due to the involvement of various governments. The United States government watches closely over what is happening with encryption technologies. There are two government agencies that control export of encryption software: the Bureau of Export Administration (BXA) in the Department of Commerce, authorized by the Export Administration Regulations (EAR), and the Office of Defense Trade Controls (DTC) in the State Department, authorized by the International Traffic in Arms Regulations (ITAR) and U.S. Department of Commerce, Bureau of

Figure 4.4

Export Administration Office of Strategic Trade & Foreign Policy Controls, and the Information Technology Controls Division. The old rule was you could not export any key size greater than 64 bits. This rule has changed and will likely change again in the future. See the following web sites for more information:

- http://www.eff.org/pub/Privacy/ITAR_export/

- http://204.193.246.62/public.nsf/docs/

60D6B47456BB389F852568640078B6C0#a

- http://www.bxa.doc.gov/Encryption/licchart.htm

- http://www.bxa.doc.gov/Encryption/Default.htm

- http://www.bxa.doc.gov//PDF/1231ERC.pdf

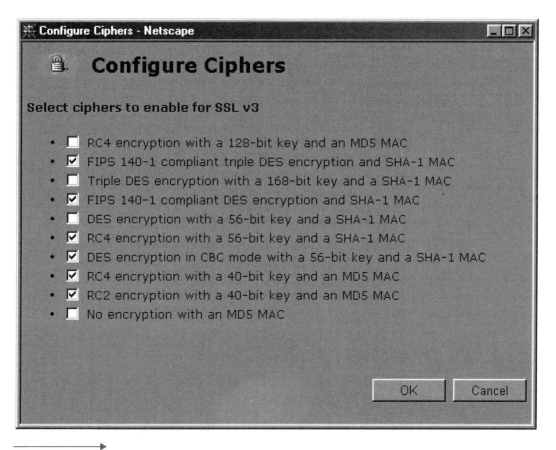

Figure 4.5

Before you start rolling out browsers worldwide, do the following.

1.   Determine in which countries you will be doing business.

2.   Check with your legal department to determine current U.S. export laws. There are some countries that you cannot export to for any reason. (See section 740.17 of the Federal Register—Vol. 63, no. 251.)[5]

3.   Determine what the import laws are of the countries in which you will be doing business. Some countries limit encryption technology; be sure to check on this. As of this writing, France and China are two such countries. For more examples see the following:

5.   http://www.bxa.doc.gov//PDF/1231ERC.pdf

- http://www.cnnfn.com/digitaljam/newsbytes/124890.html

- http://news.cnet.com/news/0-1003-200-1570561.html

So far in the process we have talked about the SSL handshake and the encryption keys and certificates. One item left to talk about is certificates and the authority used to manage the certificates.

Certificates are, in effect, signed documents. In an SSL transaction, each device will have one. We use different forms of signed documents in our everyday lives. In most countries, including the United States, there are agencies (Department of Motor Vehicles) that certify people to legally drive a car. The steps for obtaining a driver's license are very similar between all agencies:

- The user requests a license (a certificate).

- The user makes a payment (always money involved!).

- The user may have his or her picture taken and sign the document.

- The agency will "certify" that the license is good and will provide some type of unique number that only that particular license will have.

- The license will expire at some point.

- At some point, the license may need to be renewed.

- The license gives the user the right to drive a car and is used for identification purposes.

In this example, the Department of Motor Vehicles is the certificate authority, or "CA." The CA in this case will certify that holders of licenses can drive a car and that they are really who they say they are. As for identification, we trust the holder of the license that the picture and signature are those of the license holder.

Why do we trust the license? Because we trust the agency that certified the license. So we trust this third party because the third party has implemented some type of due diligence in determining the true identity of the user. If we trust the third party, then we trust the identity of the holder of the card. Get it? If not, you may want to review this section again. This is critical in order to understand the rest of the certificate process.

With Internet certificates, the process is much the same. Certificates are signed by certificate authorities (CAs). The CA will issue certificates based on a request from the user or server. A certificate authority is a commonly trusted third party (like the government agency in the license example), who is relied upon to verify the matching of public keys to the user's identity. This process can also verify items such as e-mail name, digital signature, and access privileges.

To make this process work, all parties must trust the CA. We use digital certificates instead of a card or license. Using a CA and these certificates, we can verify a user's or server's identity over the Internet. So a certificate authority, or CA, refers to either the software or service that issues digital certificates. A certificate authority acts as the third party in a digital transaction: When a user is trying to prove his or her identity to a vendor to access an account, the vendor can verify the user's identity via the certificate authority. Digital certificates work via a technology known as public key encryption. The owner of a certificate holds two keys, a public key and a private key. The public key allows anyone to encrypt data to send to a specific user. The private key, which is accessible only to the user or owner, can send signed messages and decrypt information.

The CA will issue a certificate to a user or server (see Figure 4.6). Each certificate will have the following information:

1. Certificate owner—the certificate owner is the person that has access to use the certificate. This could be protected by a password or be placed onto a smart card or other device.

2. Name—this is the name assigned to the owner of the certificate.

3. Key serial number—each certificate should have some type of number that identifies it and is unique.

Figure 4.6

A Digital Certificate

Certificate Owner
Name: Bubba Smith
Key Serial Number: #8629728212
Expires: 5/10/2002
Private Key: (Hidden)   MIIEfTCCA+agAwIBAgIQed4BZxYqg
UuPCMTE5
Public Key: (Hidden)   MDAwMDAwWhcNMDAwMjE4MjM1O
TU5WjC5

Certificate Issued By:
Name: Billy Jo Bob CA Inc.
State: Texas

Digital Fingerprint: A3:F3:68:38:AC:95

4.   Expiration date—all certificates should have an expiration date.

5.   Private key—the private key is not shared outside of the certificate.

6.   Public key—the public key is sent to other users or a shared directory service.

7.   Certificate issued by—this section has information about the CA.

8.   Name—this is the name of the CA.

9.   Digital fingerprint—this is a number that is unique to the certificate and can be used to verify a signature's validity.

As we have seen, certificates have a limited life. They are requested and created and then are either revoked or expire. Revocation is important if private keys are compromised or if there has been a change in status or policy. Revocation of a certificate is accomplished through use of a Certificate Revocation List (CRL). Someone who is going to use a certificate might want to check against a CRL to ensure the validity of the certificate. A certificate authority will sign all certificates that it issues with its private key. The corresponding certificate authority public key is itself contained within a certificate, called a "CA certificate." A browser must contain this CA certificate in its "Trusted Root Database" in order to "trust" certificates signed by the CA's private key. So the browser will have a trusted root and the server will have a certificate that is signed by the CA (see Figure 4.7).

Figure 4.7

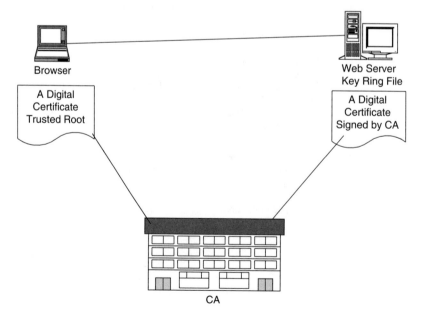

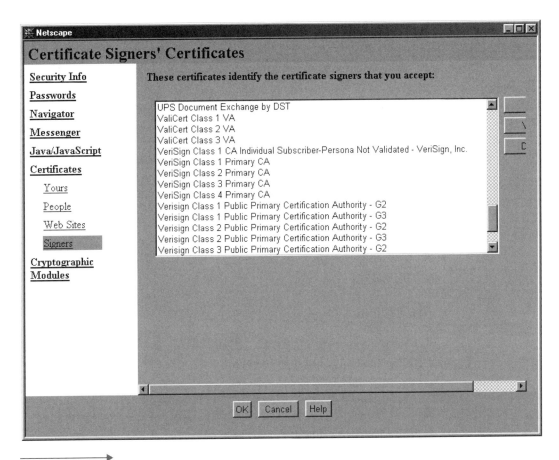

Figure 4.8

Figure 4.8 shows some examples of the root certificates that ship with a Netscape browser, where there are more than 50. If you were to use a public CA, you would use something similar to the following steps to get your server certificate (Note: These steps may vary from one software product to another.):

1. Create a key ring file.

2. Send a certificate request to the CA.

3. You may need to send identification about your company and some payment.

4. The CA will certify the request.

5. The CA will send the certified request back to you.

6.   You will then merge the certified request into your server's key ring file.

7.   Configure your software to enable SSL and open up port 443 on your DMZ.

8.   Enable your application to support SSL as needed.

9.   Hit the application with https://urlname.

Your company may choose to create its own closed, "private" certificate infrastructure for internal use. This can be accomplished with software that is provided with many web servers, you can purchase your own software, or you can have a service provider as your CA. You can also use Public CAs, such as:

- www.verisign.com

- www.entrust.com

- www.cylink.com

SSL References

- http://developer.netscape.com/tech/security/ssl/howitworks.html

- http://www.terena.nl/libr/gnrt/security/index.html

- http://www.pcwebopedia.com/Secure_Socket_Layer.htm

- http://www31.netscape.com/eng/ssl3/

- http://www.w3.org/

5

Protecting Your Intranet from the Extranet and Internet

Just walked into a Firewall.

5.1   So many choices!

A firewall is a system designed to control access to applications on a network, typically access to a private network from the public Internet. We know that when we connect to the Internet or any outside entity, we need a firewall. There are many different choices when it comes to defining the topology, selecting the vendor, and selecting the type of firewall.

There are three main types of firewall software and hardware configurations:

1.   Packet filtering

2.   Proxy server or application gateway

3.   Circuit-level gateway or generic application proxy

This chapter will help you assess the main types of firewall architectural options. In addition, an evaluation checklist exists for selecting firewall vendor solutions.

There are several reasons why we need a firewall:

- Loss of mission-critical business information

- Loss of services such as e-mail, HTTP, FTP, and EDI

- Protection of legal and confidential information

- Prevention of exposure to network servers and workstations

- Enforcement of security policies

Will firewalls solve all of your security problems? No, but they do provide a needed level of security. They do not, however, protect against users accidentally revealing a password, computers within an organization connecting to a phone that is not protected from the firewall, or insider attacks. Over 50% of all security breaches occur from insiders. Not all firewall products check incoming code for signs of viruses and Trojan horses. You will still need to implement hardware level security, OS security, application security, and solid policies and procedures. Even though they are not a 100% guarantee, you still need them in place to add additional levels of security for your enterprise's data. The question is, how much security do you really need?[1]

---

1.   Source: http://www.cert.org/security-improvement/modules/m08.html, http://csrc.ncsl.nist.gov/nistpubs/800-10/node1.html

5.1.1   Initial analysis of architectural requirements

Firewalls have traditionally been valued for the restrictions or the protection they provide. They can, however, do far more. They also act as "enablers" for an enterprise to safely interact with the Internet. Firewalls are an essential element in the infrastructure of the Internet-facing enterprise and the selection of the right components and configurations will go a long way toward not only protecting internal proprietary information but also in safely opening up opportunities for your business. By doing your homework and making the right choices, you will provide your business with a gatekeeper that screens visitors and protects the walls of your electronic community so that the modern day Billy the Kid is prevented from accessing the "town's bank."

In analyzing architectural considerations, it is important to keep in mind that many factors should be evaluated. There is no "one solution fits all" approach that is right for every business. In performing your initial analysis, and on to the final product selection, you must consider factors such as product performance, the security level desired, the availability or "dependability" desired, cost, manageability, configurability, and functional features. It will be necessary to make certain allowances or trade-offs, as not every product or architectural layout may be able to meet your every requirement. As a consequence, you must decide those factors that are most critical to your enterprise and prioritize them accordingly.

The following considerations should be included when performing your initial architectural analysis:

1.   How much traffic will be passing through the firewall system? During busier times, will a single firewall host be enough or will a multiple firewall host layout be required?

2.   Based on the nature of your proprietary data and your level of security desired, do you want to have incoming traffic pass through more than one firewall system? Are you willing to endure the extra cost and slower transaction times required in order to do this?

3.   How important is it for your enterprise to review the flow of traffic passing through the firewall system? Do you want to have the ability to screen every single message and request for linking to an external site, or are you more interested in restricting access to only certain types of sites?

4.   How critical is the dependability of your firewall system? Do you want to spend extra money on a system that is highly reliable and is available 24 hours a day, seven days a week? If you have only one

firewall device in place and it fails, what repercussions would you face? Would it affect your ability to conduct business openly and securely?

5.   Since not every product can meet your every need, do you need to consider products from more than one vendor in order to make your business less vulnerable to different types of external attacks?

6.   What unique functional features will your firewall system require based on the characteristics of the business?

7.   What is your budget for the implementation of the firewall system? Do you have carte blanche to install a state-of-the-art system, or will you have to make concessions due to budgetary constraints? Is your budget adequate to meet minimum security needs?

The answers to these questions will help guide you to the types of firewalls that are right for your enterprise.

5.1.2   Assessing the right type of firewall(s) for your enterprise

The main function of a firewall is to protect the internal proprietary data from the outside world. There are three major types of firewalls used for protecting an enterprise's Intranet, but any device that controls traffic flowing through a network for security reasons can be considered a firewall. The three major types of firewalls utilize different methods to basically accomplish the same thing—protect an internal network. The most basic type of firewall is a packet-filtering device, also known as a screening router. Packet-filtering firewalls are routers that operate in the low levels of a network protocol stack. At the higher end are the proxy-server gateways that perform proxy services for internal clients by regulating incoming external network traffic and by monitoring and providing traffic control of outgoing internal packets. The third type of firewall, known as the circuit-level gateway, relies on stateful inspection techniques. "Stateful inspection" is a filtering technique that requires a trade-off between performance and security. Let's look at the three main firewall types.

Packet-filtering firewalls

Packet-filtering firewalls provide a way to filter IP addresses by either of two basic methods:

1.   Allowing access to known IP addresses

2.   Denying access to IP addresses and ports

By allowing access to known IP addresses, for example, you could allow access only to recognized, established IP addresses, or, you could deny access to all unknown or unrecognized IP addresses.

By denying access to IP addresses or ports, for example, you could deny access to port 80 to outsiders. Since most HTTP servers run on port 80, this would in effect block off all outside access to the HTTP server.

According to a report by CERT, it is most beneficial to utilize packet filtering techniques to permit only approved and known network traffic to the utmost degree possible. The use of packet filtering can be a very cost-effective means to add traffic control to an already existing router infrastructure.

IP packet filtering is accomplished by all firewalls in some fashion. This is normally done through a packet-filtering router. The router will filter or screen packets traveling through the router's interfaces that are operating under the firewall policy established by the enterprise. A packet is a piece of information that is being transmitted over the network. The packet filtering router will examine the path the packet is taking and the type of information contained in the packet. If the packet passes the firewall policy's tests, it is permitted to continue on its path. The information the packet filtering router looks for includes (1) the packet source IP address and source TCP/UDP port, and (2) the destination IP address and destination TCP/UDP port of the packet.

Some packet-filtering firewalls will only be able to filter IP addresses and not the source TCP/UDP port, but having TCP or UDP filtering as a feature can provide much greater maneuverability, since traffic can be restricted for all incoming connections except those selected by the enterprise.

Packet-filtering firewalls are generally run on either general purpose computers that act as routers or on special-purpose routers. Both have their advantages and disadvantages. The main advantage of the general purpose computer is that it offers unlimited functional extensibility, whereas the disadvantages are average performance, a limited number of interfaces, and operating system weaknesses. The advantages of the special-purpose router are the greater number of interfaces and increased performance, whereas the disadvantages are reduced functional extensibility and higher memory requirements.

Although packet-filtering firewalls are less expensive than other types, and vendors are improving their offerings, they are considered less desirable in maintainability and configurability. They are useful for bandwidth control and limitation but are lacking in other features such as logging capabilities. If the firewall policy does not restrict certain types of packets, the packets may go unnoticed until an incident occurs. Enterprises utilizing packet-filtering firewalls should look for devices that can provide detailed logging, a simplified setup, and firewall policy checking.

Proxy-server or application gateway

Proxy servers, also known as application proxy or application gateway, use the same method as a packet filter in that they examine where the packet is being routed and the type of information contained in the packet. The application proxy, however, does not simply let the packet continue to its destination; it delivers the packet for you.

An application-proxy firewall is a server program that understands the type of information being transmitted—for example, HTTP or FTP. It functions at a higher level in the protocol stack than do packet-filtering firewalls, thus providing more opportunities for the monitoring and control of accessibility. In dispatching messages from internal clients to the external world, an application gateway acts much like a distributor and modifies the source identification of the client packets. This accomplishes two purposes: First, it disguises the internal client to the rest of the Internet, and second, it acts as a proxy agent for the client on the Internet.

By hiding the address of all internal computers, the risk of hackers gathering information about an enterprise's internal data is lessened. In the past, the use of proxy-type servers has resulted in reduced performance and transparency of access to other networks. Newer models, however, have addressed some of these issues.

Application gateways have addressed some of the weaknesses associated with packet-filtering devices in regard to applications that forward and filter connections for services such as Telnet and FTP. Application gateways and packet-filtering devices do not have to be used independently, however. Using application-gateway firewalls and packet-filtering devices in conjunction can provide higher levels of security and flexibility than using either of the two alone. An example for this would be a web site that uses a packet-filtering firewall to block out all incoming Telnet and FTP connections and routs them to an application gateway. Through the use of an application gateway, the source IP address of incoming Telnet and FTP packets can be authenticated and logged, and if the information contained in the packets passes the application gateway's acceptance criteria, a proxy is created and a connection is allowed between the gateway and the selected internal host. The application gateway will allow through only those connections for which a proxy has been created. This form of firewall system allows only those services that are considered trustworthy of passing through to the enterprise's internal systems and prevents mistrusted services from passing through without the monitoring and control of the firewall system administrators.

The advantages offered by application gateways are numerous. By hiding the source IP address of a client to external systems, additional protection is provided from the prying eyes of hackers intent on extracting information from your internal systems. The use of logging and authentication features serves to identify and authorize external services attempting to enter your internal network. Unwanted and unwelcomed guests can be recognized and kept out. This is also a very cost-effective approach, as any third-party devices for authenticating and logging only need to be located at the application gateway. Application gateways also permit the use of simpler filtering rules. Instead of having to route application traffic to several different systems, it only need be routed to the application gateway; all other traffic can be rejected.

Many types of application gateways also support e-mail and other services in addition to Telnet and FTP. Since application gateways route many forms of application traffic, they enable security policies that are based not only on source and destination IP addresses and services, but the actual data contained in the application packets can be evaluated as well.

In the case of an application gateway that is gathering and routing e-mail among an Intranet, the Extranet and Internet would view all internal users under a form based on the name of the e-mail application gateway—for example, user@name-of-email-host. The e-mail application gateway will route mail from the Extranet or Internet throughout the internal network. Internal users can send mail externally either directly from their hosts or via the e-mail application gateway that directs the mail to the destination host. Application gateways can also monitor and weed out e-mail packets containing viruses and other unwanted forms of commercial e-mail from penetrating through to the internal areas of your business.

As in the case of packet-filtering firewalls, application gateways are generally run on either general purpose computers that act as routers or on special-purpose proxy servers.

Packet-filtering devices are by and large faster performers than application gateways but characteristically lack the security offered by most proxy services.

Given the additional complexity of application gateways over packet-filtering firewalls, the additional computing resources and cost of supporting such a system should be considered when you are assessing the firewall needs for your enterprise. As an example, depending on your requirements, the host may have to support hundreds to thousands of proxy processes for all of the concurrent sessions in use on your network. As with most business decisions, the greater the performance demanded, the higher the costs that will be incurred for attaining that added performance.

Circuit-level gateways

A circuit-level gateway is similar to an application gateway, except that it does not need to understand the type of information being transmitted. For example, SOCKS servers can act as circuit-level gateways. "SOCKS" is a protocol that a server utilizes to accept requests from a client in an internal network so that it can dispatch them across the Internet. SOCKS uses sockets to monitor individual connections.

Circuit-level gateways perform the stateful inspection or dynamic packet filtering for making filtering decisions. Although circuit-level gateways are sometimes grouped with application gateways, they belong in a separate category since they perform no extra evaluation of data in a packet beyond making the approved connections between the outside world and the internal network.

The stateful inspection is a circuit-level gateway function that allows for more robust screening than that offered by packet-filtering devices, in that both packet content and prior packet history are used to establish filtering decisions. This inspection is an "add-on" function, so the circuit-level gateway device also serves as a router.

This add-on functionality provides increased performance over application proxies by compromising between performance and security criteria.

Circuit-level gateways, then, offer increased security monitoring capabilities over packet-filtering firewalls, but still rely on a well-laid-out core routing structure, and, like application proxies, can be set up to specify advanced accessibility decision making.

5.1.3   Bringing it all together using firewall evaluation guidelines

The section presented here on firewall evaluation guidelines, including the "Firewall Buyer's Assessment Form," has been used in its entirety with permission from ICSA.net.[2]

2.   Source: http://www.icsa.net/html/communities/firewalls/buyers_guide/index.shtml

Basic requirements

The exact features a firewall needs in order to effectively implement the specific policies of an organization vary. In general, however, a firewall should be able to do the following:

- Support a "deny all services except those specifically permitted" design policy, even if that is not the policy initially used.

- Support a security policy, not impose one.

- Accommodate new services and needs if the security policy of the organization changes.

- Contain advanced authentication measures or the hooks for installing advanced authentication measures if needed.

- Employ techniques to permit or deny services to specified host systems as needed.

- Log access to and through the firewall.

- Use a flexible, user-friendly IP-filtering language that is easy to program and can filter on a wide variety of attributes, including source and destination IP address, protocol type, source and destination TCP/UDP port, and inbound and outbound interface.

If users require services such as NNTP, X11, HTTP, or gopher, the firewall would do well to support the corresponding services. The firewall typically should also act as a mail gateway for Internet mail, reducing direct SMTP connections between site and remote systems, resulting in centralized handling of site e-mail. The firewall should accommodate public access to the site such that the firewall can protect public information servers while segregating them from other site systems that do not require the public to have access.

Additional requirements

The firewall should be able to concentrate and filter dial-in access (if you have that requirement). It should contain mechanisms for logging traffic and suspicious activity, as well as mechanisms for log reduction to keep logs readable and understandable. If the firewall requires an operating system such as UNIX, a secured version of the operating system should be included, along with other security tools as necessary to ensure firewall host integrity—and all operating system patches installed. Note that there is no reason for the firewall machine itself to use the same operating system as the company network.

Indeed, numerous firewalls use their own proprietary operating system, optimized for performance and security. However, managing the firewall may be simpler on a system with a familiar operating system and interface.

The firewall's strength and correctness should be verifiable. Its design should be simple so that administrators can understand and maintain it. The firewall and any corresponding operating system should be updated with patches and other bug fixes in a timely manner.

As mentioned in earlier discussion, the Internet constantly changes. New vulnerabilities can arise. New services and enhancements to other services may represent potential difficulties for any firewall installation. Therefore, flexibility to adapt to changing needs is important, as is the process of staying current on new threats and vulnerabilities. You may want to subscribe to some of the mailing lists catalogued at our web site (www.icsa.net) or consider a paid subscription to reconnaissance services such as ICSA's TruSecure Monitor.

Buy or build?

Some organizations have the capability to put together their own firewalls, either by using available software components and equipment or by writing a firewall from scratch. At the same time, plenty of vendors offer a wide range of services in firewall technology, from providing the necessary hardware and software to developing security policy and carrying out risk assessments, security reviews, and security training.

One of the advantages for a company in building its own firewall is that in-house personnel will subsequently understand the specifics of the design and use of the firewall. Such knowledge may not exist in-house for a vendor-supported firewall. On the other hand, an in-house firewall can require a great deal of time to build, document, and maintain. These costs are easy to overlook. Organizations sometimes make the mistake of anticipating only the equipment costs. When the company makes a true accounting of all costs associated with building a firewall, it could prove more economical to purchase from a vendor.

Consideration of the following questions may help the organization decide whether or not it has the resources to build and operate a successful firewall:

1.   How will the firewall be tested?

2.   Who will verify that the firewall performs as expected?

3.   Who will perform general maintenance of the firewall, such as backups and repairs?

4.   Who will install updates to the firewall, such as new proxy servers, patches, and other enhancements?

5.   Can security-related patches and problems be corrected in a timely manner?

6.   Who will perform user support and training?

Many vendors offer maintenance services along with firewall installation, so the organization can consider using those if it does not have the internal resources to perform these functions. Either way, organizations must view firewall administration as a critical job role and afford it as much time as possible. In small organizations, the task may require less than a full-time position. However, it should take precedence over other duties assigned to the responsible individual.

A firewall can only be as effective as its administration makes it. A poorly maintained firewall may become insecure and may permit break-ins while providing an illusion of security. Security policy should clearly reflect the importance of strong firewall administration, and management should demonstrate its commitment to this importance in terms of personnel, funding, and other necessary resources. A firewall should not serve as an excuse to pay less attention to site system administration. In fact, if a firewall is penetrated, a poorly administered site will be wide open to intrusions and resultant damage. A firewall also in no way reduces the need for highly skilled system administration. At the same time, a firewall can permit a site to be proactive in its system administration as opposed to reactive. Because the firewall provides a barrier, sites can spend more time on system administration duties and less time reacting to incidents and damage control.

Sites should perform the following during firewall implementation:

1.   Standardize operating system versions and software to make installation of patches and security fixes more manageable.

2.   Institute a program for efficient, sitewide installation of patches and new software.

3.   Use services to assist in centralizing system administration, if this will result in better administration and better security.

4.   Perform periodic scans and checks of host systems to detect common vulnerabilities and errors in configuration.

5.   Ensure that a communications pathway exists between system administrators and security administrators to alert the site about new security problems, alerts, patches, and other security-related information.

Given the state of the firewalls market and the speed at which the Internet is changing, nearly any organization should be able to find a commercial firewall that fits the business and security needs of the organization. Remember, a firewall can be very good at what it does, but it still is mainly a security perimeter device. Firewalls, alone, are not enough.

Further advice

Amoroso and Sharp concur that no single set of firewall features is right for all environments.[3] They recommend that each shopper select features based on the site's unique requirements. To use their example, a heavily serviced Internet connection requiring identification of all users who connect to the Internet needs user-authentication capabilities, whereas an Internet connection used only for e-mail exchange needs little firewalling at all. Amoroso and Sharp also caution against relying too heavily on grades or rankings in magazine articles and papers, as these evaluations make assumptions about site requirements. For example, speed always factors heavily in these rankings but sites with a Tl (1.5 Mbits/sec) or slower connection to the Internet will find most available firewalls fast enough to suit their needs. Further factors that could affect your choice of firewall features, according to those same authors are:

- The severity of the threat to the network

- The potential loss if an intruder breaks into the network

- Other security mechanisms already employed to protect the network and its resources

- The loss to the organization if the firewall prevents all access to and from the Internet due either to a hardware or software failure or to a successful denial-of-service attack to the firewall itself

- The services the organization wishes to support to and from the Internet

- The throughput requirements for the connection—that is, the number of simultaneous users going through the firewall

- The availability of knowledgeable firewall administrators at the site

- Potential future requirements, such as increased activity through the firewall or new Internet services requested by users

---

3.   Amoroso, Edward and Ronald Sharp. Intranet and Internet Firewall Strategies. New York: Ziff Davis. 1996.

5.2   Firewall product functional summaries

Current firewall product literature lacks true standards, a problem encountered by many firewall shoppers. Vendors naturally prepare marketing literature that puts their products in the best possible light and describes them in ways that are appropriate to the company's design and sales philosophies. However, standards have emerged in other areas of hardware and software, both in terminology and the description of features. For example, when a car brochure refers to antilock brakes or touts dual air bags, we can expect these items to fall within certain parameters.

Hoping to apply this type of standardization to firewall product descriptions, the ICSA Firewall Product Developers Consortium has supported a solution, developed by Marcus Ranum of Network Flight Recorder, Inc. (http://www.nfr.net), referred to as "Firewall Product Functional Summaries." The purpose of the firewall product functional summary program is twofold:

1.   To provide a structured format in which vendors can describe the distinguishing features and advantages of their products

2.   To provide a structured format from which potential firewall customers can compare and contrast the features and design principles of firewall products

In other words, we want vendors to provide product information in a format that allows potential firewall customers to make meaningful comparisons between products. Over the past three years, ICSA has collected Firewall Product Functional Summaries from members of the Firewall Product Developers Consortium and posted them on the ICSA web site. Copies have also been made available on the Third Annual Firewall Buyer's Guide CD. The summary format used in the program was derived through an open process including firewall vendors, agencies of the computer-security community, and the firewall customer community. Marcus Ranum coordinated this cooperative industry effort.

The next two paragraphs describe the thinking behind the Firewall Product Functional Summaries. The remainder of this section provides an overview of what firewall shoppers will find in Firewall Product Functional Summary documents.

Computer-security systems, like other mission-critical systems, must have sound basic design principles, and the implementation of those principles must be of high quality. When choosing a computer-security system, then, the customer must have a means to judge the capabilities and design principles of the system in terms of the protections required by that customer's intended deployment of the system. The Firewall Product Functional Summary program permits manufacturers of computer-security products to present their products and designs in the best possible light, while adhering to a format that encourages accurate product comparison. The summary format requests information from the vendor about design decisions made in a number of important areas, yet tries to permit the response to be as free-form as necessary so as not to constrain the vendor within the bounds of a narrow definition of what constitutes a firewall. Since the network security field is dynamic and rapidly growing, new techniques and terms are constantly brought into use. To provide a basis for clear communication, the summary format includes a simple glossary of terms and definitions. Vendors are welcome to define their own terminology, distinct from the terms in the glossary, but are requested to provide definitions in the glossary section for new terminology that is coined, and to annotate them as such. Readers are encouraged to peruse the glossary section for annotations and definitions of such new terms as may appear.

The following overview describes the contents of the sections included in the Firewall Product Functional Summary documents.

5.2.1   Product summaries

Product description

This section includes basic identifying information, such as the corporate name of the vendor and the product version to which this summary applies. The purpose of this section is to prevent confusion and to allow the vendor to supersede a version of the summary as a product is updated. The date of publication of the summary is also given.

Executive overview

This section provides a one-paragraph summary of the product: what it does and its distinguishing characteristics. The executive overview section should be relatively free of technical jargon.

Description of firewall product functional summary

This is the standard text describing the purpose of the document, as paraphrased above. It is included in each summary to explain to readers the philosophy behind the document.

Product overview

This section offers a brief description of the product's primary features. It should be more detailed than the executive overview and should include information about the types of services supported by the product, the hardware or software platform of the product, the basic overall design approach, and any distinguishing characteristics.

Vendor information

This section tells how to contact the vendor and provides an opportunity for vendor companies to describe themselves in their own terms. This section will usually include information about the size of the company, its geographical coverage, and so on.

Product security architecture

This section explains how the firewall protects itself and the systems connected to it. In cases where additional protections are provided or additional protective relationships are provided, this will include an explanation of the design principles and operation of these protective relationships.

Security architecture

This section provides an overview of the basic security architecture and philosophy of the product. This gives the vendor an opportunity to indicate why the company's chosen approach is valid, unique, and desirable, and how the overall architecture of the system enhances its security properties.

Product default operations

This section briefly describes the assumptions that the product makes on behalf of the user when the product is initially installed. This helps the customer understand the firewall's security properties as well as how much configuration the customer will have to perform on his or her own. Explaining the default options that a firewall supports gives customers a better idea of how much effort is needed to make it operational. Since a firewall implements policy, the firewall's defaults are its default policy.

Topics likely to be found here include whether services are enabled by default; whether transactions get logged by default; whether the firewall requires individual authorization at a level of users, hosts or networks; and how much help the firewall requires to tailor a policy to a specific organization's requirements.

Protection of the firewall system

This section provides a description of how the firewall system protects itself against attack. The goal of this section is to explain to potential customers why the product is secure and why the vendor believes its firewall is resistant to attack. The vendor can explain the firewall system's software design and how it enhances the firewall's resistance to attack. In addition, the vendor might discuss here how the system uses high-integrity media, operating-system technologies, access control, intrusion detection, and response capabilities to provide protection.

Protection of attached networks and hosts

This section offers a description of how the firewall system protects connected systems against attack. The goal of this section is to explain to potential customers how the product protects hosts that reside behind it and why the protective controls it implements are resistant to attack. Some topics that might appear here include how the firewall decides what to block or permit; how it implements blocking and permitting; how it protects against network spoofing; and how the firewall performs authentication, including any standards it supports.

Protection of individual hosts

This optional section describes how the firewall system interacts with individual hosts inside or outside of the firewall, if there is some kind of interaction that improves or bolsters the security of the firewall or the individual hosts. The goal of this section, if it is appropriate to the product, is to explain to potential customers what extra security-related interactions the product may provide for systems it protects and how these mechanisms resist attack. This can include discussion of the use of cryptographic protocols between the firewall and the protected nodes for authentication or confidentiality, and the use of specialized software between the firewall and the protected nodes to improve security and integrity.

Other protective relationships

This is another optional section, in the same format as above, to be used if a firewall maintains a protective relationship with some other network or system. The goal of this section, if appropriate to the product, is to explain what extra protective capabilities the firewall provides to improve the security of networks and how the additional mechanisms resist attack. Examples include protection against viruses on the internal network and protection against network outages.

Services provided

If a firewall provides service-based controls, this section lists the services that it supports. This will normally appear in the form of a relatively simple list, since more details can be found in the per-service information following. If the product does something unique in its handling of network services and security, that will be described here, together with how and why it works and how it resists attack. This section may be extended as appropriate to explain design and service philosophy. The goal of this section is to describe how the firewall provides security for services and how the chosen approach is resistant to attack and easy to manage. Also appropriate here are any default behaviors applied to this service—for example, whether it is initially disabled and if it logs all transactions by default. For each service, if appropriate, this section describes the controls that the firewall provides on that service, as well as service-specific logging, auditing, access control, authentication, and other capabilities. Service-specific residual risks will also be explained here.

Product audit/event reporting and summaries

This section describes the kinds of events the firewall logs and audits, explaining how the product reports and summarizes the events. This section aims to demonstrate to potential customers the types of information that the product will provide to the administrator and the types of operational summaries that will be available. Sample report formats or alert messages may be included as appendices to the document. Topics of interest here include log reduction, log reporting, log configuration, types of events logged, active trouble detection, and alert channels such as e-mail, pagers, and sirens.

Product testing methodology

In this section the vendor describes procedures for product testing and quality assurance, demonstrates the tests and procedures applied as part of the release/test cycle for the product, and shows how they provide reliability and integrity. Topics of interest here include test methodology, outside evaluators, formal methods used, and testing tools used.

Product performance attributes

This section provides a description of the product's estimated or measured performance range. The goal is to give potential customers enough information to estimate whether the firewall will support their current workload, bearing in mind that most sites have no idea what their workload resembles. Vendors provide information in this section that can relate measures used to an average workload to help customers size their system. This section addresses product-performance questions such as: What is the highest throughput connection supported at its full rate? If the product performs network-level encryption, what is the latency induced by encryption? What performance tests have been performed and with what results? And if maximum load is estimated in simultaneous users, approximately how many are supported?

Product operational assumptions

A brief description of the product's operational and environmental assumptions appears in this section. Topics of interest include reliance on extended hardware configurations, dependence on particular network topology, and requirements for specialized network or power interfaces.

Product operational/management requirements and interface

This section provides a brief description of operational and management requirements to inform the potential customer of the amount of maintenance the product requires, how to manage the product, what the management interface is like, and whether the product supports separation of management roles or delegation of management.

Product customer support

This section offers a description of product and customer-support policies and services, including the policy and mechanisms for upgrades and patches. Information on product warranties, maintenance contracts, support on-call hours of operation, and support response-time commitments can be found here as well.

Product interoperability considerations

If appropriate, vendors can include here a discussion of any interoperation concerns or features. Topics of interest here include support for other network protocols; network address translation, masking, and hiding; client-side software requirements; connected host software requirements and platforms supported; support for customization of the product; and support for any relevant standards, particularly concerning use of encryption.

5.3   Firewall buyer's assessment form

The purpose of this form is to aid the potential buyer in collecting the necessary information to help in specifying a firewall. It asks for information about your business environment, information systems, Internet connection, what you think you'd like in a firewall, and other considerations.

This guide requests information in generic terms. Buyers should complete the information to the best of their ability, ignoring sections that do not apply. If you come across sections that you haven't thought about—good! The investigative work that you put into this process up front will ultimately result in fewer headaches after your purchase and a firewall solution that better fits your company's real needs.

When you've done your homework, you can then present this information to the commercial firewall vendors in whose products you are interested. This will help them provide you with better solutions and you will have eliminated a lot of guesswork.

A basic process

1. Read and understand Part I of the Third Annual Firewall Buyer's Guide. You might also want to read *How to Pick an Internet Firewall*, by Marcus Ranum. It has some good tips on dealing with vendors and other issues.

2. Complete this assessment form.

3. Review product information to narrow the field to a group of products in which you're interested. Product Functional Descriptions (PFDs) of ICSA consortium member products are included in Part II of the Third Annual Firewall Buyer's Guide.

4. Get the contact information of all the vendors in which you're interested.

5. Send/fax the vendors this form and tell them what you're looking for.

6. Based on their feedback, make further comparisons.

7. Finalize your decision.

*Name*_____

*Title*_____

*Company*_____

*Address*_____

City _____*State*_____*Zip* _____

*Phone#*_____*Fax#*_____

E-mail address _____

Other contact info: _____

I. Business Environment

Because of differences in firewall products, it is essential to establish both the present and the projected scope of your network. This must be established early in the specification process.

A. Existing Environment

1. What is the physical/geographic scope of your organization?

Number of physical building sites_____

Location(s) of site(s)_____

2. Internal Operational Issues

—Business units that have special information access restriction needs (list)

—Business units that have special information access availability needs (list)

—Geographically separated business units that have special data sharing/interoperability needs (list name and geographic locations)

3. External Operational Issues

External VAN requirements (e.g., ANX) (describe)

Business partner interoperability requirements (list and describe)

_____

_____

4. Public Operational Issues (Services offered to the public) (list and describe)

_____

_____

5. Remote access requirements (list and describe)

_____

_____

6. Internet commerce/transaction service plans (list and describe)

_____

_____

B. Planned Environment

List and describe all foreseen changes to each item in Section A.

II. Information Systems Environment

For reasons of interoperability, a description of the computing environment into which the firewall will be deployed is helpful. Details of this section should be limited to technologies that are currently deployed. Items in this domain (II) may overlap with items in III.

A. Existing Environment

1. End-User Workstations

> *Operating system(s) used* _____

> *Hardware types* _____

> *Deployed software* _____

> *Number of total workstations* _____

2. Network

> *Media* _____

> *Devices* _____

> *Protocols (include addressing)* _____

> *Topology Diagram (map your network architecture on a separate paper, and attach as an exhibit). Be sure to include both LAN/campus and WAN/site mapping.*

3. Remote Access Facilities

> *What equipment do you employ?* _____

> *What authentication methods are in place?* _____

4. Servers

> *Number of servers* _____

> *Operating systems* _____

> *Hardware types* _____

> *Deployed software* _____

5. Existing Maintenance/Support Arrangements with Vendors and Consultants (describe limits of coverage)

> _____

> _____

> _____

> _____

6. Antivirus/Malware Control Technologies (list programs and where they reside)

_____

_____

_____

7. Network/System Management Technologies (list and describe)

_____

_____

8. Authentication Technologies (list and describe)

_____

_____

_____

B. Planned Environment

In this section, please note any planned changes to Section II A that modify the above.

_____

_____

_____

_____

III. Internet Connectivity

If Internet access is currently in place, details of connectivity, services, and existing custom development will be of great assistance in determining compatibility and customization requirements associated with the new product.

A. Existing Environment

1. Type of Internet connection (ISDN, T1, T3, etc.)_____

2. Existing firewall (if any—list product name, version number, and vendor)

_____

_____

3. Means of connection used by internal systems (list and describe)

_____

4. *Externally accessible servers/services (list and describe)* _____

_____

_____

5. *Electronic commerce/transaction servers (list and describe)* _____

_____

6. *Internet Security/Access Policy (see Chapter 4)*

Do you have a written corporate Internet access policy? _____

*Has it been reviewed and adopted by management?*_____

B. *Planned Environment*

1. *List items that differ from Section III A (existing environment), particularly changes to the Internet Security/Access Policy.*

_____

_____

_____

2. *Protocols to Be Supported*

The six protocols listed are the ones required for ICSA certification. This is not meant to be a complete list nor does the list imply that these are the only protocols you will/won't need. Users must research their existing and planned applications and fill out the table accordingly.

Some sources of other protocols include the /etc/services (UNIX file) and ftp:// ftp.isi.edu/in-notes/iana/assignments/port-numbers.

Protocol Services for Internal Users

Services for public

Services for remote users, special conditions

Telnet

FTP

HTTP

SSL or SHTTP

SMTP

DNS

IV. Firewall Features

Will you need the following features? (Check all that apply and describe where appropriate.)

- *Access Control*
- *Time Based*
- *Address Based*
- *Authenticated*
- *Alerts/Alarms*
- *Visual*
- *Audible*
- *Paging/Phone*
- *E-mail*
- *SNMP*
- *Syslog*
- *Authentication*
- *Token*
- *One-time*
- *Password*
- *Configuration Management*
- *Profile-Based Configuration Management*
- *Ability to Manage Multiple Configurations*
- *Verification of Configuration Consistency*
- *Content Control*
- *Active Content management*
- *Java*
- *ActiveX*
- *Virus/Malware Control*
- *Onboard*
- *Outboard*
- *Third Party*
- *WWW Access Control*
- *URL Filtering/Blocking*
- *Access Logging*
- *Log Management—define any reporting requirements and existing reporting/ event analysis products you are currently using, if any*
- *Log Summary*

- *Intrusion Detection*
- *Network Options*
- *Interfaces*
- *Maximum Number* _____
- *Interoperability of Different Media Types (list)*
- *Granularity of Rulebase by Interface*
- *Media*
- *Ethernet*
- *10BaseT*
- *100BaseT*
- *Gigabit*
- *Fiber Optic*
- *FDDI*
- *Token Ring*
- *NAT (Network Address Translation)*
- *Remote Administration*
- *Console Only*
- *HTTP/Browser Based*
- *Remote GUI*
- *Single Console/Multiple Firewalls*
- *SNMP*
- *System Attributes*
- *Turnkey*
- *Ability to Incorporate Third-Party Servers/Products on Platform*
- *VPN*
- *Compliant with:*
- *IPSEC*
- *S/WAN*
- *SKIP*
- *Others*
- *Firewall to Firewall*
- *Firewall to Client (internal and external)*
- *Key Management/Exchange*

V. Other Considerations

My price range for a firewall is $_____ –$ _____

I expect/need to have a firewall purchased, up,

and running by (date) ___/___/___

I need to have a firewall that is ICSA certified. _____

Other testing/certification/reviews required (list): _____

Deployment of the firewall will come under the job function of (title)

_____

Maintenance of the firewall will come under (title)'s job function (title)

_____

I need the following features in a service contract:

_____

_____

_____

_____

_____

Any other special requirements not covered in this form:

_____

_____

_____

_____

_____

5.4   Firewall vendors: Picking the products that are right for you

ICSA conducts certification tests on firewalls to determine if they meet their Firewall Product Certification criteria. If a firewall product success-fully completes the testing, it is posted on their web site.

ICSA tests firewall products on the following: required services security policy; logging; administration; functional testing; security tests; and docu-mentation.

ICSA periodically retests the certified firewall products to make sure that the firewall vendor has continued to develop a secure product that meets their Firewall Product Certification criteria.

The following firewall vendors and their products have met ICSA's Firewall Product Certification criteria.

Vendor Name Certified	Product Names
3Com Corporation	OfficeConnect Internet Firewalls OfficeConnect NETBuilder
Alcatel Fort Knox Policy Router	OneStream Fort Knox
Axent Technologies	AltaVista Tru64 UNIX Raptor NT Raptor Solaris
BorderWare Technologies	BorderWare Firewall Server Check Point SoftwareFirewall-1 NT Firewall-1 Solaris
Cisco Systems PIX	Com21 Cable Modem ComPort 5000
Computer Associates GuardIT	Unicenter TNG Network Security Option
CyberGuard Corporation	CyberGuard NT CyberGuard Unixware
Elron Software Inc.	CommandView Firewall for NT
eSoft	Instagate
GenNet	WebGuard Solaris
Global Technology Associates, Inc.	GNAT Box
IBM	SecureWay AIX SecureWay NT
Intel	LANRover VPN Gateway
Internet Dynamics	Conclave
Lucent Technologies	Lucent Managed Firewall SecureConnect Firewalls
Marconi Communications	Firewall Switching Agent for ESX/ Firewall1

NetGuard	Guardian Firewall
Netopia	Netopia S9500 Security Appliance
NetScreen Technologies	NetScreen Family Network-1 Security Solutions CyberWall PLUS-IP
Network Associates	Gauntlet NT
Nokia	Nokia IP Series Routers
Nortel Networks	BaySecure/Firewall-1 Shasta 5000 Broadband Service Node BSN
Novell BorderManager Enterprise Edition	Novell FireWALL for NT
Progressive Systems	Phoenix Adaptive Firewall
Secure Computing	Sidewinder SecureZone
SonicWALL, Inc.	SonicWALL Family
SLMSoft.com	SecureIT
Sun Microsystems	SunScreen EFS
Tiny Software	WinRoute Pro
WatchGuard Technologies	Firebox II

The following sections provide 3 different solutions to protect servers and services in a DMZ.

5.5   SSL network appliance overview[4]

SSL appliances offload public-key cryptographic functions from servers. By generating keys with a dedicated appliance, the risk of overloading the web server with secure sessions is minimized and the SSL transactions are only a few milliseconds faster. However, since key generation time is a relatively small portion of total object access time, most SSL appliances increase the SSL capacity of a system but do not provide any noticeable acceleration of the SSL transaction.

---

4.   This section reprinted with permission from Redline Networks—(Author: Sarah Z. Stanwyck).

5.5.1   Deployment

SSL appliances are often deployed behind a server load balancer (see Figure 5.1). One-arm mode installation is not recommended with an SSL appliance due to the limitations in scalability and availability.

Installation is easier and security is improved if the SSL appliance includes internal load balancing and intelligent failover and can be deployed as shown in Figure 5.2.

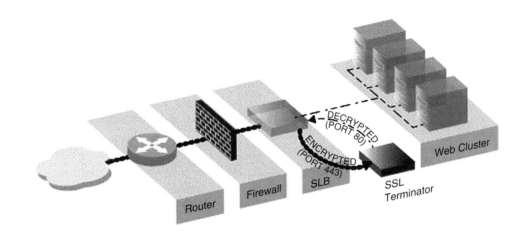

Figure 5.1

Figure 5.2

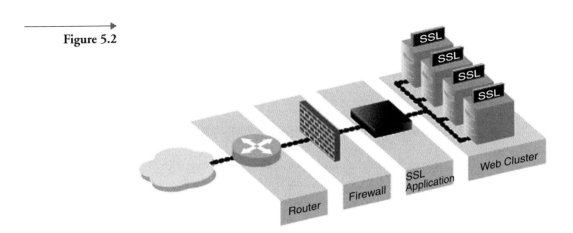

5.5.2   One-way vs. end-to-end SSL

The SSL appliance may support one-way SSL to clients, end-to-end SSL to clients and internal servers, or both modes of operation.

In one-way SSL, the SSL appliance and client exchange a key, then the client can send an encrypted request to the SSL appliance where it is decrypted and sent to the server for processing. The unencrypted response comes back from the server, is then encrypted by the SSL appliance, and sent back out to the client.

In end-to-end SSL, the SSL appliance must exchange a key with the client, and, in a separate transaction, exchange a different key with the web server. Similar to one-way SSL, the client sends an encrypted request to the SSL appliance where it is decrypted and information such as the header or cookie is read. In end-to-end SSL, the appliance then re-encrypts the request for secure transfer to the web server. At the web server, the request is first decrypted, then a response is generated, and finally the web server must encrypt the response before sending it to the SSL appliance. The SSL appliance must decrypt the server's response and then, using the key information for the client, re-encrypt the response for secure transfer to the client. This end-to-end SSL method is necessary to ensure total transaction security, but the additional rounds of encryption and decryption can burden the web server and slow SSL transaction time.

5.5.3   Key generation capacity

The most commonly cited specification for SSL appliances is RSA keys—the number of keys the appliance can generate in one second. If the SSL appliance supports session reuse, a single SSL key can be used for multiple requests from a single client, increasing the utility of each key and decreasing the overall need to generate keys. Key generation capacity is an often quoted specification, but there are other features of an SSL appliance to consider when determining the right SSL solution for a site or enterprise including deployment options, load balancing, support for end-to-end SSL, and transaction acceleration.

5.5.4   SSL transaction acceleration

Regardless of the number of new keys per second an SSL appliance can generate, the SSL transaction time will be slower than a similar clear text transaction unless the SSL appliance includes specific acceleration functionality. Even top of the line SSL appliances claiming thousands of keys per second cannot speed end-to-end SSL transactions without acceleration technology.

Figure 5.3

SSL key generation time in milliseconds.

SSL Key Generation Times	
Keys/sec	**Key gen time (ms)**
200	5.00
400	2.50
600	1.67
800	1.25
1,000	1.00
1,600	0.63
2,000	0.50
5,000	0.20
10,000	0.10
100,000	0.01

Figure 5.3 shows the number of milliseconds it takes to generate a key. At best, the large key generation capacity of these appliances provides a few milliseconds of acceleration, something a user would never notice.

It is possible to truly accelerate SSL transactions, but it requires an approach that includes advanced Layer 7 intelligence. To accelerate SSL transaction time more than a few milliseconds, it is necessary to optimize and compress the response data in real-time. If it takes too long to do the optimization and compression work, then the SSL appliance will provide no acceleration benefit. However, if the acceleration work is done at high speed, the response can be optimized, compressed, and encrypted so the amount of data sent to the user is reduced, and user access time is accelerated.

Simply adding compression to an SSL appliance does not ensure faster response time. Layer 7 optimization and compression is intense work that can only be done quickly and at high capacity when run on a purpose-built I/O optimized platform. Additionally, there are hundreds of edge cases that must be dealt with properly to ensure optimal rendering for all content and all users.

5.5.5 Summary

SSL appliances were initially deployed in the network to offload SSL work from servers so the server resources could be dedicated to generating content. While key generation capacity differentiated early SSL appliances, advances in ASIC development have steadily increased key generation capacity and allowed other features such as support for end-to-end SSL, load balancing and transaction acceleration to become the key differentiation among SSL appliances.

For the best in availability, scalability, ease of deployment, and performance, an SSL appliance solution should:

- Be deployable in one arm mode on the same subnet as the web servers or deploy in-line with advanced failover functionality

- Include load balancing traffic management functionality with Layer 4 and Layer 7 health-checking, and sticky cookie support

- Support both one-way SSL and end-to-end SSL

- Generate enough keys to support traffic load

- Accelerate secure transactions with high speed content optimization and compression

5.6   Secure access—SSL based extranet appliances[5]

The ability to provide remote access to corporate applications has always been a challenge. Virtual Private Networks (VPNs) have addressed this challenge, but not without a cost. VPNs require the installation of software on a client PC, ultimately resulting in increased calls to an already overburdened Help Desk. VPNs are also time consuming to deploy, so the lead-time to deliver access to a corporate application from the Internet can be quite long. Historically, VPNs have been adopted by employees and corporate partners for remote access. VPNs have not addressed access for kiosk users, retiree access, disaster recovery or access from locations where VPN connectivity is disabled.

An emerging market has developed for products that provide secure access for all client "profiles," meaning employees, retirees, corporate partners, kiosk access, and disaster recovery usage regardless of client location. Essentially, this market provides "anywhere, anytime, any-client" access to corporate applications. This market leverages existing desktop functionality to provide remote access to all applications, including Web, Client/Server, Terminal Services, Messaging, File Services, and Terminal Emulation Applications. These remote access technologies take advantage of the onboard security (SSL) built into a web browser, as well as the ease of use that a

---

5.   This section reprinted with permission from Neoteris, Inc. (Author: Ken Spinner).

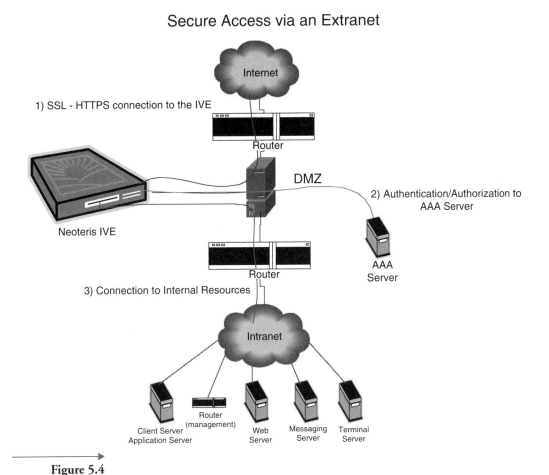

Secure Access via an Extranet

Figure 5.4

browser provides. By using a browser for connectivity, companies will avoid the cost of maintaining and deploying client software and provide a familiar interface for the end-user. These technologies are therefore referred to as clientless, as client VPN software is not required (see Figure 5.4).

Clientless solutions enable enterprises to provide access to all of their internal IT resources over the public Internet, thereby creating what is often referred to as an Extranet. In the past, Extranets were typically implemented as distinct network elements to service a corporation's business partners. Rather than compromising security by opening up communication directly with internal production resources, IT managers prefer to offer limited access to an Extranet, which is deployed in a DMZ to ensure the security of critical production servers. The downside of such Extranet deployments is that they are customized for each application, so each deployment incurs a significant expense. Capital expenditures are required for each additional Web and application server, as well as authentication, and access control software. In the past, IT Departments would incur incremental charges every time they needed to customize and integrate a new service or application into the Extranet. As each discrete Extranet component is added, the risk of a security violation also increases.

When developing an Extranet, security is always a top priority. Regardless of the type of Extranet that is being developed, companies must ensure that each Extranet component has been rigorously tested to eliminate security vulnerabilities. Custom, nonappliance based Extranet components must go through a hardening process which should involve hardening web servers, operating systems, network components, and applications. The hardening process is a tedious, time-consuming process. The hardening of any device involves the removal of all unnecessary services and the application of all known security patches. SSL based Extranet Appliances should also be evaluated for Security integrity, however many are pre-hardened by the manufacturer. This eliminates the ongoing hardening process required by traditional Extranet components.

Because of the broad accessibility of Extranets (tens of thousands of people may have access to a large enterprise Extranet), the need for authentication, authorization, and accounting controls are very important. Authentication controls are important to ensure the user is who he claims to be. Static user names and passwords are easy to hack; therefore, most organizations require two-factor authentication technologies for Extranet remote access. These two factors include something that you possess (e.g. a random number generator token or digital certificate) and something you know (a PIN or password). Authorization controls (sometimes referred to as entitlement) provide each user or user group permission to access specific applications or resources. Each user profile has different requirements. For example, a retiree may only need to access an HR benefits web site; a clerical worker may need access to e-mail; and an executive may need access to ERP, Sales Force Automation, and Executive Information Systems applications. Accounting or auditing is important as it provides a trail of remote access activity. This is particularly important where customer privacy and regulatory compliance is an issue. In many cases system logs must provide information that allow a system administrator to re-create exactly what a remote client did while accessing a specific application.

Instant Virtual Extranet (IVE) appliances from companies like Neoteris, Inc. simplify the deployment of Extranets. They reduce the complexity and security implications of delivering internal applications to remote users.

IVEs integrate with industry standard authentication databases, they provide access to a large number of IT applications, with robust application-layer security that allows for granular group-based authorization down to the URL and file level. Extranets that include an IVE do not require new servers or duplicated application software licenses or software plug-ins/APIs to be integrated with existing infrastructure. They give companies the benefit of being securely connected to all clients instantly, without the upfront and ongoing maintenance costs of custom Extranet installations.

5.7   Understanding air gap-based filtering proxies and their benefits when used for deploying web applications[6]

For several significant reasons, web-based information systems present unique challenges from a security standpoint.

First, web-based systems often force organizations to violate some of the most basic tenets of information security. For example, many e-Business applications require that unknown—and, therefore, untrusted—users be allowed to interact with critical information systems on internal networks. Anonymous prospects must be able to browse catalogs, check inventory and prices, and even fill "shopping carts." From a technical perspective, not only must firewall ports be opened to allow such communications, but web servers performing real-life business functions must process application-level requests emanating from unidentified sources. If not properly implemented, remote access web-based systems such as SSL VPNs—designed for mobile employees to access key systems and file repositories while out of the office—require communication channels to be created from the Internet to sensitive systems and data such as e-mail and corporate directories—again often forcing organizations to violate sound security policies.

Additionally, web-based systems are accessible from public Internet kiosks, shared or borrowed computers, and other machines over which no organizational control exists—generating a whole slew of previously unconsidered problems related to access from "insecure" locations. Temporary files, user credentials, and other sensitive data is often left on machines after users complete their activities. Through the exploitation of various

---

6.   Reprinted with permission from Whale Communications (Author: Joseph Steinberg).

weaknesses, hackers can sometimes even reinstate user sessions—that is reestablish sessions of legitimate users who previously used the same computer—and wreak tremendous havoc by accessing, modifying, or creating data on behalf of that user (e.g., sending an e-mail on behalf of the legitimate user).

Finally, common security technologies—including firewalls, intrusion detection systems (IDSs), and even standard reverse-proxies—are often ineffective in protecting web-application infrastructure. Attacks exploiting application-level vulnerabilities such as buffer overflows can traverse proxies, SSL-encrypted communications easily bypass IDSs, and open ports seriously compromise the effectiveness of firewalls. Worse yet, reverse proxies may introduce new weakness in the stability and security of the architecture. Reverse proxies are, themselves, often subject to compromise by hackers, since they are typically implemented using web-server software with some added code to handle the proxying capabilities. A hacker can easily transform a hacked reverse proxy into an effective host to use in staging attacks against internal systems.

The security risks described above are serious—and real. To combat these threats, and to address the shortcomings of the individual staples of classic IT security infrastructure (as described above), organizations have designed various complicated, proprietary architectures—utilizing multiple security technologies, often implemented in part on actual application servers. As a result, many face serious issues of integration, complexity, and scalability. Upgrades of one component of the security architecture may cause another component (or even the main web application) to cease functioning. For enterprises with large numbers of web servers, implementing and managing security systems on each individual machine has proven impractical.

In addition, many of the complicated solutions developed for securing web systems do not fully address the security concerns of web access—especially those emanating from the issue of access from insecure locations. Often the security remains inadequate; sometimes it is also implemented at a cost to the application's business functionality or in some other manner that seriously hinders user experience and productivity.

Air Gap Based Filtering Proxies were created specifically to address the aforementioned security issues, and to enable secure deployment of web-based systems. By offering both inbound filtering to ensure that no attacks reach sensitive systems and outbound filtering to ensure that no sensitive data remains on insecure machines, and by doing this on a secure Air Gap platform, these systems offer a viable, simple, scalable solution to the problem of securing web applications.

5.7.1   The solution

A detailed description of the architecture of Air Gap based filtering proxies and how they successfully address the aforementioned issues follows.

The underlying concept in Air Gap design is that sensitive systems must never be connected to the Internet (or any other insecure network)—and that any requests made from the Internet to internal servers must be subjected to thorough inspection before being relayed to destination machines. Air Gap works much like a drop box—requests from the Internet are dropped into a bucket where—after the bucket is physically isolated from the Internet—internal servers can retrieve the requests, check their appropriateness, and process accordingly.

Air Gap architecture consists of three components (often implemented within one box as seen in Figure 5.5):

5.7.2   An "external" server

This machine serves as the "face" of the Air Gap proxy—the address to which users wishing access to web-based applications go. Its IP address and DNS name are published to the world, and users interact with it as if it

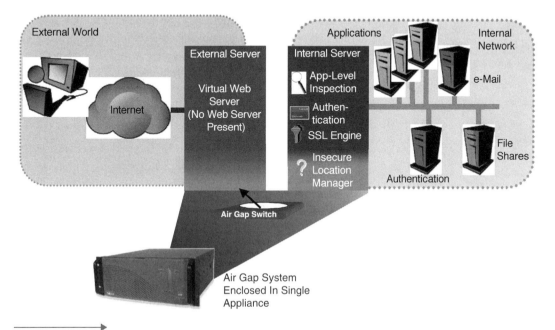

Figure 5.5

were an actual web server. In actuality, all that this machine does is receive encrypted user requests, strip off any networking information, and load the encrypted application-level information from the original network packets onto an Air Gap switch. By removing destination IP information, Air Gap technology eliminates a hacker's ability to address systems not intended to be externally addressable. The external server is typically networked to an organization's DMZ. It is important to understand that despite any hardening performed on the external server, the Air Gap model assumes that this machine may not be secure—so no configuration information or the like is stored on it.

5.7.3   Air gap switch

An Air Gap switch is some form of solid-state device (not a computer or any other programmable device) consisting of a memory bank and a high-speed switch that can be connected to only one server at a time. After the external server loads the application-level information onto this hardware device, the analog switch disconnects from the external server, switches sides, and connects to the internal server.

5.7.4   Internal server

This server is connected to the internal LAN (or some more internal DMZ than the External Server). It pulls the application-level information from the Air Gap switch, decrypts any data that is encrypted with SSL, and performs security checks on all requests. When user requests are deemed to have passed the necessary security tests, the internal server determines to which destination server the request must be sent, builds a TCP/IP communication channel to that server, and relays the request across the internal network.

Responses work in a similar fashion, with the internal server translating and encrypting traffic from the various application servers prior to transmission across the Air Gap switch.

All of the security functions of the Air Gap architecture are carried out on the internal server. This includes:

SSL management

Air Gap enables organizations to establish a single location for handling SSL, which is clearly ideal. If each individual web server would handle SSL, not only could application performance suffer, but security concerns could arise. SSL encrypted requests are not readable by IDSs, and any attacks sent in encrypted form could reach their intended targets unobstructed. Additionally, from a business perspective, centralizing SSL processing allows for optimization—both in terms of number of SSL certificates needed (one for the proxy rather than one for each server), as well as in terms of accelerators (if acceleration is needed only one accelerator can be installed at the proxy rather than one on each server). By performing SSL management at the proxy we eliminate this problem. Also note that the Air Gap architecture allows the SSL certificates (and decryption private keys) to be stored on the internal server—where it physically cannot be reached by hackers on the Internet. The risk of a hacker stealing the certificate and associated key and setting up a rogue web site that impersonates the organization, are dramatically reduced when using the Air Gap solution. Also, the Air Gap system can utilize various techniques to check that the SSL packets are properly crafted, have not been tampered with, etc.

Authentication

For those sections of a web site where authentication is necessary, authentication—including two-factor-based strong authentication—should be carried out at the network perimeter, not on the actual application server. Systems that require authentication should not be accessed by unknown users— even to receive a login page. By offloading the authentication to the perimeter, Air Gap solutions both improve security (by ensuring that unknown users cannot attempt to attack the system by responding to login requests with buffer overflow attempts and the like), as well as performance (by ensuring that the server need not dedicate resources to receiving, processing, and rejecting random "junk" requests generated by worms such as Code Red, Nimda, etc.).

Inbound filtering

All inbound requests should be inspected to ensure that only legitimate application requests—and not attempts to attack internal servers—pass. Filtering should always be done using positive logic (i.e., maintaining a rule base of acceptable request and rejecting all others), as negative logic (i.e., maintaining a list of exploits that should be rejected) will not protect an organization from as-of-yet undiscovered vulnerabilities. Web requests consist of URLs, parameters, and methods—and an Air Gap based proxy should include a filtering engine that can inspect all requests based on values and combinations of these items.

The Internal server also must manage all issues related to outbound data modification and manipulation—that is, to ensure that outbound data is handled in such a fashion that both meets the needs of remote users, as well as ensures that no security issues arise because a user is accessing the system from an Internet kiosk or other "unsafe" machine. Among the tasks it performs in this regard are:

- Instruct the browser not to cache any data and to expire any data that must be cached.

- Replace any uses of vulnerable HTTP Basic Authentication with safe authentication

- Overlay stronger forms of authentication (such as SecurID) when appropriate

- Ensure that any user logouts actually terminate sessions on the proxy and the back office in such a fashion that they cannot be re-established

- Ensure that no user credentials are ever cached on the browser machine

- Ensure that all temporary files (generated, for example, by opening an e-mail attachment) are erased when the user logs out

- Implement timeouts to ensure that if a user neglects to log out, his session will be terminated—but, do so in a fashion that does not time out legitimate users who are typing long e-mails or performing other activity that the server cannot detect.

- Implement periodic reauthentication schemes—so that the damage is contained in situations in which a user walks away from an Internet kiosk without logging out of the web application and another user walks up to it shortly thereafter (before a timeout occurs).

5.7.5 Security benefits

The Air Gap solution offers numerous security benefits:

First of all, Air Gap maintains a constant disconnection between the External and Internal servers—and the External and Internal networks. This allows organizations to adhere to policies forbidding exposure to the Internet, a sensible rule that reverse-proxy solutions force organizations to violate. It also keeps the security engine of the Appliance safe from tampering. Even in the worst-case scenario, if a hacker were to gain administrator-level control of the external server, all he could do is load bad data onto the Air Gap Switch—which would be rejected by the authentication, application filtering, and SSL inspection engines on the internal server.

Also, unlike standard reverse proxies, Air Gap based proxies do not allow external users to access any machines that have access to the internal network. A typical proxy—which is a computer with multiple network interface cards each attached to a different network—suffers from an innate problem that untrusted users are able to communicate with a machine that can communicate to internal networks. If a hacker, for example, attacks the proxy via the NIC facing the Internet, he can then use the proxy as a staging ground for attacks to the internal network through another network-interface card. Air Gap technology ensures that any machines that can be reached by untrusted users do not have access to the internal network, and that the staged-attack technique described above is rendered powerless.

When using an Air Gap solution, the only holes necessary to keep open in corporate firewalls in front of the Air Gap based proxy are the ports used for web access—normally TCP/80 & 443—while all others can be shut off. Unlike the case with other solutions, however, no ports need to be open between the proxy and the back office (from the DMZ to the internal network). This minimizes network exposure, and provides a single point of management for security personnel. Of course, this also allows organizations to adhere to sensible corporate security policies prohibiting the opening of firewall ports from the untrusted world into the internal network.

As discussed earlier, TCP connections are terminated on the external server side (i.e., on the DMZ-side) of the Air Gap architecture. The proxy plucks the application-level payload out of network packets it receives and loads only this data onto the Air Gap switch. No network protocols or packets are transmitted. New TCP packets are generated by the Appliance server on the internal LAN after the rigorous security checks described throughout this document are performed.

Unlike standard reverse proxies that rely on the stability and security of operating systems and which can be compromised through the exploitation of o/s vulnerabilities, Air Gap switches are implemented with firmware—they run no software, no operating system, and are completely stateless. In short, there is nothing to compromise. Without an operating system running, there is no operating system to attack—and there is no chance of exploiting an operating-system vulnerability to compromise the proxy or break through to the internal network.

Eliminates plain-text sensitive information in insecure locations—Enterprise security policies normally mandate that no sensitive information be maintained in DMZs; reverse-proxy architectures almost universally force organizations to violate such regulations; SSL certificates and decryption keys, authentication information, and security configuration and enforcement mechanisms are maintained in the insecure DMZ or made accessible to the DMZ via the opening of (even more) firewall ports.

Air Gap architecture allows all sensitive data to be stored on the internal network—no SSL certificates, decryption keys, etc. are stored in the DMZ. Additionally, SSL decryption occurs on the internal LAN—not on the DMZ. Without Air Gap technology, decryption normally takes place on the DMZ and important information is transmitted in plain-text to the back office over the insecure DMZ network wire.

Because all requests are inspected, buffer overflows and other attempts to exploit system vulnerabilities do not reach internal systems. Organizations are protected against not only vulnerabilities known at the time the Air Gap system is deployed, but against problems that are discovered in the future for which no patch or other remedy exists. In fact, deploying a filtering proxy can reduce the urgency to patch web and application servers—because in most cases even without patching the systems are secure because of the filter protecting it. It is important to realize that the lack of robust filtering is one of the more serious vulnerabilities in most reverse-proxy architectures—as if a user sends an application-level attack to an unprotected proxy, one of two things is likely to happen. The attack may successfully compromise the proxy—in which case the hacker would gain access to a machine that can reach servers on the internal network. Alternatively, the attack may have no adverse effect on the proxy, but the proxy may relay the attack to servers on the internal network and inadvertently compromise them on behalf of the hacker. In such a fashion, hackers and other mischievous folks can achieve successful security breaches against internal systems protected by reverse proxies.

Quite significantly, the solution described earlier includes functionality to eliminate the threat of access from insecure locations developing into a problem of unauthorized access. Even the greatest security system is worthless if it has "back doors" that allow unauthorized users to "spoof themselves" as legitimate users.

6

Authentication and Authorization

Hand over your credit card and social security numbers—now!

6.1   The basics

Let's imagine that I worked for NASA (spaceships are cool). I would get a key card and a nametag that I could show off to other people and use as bragging rights. Additionally, the keycard and nametag would tell everybody how important I was within NASA. This might work for me and against me, in that I'd be authenticated to enter the building, but not authorized to enter every room. This is essentially the same way in which the internet works. As businesses implement networked information strategies that call for controlling access to information resources in the networked environment, authentication and access management are emerging as major issues that must be developed, implemented, and supported. There are two primary access issues that must be dealt with: authentication and authorization. Authentication and authorization have very specific definitions.

"Authentication" is the process where a user (via any type of physical access—PC, network, remote) establishes a right to an identity. I log in to a system with my user name and password, and the system now knows who I am.

User name = Bubba Joe Smith

"Authorization" is the process of determining whether a user is permitted to perform some action or access to a resource. I log in to a system with my user name and password, and the system knows who I am and now can grant or deny access to certain databases.

User name = Bubba Joe Smith

Access to the Fishing Database = Bubba Joe Smith

Figure 6.1 shows you the difference. Bubba Joe has authenticated with the server, and the server now knows who Bubba Joe is. With this information the server can control access to each resource. Within each database (DB) the server administrator can control via "authorization." Bubba Joe is not authorized to open the payroll and accounting DB, but he is authorized to open the fishing DB.

This whole process sounds really simple but, unfortunately, it is not. Authentication and authorization are very complex subjects that take a lot

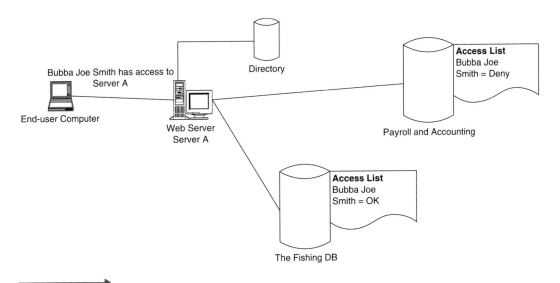

Figure 6.1

of time and money to implement and support. So our job (and we do choose to accept it) is to help you understand the issues and complexity of authentication and authorization.

One issue that we have not covered is the "directory attack" (aka "dictionary attack"). The directory attack is one of the simplest types of hacker attacks. Using a "footprinting" process, a hacker will get a list of user names. Then, using a tool with a directory word list (e.g., from a dictionary), the hacker will start accessing the URL with a list of possible passwords. This type of attack is a general threat to all passwords. Since passwords are typically short (in character length), the password can often be determined by brute force. Depending on the system, the password, and the skills of the hacker, such an attack can be completed in days, hours, or perhaps only a few seconds.

6.2   **Authentication**

There are many different methods that can be used to authenticate a user.

- User name and password
- Certificates (x.509v3)
- Biometric techniques (more on this later)

- Smart cards

- Anonymous (Yes, there is such a method—and we will discuss it in this chapter.)

6.2.1   User name and password

Overall, a user name and password are easy to set up and implement. Most operating systems and web servers will have some type of user name and password authentication system. Most of these systems will have some type of mechanism to manage the user name and password architecture—for example, account expiration, password expiration, password length, and/or quality of password. Currently, this is the access method of choice for most pages on the Internet.

Advantages

- Easy to implement and manage

- Inexpensive—provided with most operating systems and web servers

- Only minimal training required for end users

Disadvantages

- User name and password sent in the clear for basic authentication (although not in all cases, and SSL can encrypt at the Network level)

- User name and password subject to directory attacks

- On the Internet, users may have many different user names and passwords (which can be a real headache to maintain)

6.2.2   Certificates (x.509v3)

User certificates can be used by end users to assure their identity; Lotus Notes has a built-in certificate system using a physical ID file. You can have an x.509v3 certificate in your browser and it will allow you to access various web applications that support this type of authentication. Access to the certificate is normally controlled by a password that is local to the certificate. For example, on Netscape you can open the certificate database with a password, which then allows you to use the certificate. With the exception of x.509v2 and SSL, thus far this technology has not been widely used on the Internet. Many companies are starting to implement user certificates on their internal network.

Advantages

- Binds the certificate to the user

- Ability to encrypt data and digitally sign messages

- Supported by most web browsers and e-mail packages

- Offers some mechanisms for a single sign-on solution

- Difficult to stage a directory attack

- Allows roaming users, i.e., users moving from one location to another (if your vendor supports this feature)

- Can encrypt data, e-mail, and sign with only one certificate (actually, it is better to have separate certificates for signing and encryption)

Disadvantages

- Cost—implementing a PKI can be expensive

- Extensive user training is required

- Requires a support structure

- Roaming users, i.e., users moving from one location to another (not many vendors support this feature—but this is getting better)

- Vendors are only now developing tools that can handle large-scale implementations

6.2.3   Biometric techniques

A biometric authentication system will use devices such as fingerprints or eye scanners to allow access. This type of device can ensure greater security for high-risk environments that need to limit and control access to sensitive systems. Using this type of system, you could limit "tailgating," or, allowing users to use another person's user name and password.

Advantages

- The person is the authentication—very difficult to impersonate

- Directory attacks are nearly impossible

- Offers some mechanisms for a single sign-on solution

Disadvantages

- Not many vendors support this technology

- Expensive to implement

- Very few examples of this technology exist

(Check out http://www.microsoft.com—Microsoft is working with I/O Software for a solution to run on Windows.)

6.2.4 Smart cards

A smart card is typically a credit card–sized plastic card that has an embedded integrated circuit (IC) chip. This chip is what makes the card "smart." The smart card can store all types of information, which can be transferred via an electronic interface that connects to a computer. This smart card can store information about who you are and cryptographic keys and perform cryptographic algorithms, like encryption. Access to the smart card is controlled via a PIN or a password.

Advantages

- Easy to bind the card to the person
- The card can hold keys and other information about the user
- If keys are included, then it is easy to encrypt data and e-mail
- Easy to train users on the technology
- Great solution for roaming users; the certificate can easily be transported

Disadvantages

- Very expensive, although the cost of this technology is dropping
- Still easy to give the card and PIN to another user i.e.,"tailgating"
- Requires a support system and may require more hardware on each PC

6.2.5 Anonymous

The argument may be made that "anonymous" is not an authentication method. An anonymous user name is a method for giving users access to files so they don't need to identify themselves to the server. The user enters "anonymous" as a user ID. Usually, the password is defaulted or furnished by the server. Anonymous identification is a common way to get access to a server to view or download files that are publicly available.

Through the use of a control anonymous setting, anonymous is both an authentication method and an authorization method. By accessing a system via a control anonymous setting, you can be sure that you know where users are and what data they are accessing. This can be accomplished by use of Access Control Lists (ACLs) and audit logging. There will be cases where you want and need anonymous access to a data source. Never assume that anonymous should be a "default" access. This is dangerous. Make sure you limit anonymous access to the data sources that really need to gain access.

Advantages

- Easy to implement
- Little to no user training required
- Ability to conduct secure transactions without registering a user with a user name and password. How? Have you ever purchased a book online and used a credit card? Not all companies will require you to create an account. All you need to do is enter your credit card information (and hopefully you used SSL!)

Disadvantages

- Clearly, there is no binding to a specific user. Consequently, you don't know who accessed the data
- Cannot block access on a "per-user" basis
- Potentially open to "spam" attacks, where garbage is dumped onto your site
- No logging or audit trail

At this point, we are going to focus on basic authentication, a process widely used by browsers on the Internet. Basic authentication uses a series of status codes to communicate with a browser. See ftp://ftp.isi.edu/in-notes/rfc2617.txt and ftp://ftp.isi.edu/in-notes/rfc2616.txt for details.

"Status code" is one of the primary mechanisms that alerts the browser to the fact that credentials are needed (i.e., user name and password). The user will type in a URL, and that URL will access a page that is "secure." The server will return a status code; one of the codes may be 401. The browser will then prompt the user with a dialog box and enter his or her user name and password, which will be submitted back to the server. There are many different status codes. Here is an extract of the status codes from RFC 2616.

Status-Code =

```
|  "101"; Section 10.1.2: Switching Protocols
|  "200"; Section 10.2.1: OK
|  "201"; Section 10.2.2: Created
```

```
| "202"; Section 10.2.3: Accepted

| "203"; Section 10.2.4: Non-Authoritative Information

| "204"; Section 10.2.5: No Content

| "205"; Section 10.2.6: Reset Content

| "206"; Section 10.2.7: Partial Content

| "300"; Section 10.3.1: Multiple Choices

| "301"; Section 10.3.2: Moved Permanently

| "302"; Section 10.3.3: Found

| "303"; Section 10.3.4: See Other[1]

| "304"; Section 10.3.5: Not Modified

| "305"; Section 10.3.6: Use Proxy

| "307"; Section 10.3.8: Temporary Redirect

| "400"; Section 10.4.1: Bad Request

| "401"; Section 10.4.2: Unauthorized

| "402"; Section 10.4.3: Payment Required

| "403"; Section 10.4.4: Forbidden

| "404"; Section 10.4.5: Not Found

| "405"; Section 10.4.6: Method Not Allowed

| "406"; Section 10.4.7: Not Acceptable

| "407"; Section 10.4.8: Proxy Authentication Required

| "408"; Section 10.4.9: Request Time-Out

| "409"; Section 10.4.10: Conflict

| "410"; Section 10.4.11: Gone

| "411"; Section 10.4.12: Length Required

| "412"; Section 10.4.13: Precondition Failed

| "413"; Section 10.4.14: Request Entity Too Large

| "414"; Section 10.4.15: Request-URI Too Large

| "415"; Section 10.4.16: Unsupported Media Type
```

1.   This code is the same as 302, except that the client should make a GET request for the new URL, regardless of the original request method.

| "416"; Section 10.4.17: Requested Range Not Certifiable

| "417"; Section 10.4.18: Expectation Failed

| "500"; Section 10.5.1: Internal Server Error

| "501"; Section 10.5.2: Not Implemented

| "502"; Section 10.5.3: Bad Gateway

| "503"; Section 10.5.4: Service Unavailable

| "504"; Section 10.5.5: Gateway Time-Out

| "505"; Section 10.5.6: HTTP Version Not Supported

This extract shows the actual process that the server will implement to send the status code back to the browser.[2] If a server receives a request for an access-protected object and an acceptable authorization header is not sent, the server responds with a "401 Unauthorized" status code and a "WWW-Authenticate" header as per the preceding defined framework, which, for the digest scheme, is utilized as follows:

```
challenge = "Digest" digest-challenge

digest-challenge = 1#(realm | [domain] | nonce |

[opaque] |[stale] | [algorithm] |

[qop-options] | [auth-param])

domain = "domain" "=" <"> URI (1*SP URI) <">

URI = absoluteURI | abs_path

nonce = "nonce" "=" nonce-value

nonce-value = quoted-string

opaque = "opaque" "=" quoted-string

stale = "stale" "=" ("true" | "false")

algorithm = "algorithm" "=" ("MD5" | "MD5-sess" |

token)

qop-options = "qop" "=" <"> 1#qop-value <">

qop-value = "auth" | "auth-int" | token
```

Figure 6.2 shows a 401-status code being returned back to the browser.

2.   Source: ftp://ftp.isi.edu/in-notes/rfc2617.txt

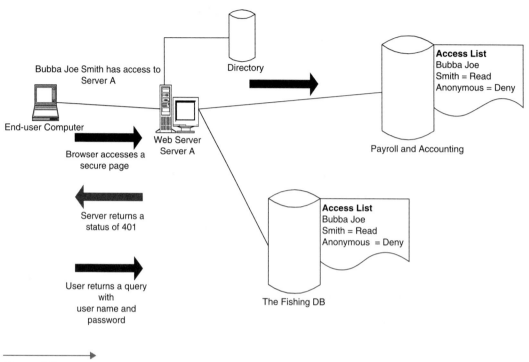

Figure 6.2

6.3   **Authorization**

Authentication is only part of the story. Authorization comes next; access control uses the HTTP FORBIDDEN status code (403). When a user attempts to access a URL that is restricted in this way, the server returns this status code to tell the user's browser that access is not allowed. Cached information in the browser is reissued with each request in a WWW-Authenticate header. The browser now issues a second request for the URL containing the information necessary to establish the user's credentials. The server checks the contents of the information, and, if it validates successfully, the request is passed on to the authorization phase of the transaction, where the server will decide whether the authenticated user has access (ACL) to the requested URL. On future requests to this URL, the browser remembers the user's authentication information and automatically provides it with each query. This way the user doesn't have to provide his user name and password each time he or she accesses a secure page.

Now we will confuse all of this with a concept known as "realms." A realm is a directive that is sent with the browser each time it tries to authenticate with a server. The realm directive is required for all authentication schemes that issue a challenge to a URL. The realm value is normally a string, and it is assigned by the web server. (See ftp://ftp.isi.edu/in-notes/rfc2617.txt for more information about realms.) If the authentication information becomes invalid, the server can again issue a 401-response status code, thus forcing the browser to request the user's credentials all over again. There are several methods to enhance this process that are server dependent and specific, including use of browser cookies.

6.3.1   Passwords

In a system that uses user names and passwords, you should make sure that your users use hard-to-guess passwords. Following are some general guidelines for passwords.

- The password must not contain a word, name, or number that has some significance, such as a telephone number, address, or Social Security number.

- Passwords should be six to eight characters in length. (This requirement can be different from one company to another.)

- The password should be a mixture of letters, numbers, and special characters (which could include *, ?, @, !).

- Do not share the password with anyone else.

- Do not use the default password that is given to you. Change it as soon as possible.

- Do not write down your password.

- Do not use "password" as a password.

- Try not to use any word from a dictionary. (We already discussed directory/dictionary attacks.)

- Do not use any names as your password, like Bubba, Mike, or Billy Joe Bob.

- Never tell anyone your password—not even your system administrator or account manager. Make sure you have chosen a password that you can remember.

- Don't use the same password for all of your Internet accounts.

- Try to change your password on a regular basis.

- If someone calls you on the phone and says, "Yes, and we are with the Network Password Police, and we need to know your password," don't give it to them! But if you *do* give your password out over the phone, take the following steps:

1.   Create an e-mail message.

2.   Put your credit card number in the subject line.

3.   Put your cash PIN number in the body of the message.

4.   Mail this message to the authors of this book.

5.   We will have fun shopping on your credit card.

Password management should not always be left up to the user. Most operating systems and web servers will have some built-in mechanism to manage the password policies that you will put in place. If possible, take the following steps:

1.   Enforce a reasonable minimum password length, which increases the number of permutations needed to randomly or programmatically guess someone's password. You should also enforce an alphanumeric password combination.

2.   Enforce maximum and minimum password age. A maximum password age forces the user to change the password after a period of time, preventing someone else from discovering it. A minimum password age prevents a user from immediately reverting back to a previous password after a change.

3.   Enforce password uniqueness and maintain password history. These steps prevent users from bouncing between their favorite passwords. You should specify the number of unique passwords that a user must have before that user can use a password that has previously been used.

6.3.2   Tokens

One authentication method is to use a concept known as "tokens." Tokens can be hardware and/or software. One mechanism that tokens provide is to authenticate at a central point and receive a token. That token is then used via a session to access several secure resources. NT uses a similar system with its System Account Management (SAM) DB. Another type of token is a computerlike card, which is effectively a password calculator. In this case, there is no physical connection to the client computer. In essence, no software or hardware is required of the client. The token contains a secret value, which is used to respond to challenges. Some of the best-known tokens cards are from ActivCard and from Security Dynamics (Secure ID).

Token cards can also protect against both passive attacks and instant replay attacks, in which one of the "bad dudes" records valid authentication information exchanged between one of the computers and then attempts to replay it later to gain entry. Sorry, Charlie, but this won't work, because token cards provide "once only" passwords. The password can change many times during a day, making replay nearly impossible.

There are software token cards. These tokens allow a person who travels frequently to various locations, and who uses a personal computer or laptop, to access various services. The disadvantage of using the software token cards method is that some specialized software normally needs to be loaded onto one personal computer for its use. Also, you may be limited to one personal computer, whereas the hardware token card can be used on any personal computer. In the best case, you will need to load the software again on each computer you use or carry some type of token software with you.

The use of token-based authentication systems is becoming an efficient and cost-effective means to implement security. If you are on the road and need access to your company's network, you can do so just by plugging your laptop into any network-enabled Ethernet connection. Here is how it works: You will use a simple device known as a "KEYFOB," which has a numeric display that shows a series of numbers. The numbers change every 60 seconds. You enter the number from the token card and a PIN. Now you can access your network. In 60 seconds, the numbers that you used to get into the network will not work.

Token-based security systems have been on the market for more than 10 years. Using these types of systems, you can secure most types of hardware and software. The goal of these authentication systems is to provide strong authentication not only to your network but to the desktop as well. So watch out for future enhancements and new products.

One process that we have not discussed is using browser cookies. You can use cookies as a token. The process, as follows, is simple and effective.

1. The user will access a web server via a browser.

2. The server will issue a cookie to the browser. The cookie is encoded and time stamped, for example, for 30 minutes.

3.   Using the cookie, the browser now can access other servers and access data using the cookie as credentials.

4.   The server can then monitor the cookie and track its user and expiration. If the cookie is not used in 30 minutes, it is declared invalid.

Advantages

- Only one prompt per authentication is necessary. HTTP realms can be bypassed or managed via this type of system.

- It is easy to track each cookie as it authenticates into each application.

- Using this type of system, you can "time out" users due to inactivity.

Disadvantages

- The user must enable cookies. If not, the user could go crazy with prompt warnings about cookies from the browser.

- Specialized software is necessary that can communicate between servers to pass "validity" information about current and authorized users.

6.3.3 Kerberos (guard dogs)

"Kerberos," named after the dog in Greek mythology that guarded the gates of Hades, is software that is used in a network to establish a user's identity. Developed by MIT (Massachusetts Institute of Technology) in the mid-1980s, Kerberos uses a combination of encryption and distributed databases so that a user can log in and start a session from any computer on the network. This can be a real advantage on a network with a lot of roaming users. The Kerberos protocol uses strong cryptography so that a client can prove its identity to a server across a network connection. After a client and server have used Kerberos to prove their identity, they can also encrypt all their communications for privacy and data integrity. Kerberos is freely available from MIT under a copyright permission notice very similar to the one used for the BSD operating and X11 Windowing system. MIT provides Kerberos in source form.

Kerberos is a network authentication system targeted for use on physically insecure networks. It is implemented by communicating over networks to prove their identity to each other while preventing eavesdropping or replay attacks. Data stream integrity is provided. Users or systems are given "tickets" that can be used to identify themselves to other systems, and secret cryptographic keys are provided for secure communication with other systems. A "ticket" is a small sequence of a few hundred bytes. Using this ticket system, a ubiquitous access system can be designed allowing a single ticket to authenticate with many different security mechanisms. Overall, Kerberos is used in application level protocols. Remember the OSI reference model? Kerberos lives on level seven.

The Kerberos protocol is composed of three subprotocols: authentication service (AS) exchange; ticket-granting service (TGS) exchange; and client/server (CS) exchange.

Authentication service (AS) exchange

The user accesses the network by typing a log-on name and password. The Kerberos-enabled client converts the password to an encryption key and saves the result in a variable. The client then requests credentials from the Kerberos Key Distribution Center (KDC). When the KDC receives the request, it looks up the user in its database, gets the user's master key, decrypts the preauthentication data, and evaluates the time stamp inside. Once the user's identity has been validated, the KDC creates credentials that the client can present to the ticket-granting service.

Ticket-granting service (TGS) exchange

The Kerberos client on the user's workstation requests credentials for the service by sending a message to the KDC. This message consists of the identity of the service for which the client is requesting credentials and an authenticator message encrypted with the user's new log-on session key. The KDC uses the log-on session key to decrypt the user's authenticator message and evaluates it for validity. If the authenticator passes the test, the KDC extracts the user's authorization data and creates a session key for the user to share with the targeted server. The KDC encrypts one copy of the service session key with the user's log-on session key. The KDC embeds another copy of the service session key in a ticket, along with the user's authorization data, and encrypts the ticket with the server's master key. The KDC sends these credentials back to the client. When the client receives the reply, it decrypts the service session key with the user's log-on session key and stores the service session key in its ticket cache. The client extracts the ticket to the server and stores that in its ticket cache.

Client/Server (CS) exchange

Once a user has a ticket to a server, the workstation client can establish a secure communications session with that server. The client sends the server a message containing an authenticator message encrypted with the key sent by the KDC for the session with the server. Also sent is a ticket for sessions with the server, and a flag indicating whether the client requests mutual authentication. The server receives the request, decrypts the ticket, and extracts the user's authorization data and the session key. The server uses the session key from the ticket to decrypt the user's authenticator message and evaluates the time stamp inside. If the authenticator message is valid, the server checks the mutual authentication flag in the client's request. If the mutual authentication flag is set, the server uses the session key to encrypt the time from the user's authenticator message and returns the result in a message of type Kerberos Application Reply. When the client receives the reply, it decrypts the server's authenticator message with the session key it shares with the server and compares the time sent back by the service with the time in its original message. If everything matches, then the client is assured that the service is genuine, and the connection is validated.

There are several different versions and distributions of Kerberos. Most of them are based on an MIT distribution.

Versions of Kerberos V4

- MIT Kerberos V4

- Bones

- Transarc

- Digital Unix

Versions of Kerberos V5

- MIT Kerberos V5

- OSF DCE Security

- Microsoft Windows 2000

In the United States and Canada, Kerberos is available via anonymous FTP from athena-dist.mit.edu (18.71.0.38).[3]

6.3.4   Single sign-on

Single sign-on programs allow a user to authenticate one time and, thereafter, be able to access additional network resources and systems without having to reenter passwords during future log-ins.

---

3.   http://www.securitydynamics.com; http://www.ibm.com; http://msdn.microsoft.com/library/default.asp?URL=/library/psdk/
        secspi/aboutsspi_302t.htm

In use, many single sign-on (SSO) systems operate as follows:

1.   The user enters a user name and password to a primary log-in program. The program then authenticates the user against a master system.

2.   After this one-time authentication, the user may then request access to additional systems. Each time he or she does so, the single sign-on system will retrieve the user's password to use in the new system and will start a session using that password.

The main purpose of single sign-on, therefore, is to enable authorized users to perform one initial sign-on to access a variety of networks, systems, and applications. From the user's point of view (fewer user IDs and passwords to remember), single sign-on is a desirable feature.[4]

Advantages of Single Sign-On Systems

Through use of a secure single sign-on system, a business enterprise and its users can realize the following benefits.

■   Greater security is achieved for the enterprise without having to modify or replace applications.

■   Costs are reduced due to eliminating user downtime and administrative costs due to contacting help desks for aid in recovering forgotten or lost passwords.

■   User productivity is increased as less time is spent logging on to multiple systems.

■   The system allows for a more cohesive security infrastructure that can manage stronger authentication mechanisms (such as digital certificates, tokens, or smart cards) and new applications, as needed.[5]

Disadvantages of Single Sign-On Systems

■   Without secure authentication, the single sign-on can provide a "one-stop shop" for hackers.

■   If the single sign-on system is authenticated from a central server, a failure or denial-of-service attack can be devastating.

■   Due to the various operating systems and platforms that may be in use, a true single point of administration may be difficult to implement.[6]

4.   Source: http://www.m-tech.ab.ca/papers/ps_sso/node2.html
5.   Source: http://209.140.121.231/ssso.htm
6.   Source: http://www.gocsi.com/sso_ft.htm

The single sign-on selection process

When determining which single sign-on system may be the best for your enterprise, the following points should be evaluated:

- Will it be easy to use and administer the SSO?

- Will the SSO reinforce existing security?

- Is the SSO start-up/log-on integrated with that of the operating system?

- Is the operation of the SSO consistent with that of the operating system and OS platforms?

- Can new applications be added without having to make changes to the SSO?

- Does the SSO tie in with the existing security infrastructure?

- Does the SSO support public and private key technologies?

- The defining architecture and interface set for SSO is XSSO (developed by the Open Group). Does the SSO conform to XSSO architecture?

- Can a user log on not only from his or her own machine but also from any other machine equipped with SSO?

- Does the SSO utilize computer-generated, one-time-use passwords?

The growing number of user names and passwords that users need to memorize in order to do their jobs continues to grow. SSO allows users to access many applications through the use of a single password log-on. The benefits of SSO include cost reduction due to reduced user downtime and administrative costs associated with contacting help desks to recover forgotten passwords; increased productivity; and a strengthened security infrastructure. When selecting an SSO, due consideration should be placed on selecting a system that is easy to use and administer, is compatible with existing operating systems, and allows for the addition of new applications without having to make changes to the SSO.[7]

6.4   Smart cards

A smart card is a device the size of a credit card containing an integrated central processor that is capable of storing information such as the cardholder's personal information (birth date, bank account information, medical records, etc.). Security is maintained through a combination of measures

7.   Source: http://www4.ibm.com/software/network/globalsignon/library/whitepapers/white-overview.html

such as PIN numbers, public and private keys, and passwords. Smart cards are known by different terms such as "chip card," "integrated circuit card," "PC in your wallet," and "DB on a card." These cards provide a great deal of security for the data stored inside them. Some models of smart cards can hold over 100 times the amount of information that is contained in a standard magnetic-stripe card. The security and mobility of smart cards have made them increasingly popular, mainly for financial applications. Uses of smart cards include establishing identification when logging on to ISPs or on-line banks; providing health information that can be used by hospitals or doctors; and making on-line purchases without the use of traditional credit cards. Companies such as Cylink, Motorola, and IBM are continually improving the technology and security features of their smart card solutions. Cylink, for example, has designed a smart card called "MiniKey" that contains several advanced security and authentication features. MiniKey connects to the USB port directly, without additional hardware requirements. In addition, MiniKey has 1024-bit RSA capabilities, which are provided by an internal cryptographic smart card. There are hundreds of smart card operations in use worldwide, with over a billion in use. Currently, they are most widely used in Europe, but their use is expected to increase, as Ovum, a research firm, predicts that 2.7 billion smart cards will be shipped annually by 2003. Some cards can be programmed to support multiple applications and application updates. Smart cards can be designed to be inserted into a slot and read by a special reader or to be read at a distance, such as at a tollbooth. The cards can be disposable or reloadable. Smart cards are covered under the International Organization for Standardization (ISO) 7816 standard. The standard entitled "ISO 7816 Identification Cards—Integrated Circuit(s) Cards with Contacts" consists of eight documents that describe all physical aspects of the cards.

The business enterprise looking to incorporate smart cards into its security systems may consider them for many applications, including the following:

- To replace traditional employee ID badges (Smart cards provide picture identification; access to company facilities, including secure areas; and an electronic wallet for company cafeteria and vending machines.)

- Storage of employees' digital signatures, including certificate authority and private keys

- Network access identification, including single sign-on

- Employee medical and health information

- Employee business travel profile, including the company's preferred airlines, hotels, and car rental agencies

Due consideration should be made for the system and infrastructure requirements that would support the implementation of the smart cards.

In making the card selection process, the following issues should be considered:

- Compliance with standards, including ISO 7816

- Compatibility with operating systems

- Ability to implement digital signature applications

- Storage size of the EEPROM (electrically eraseable programmable read-only memory) required to support designated applications

- Material of the card (Can it accept printing for applications such as employee photos?)

- Does the card vendor have an established support presence?

7

E-Commerce: Public Key Infrastructure

He lost his x.509 private Key.

7.1   PKI and you

In Chapter 6, we briefly covered Public Key Infrastructure (PKI). This chapter is devoted to this topic. We have discussed SSL, encryption, and certificates. Now we are going to focus on Public Key Infrastructure. PKI is slowly immersing itself into the business enterprise. Lotus Notes has had a PKI since Release 1.0. For an effective PKI to be implemented, however, you will need to have some idea of what this beast is. As you might guess, public key cryptography requires a public key infrastructure. What is driving this use of PKI are applications and access to those applications. Businesses around the world are deploying new generations of business-critical applications, and in many cases, these are distributed applications. These applications are serving the following types of environments: customer to business; business to business; and employees to business.

7.1.1   Customer to business

This environment is one in which the customer will use the Internet to interact with a business. Customer-to-business access is not only to "buy" something. Following are a few examples of other uses this type of access provides. It can:

- Look up information on a product or service

- Inquire or make a change to an order

- Place an order

- Send an e-mail with a question regarding the company's offerings

There are a lot of reasons for a customer to use the Internet. Do you have to authenticate with each of these reasons? No, you only need to authenticate in those areas where you need to identify the user. Interestingly enough, implementing a PKI for the general public is somewhat difficult. You will see why a bit later.

7.1.2   Business to business

This environment is where PKI can really shine. You will see that by using some type of PKI, you can determine whom you are doing business with and use that information to track and verify transactions. PKI can be very useful in the high-volume transaction and mobile world of Internet commerce. It provides risk management control for business systems.

7.1.3   Employees to business

This environment is another example of how PKI can help an organization. PKI can provide a secure mechanism to transfer mail not only inside the organization but also outside the organization. Also, there are the benefits of being able to have a secure transaction and access based on a certificate. You could even set up a central certificate database (LDAP) and authenticate using it as your authoritative source.

7.1.4   PKI components

With all that said, let's review: PKI is the use of public key cryptography via some type of network (for our discussion—the Internet). In most cases, a standard public-private key system will be used. This PKI will include several components.

Certificate authority (CA)

The CA issues, verifies, renews, and revokes digital certificates. A certificate includes the public key or information about the public key and may even offer a directory to store the public key.

The management system

There are many different implementations of PKI in the marketplace. Many of these systems are shipped with a web server or are offered as a stand-alone program. The keys are typically created simultaneously using the same algorithm by a certificate authority.

Features

Following are some of the features that we will be working with when using a PKI.

- Certification—Remember when we talked about binding a user to a certificate? This is certification, the process of binding a public key value to a person or system.

- Authentication—Again, we already talked about this. This is the process of allowing access into a system based on a set of credentials. This does not guarantee authorization. Once we know who you are, then we can authorize you. Do you see the relationship between the certificate and binding? We bind you to a certificate via certification, then we authorize into the subsystem. Then you are authorized to perform a function (access, read, write, etc.).

- Validation and Expiration—This is the process of verifying that a certificate is valid. We used the analogy of a driver's license that has an expiration date. The CA and the "stamps" that have been placed on the certificate by the CA verify the certificate.

- Nonrepudiation—This is a scheme in which there is proof of who sent a message, the recipient can show this proof to a third party, and the third party can independently verify the source.

- Digital Signatures—When a public-private key is issued, the CA generates two separate pairs of public and private keys for each user or server. One pair is used for encrypting and decrypting information, and the other is used by client applications to create a digital signature on a document or transmission.

- Encryption of e-mail—Using PKI, we can encrypt documents, files, and e-mail. S/MIME can be used to send encrypted e-mail.

7.2   X.509

To understand X.509, we need to discuss something called X.500. Think of a telephone directory; X.500 is much like your local phone directory. You start with a person's name and, using that name, you can look up information about that person, such as his or her phone number and address. In the case of X.500, you can access many different items about that person, including his or her e-mail address. The concept of an X.500 directory is that the displays can represent any system entity, not just people but computers, businesses, and governments. The entry can also contain the certificate specifying the person's public key. Both X.509 and X.500 were designed in the mid-1980s, before the advent of the Internet.

The lookup method to X.500 is based on a property known as a DN. (Just what we need—another acronym!) DN, which stands for "distinguished name," is a method to look up entries in a directory. The DN must be unique in the directory and will be arranged using a hierarchical methodology. This seems to be more confusing terminology. Actually, here is what all this means. A directory (of names) will be organized into a logical structure that someone who is looking for a name could follow. Using an X.500 directory structure, all information held in the directory would be known as the "directory information base," or DIB. The DIB contains entries that are related hierarchically to each other.

Now your next question would be, "What is an entry?" Every entity has attributes associated with it. An attribute comprises an attribute type and

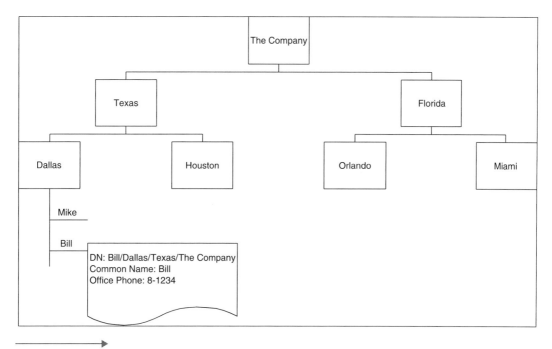

Figure 7.1

one or more associated values. One example of an attribute type would be "office phone number," and the attribute value might be "8-1234." The entries held in the DIB are formatted using a tree structure, which is similar to a structure chart used by most hierarchical organizations. The DIB would be similar to looking at a tree from the top down. In this example you may want to know Bill's office phone number. The problem is that there are 200 Bills in the Company. Looking at the tree from the top down, you can then follow the structure. You may know that Bill works for the Company. You may also know that Bill works in Dallas, Texas. With that information you can find Bill and then read his phone number. In Figure 7.1, Bill's DN is "Bill/Dallas/Texas/the Company." This name format is known as a "canonical" name. If there were a country identifier, then you would have an additional display shown, such as "C = US." These identifiers show each component of a name.

- CN = Common Name

- OU = Organization Unit

- O = Organization

- C = Country

Using the X.500 directory we can now find our way around and manage names within our organization. This is where X.509 arrives. As we said, each entry in an X.500 directory will have attributes and values. One of those attributes can and will be an e-mail address, and a place for a public key. Using these attributes, we can do several tasks: send e-mail; send encrypted e-mail; validate a signature; and authenticate against a directory.

This is very powerful, so place a mental bookmark here. We will be discussing directories more as we go on.

X.509 focuses on defining a mechanism by which information can be made available in a secure way to a third party and it supports the authentication of the entries in an X.500 directory. Every X.509 certificate will be "signed" by a certificate authority, or CA. The main purpose of a CA is to bind a public key to the name contained in the certificate, which will provide assurance to third parties that some measure of care was taken to ensure that this binding is valid. Figure 7.2 shows the features of an X.509v2 certificate.

Version

This identifies which version of the X.509 standard applies to this certificate and impacts what information can be specified in it.

Serial number

This number is unique and is assigned to the certificate by its issuing CA. This information can be used in several ways—for example, when a certificate is revoked, its serial number is placed in a certificate revocation list, or CRL. We will describe the CRL later.

Signature algorithm identifier

This identifies the algorithm used by the CA to sign the certificate.

Issuer name

This is the name of the entity that signed the certificate (typically the CA).

Validity period

This is a pair of dates/times for which the certificate is considered valid. Each certificate is valid only for a limited amount of time. A start date and an end date define this time period.

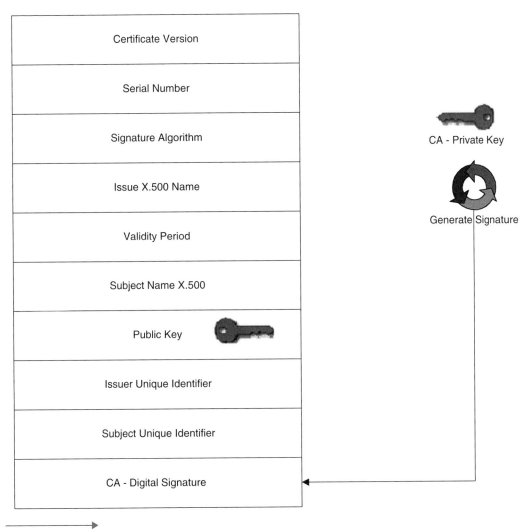

Figure 7.2

Subject name

The subject name sees the X.500 standard, so it is unique across the directory, or DIB. The entry will be in the format of a distinguished name (DN) of the entity—for example, "CN = Bill/OU = Dallas/OU = Texas/OU = the Company/C = US." (Each of these refers to the subject's common name, organizational unit, organization, and country.)

Public key

This is the value of the public key, along with an algorithm identifier, which specifies the public key cryptography system to which this key belongs.

Issuer unique identifier

This is an optional bit that is used to make the issuing certification authority name unambiguous in the event that the same name has been reassigned to a different entity. This field is not widely used, since it has turned out to be difficult to manage and is ignored or omitted in most implementations.

Subject unique identifier

This is an optional bit string used to make the X.500 name of the subject unambiguous.

Certification authority CA—Digital signature

The CA will 'stamp' the certificate with a signature. This signature binds of all the other fields (listed above) into the certificate. The certificate identifies the CA via a digital signature but also by the name of the certificate. Certificates are issued by a CA which, by design, is a trusted party that vouches for the identity of those to whom it issues certificates. In order to prevent faked certificates, the CA's public key must be trustworthy. The CA can publicize its public key or provide a certificate from a higher level CA which attests to the validity of its public key.

Now you have seen what an X.509v2 certificate looks like. More information can be gained at http://www.ietf.org/html.charters/pkix-charter.html.

Figure 7.3 shows an X.509v3 certificate. "Extensions" are new fields that have been added to X.509v3. These are significant changes to the X.509 standard. One of the fundamental changes was to make the certificate and CRL formats flexible. These extensions are fully described in RFC 2459.

We will review some of these new extensions: key usage; certificate policy; alternative names; and certification path constraints.

Key usage

This field indicates the purpose for the key—for example, digital signature, certificates signing, and CRL. This is becoming very important in the maintenance of keys, because keys that encrypt data may need to be recoverable and keys for nonrepudiation may be defined as "nonrecoverable."

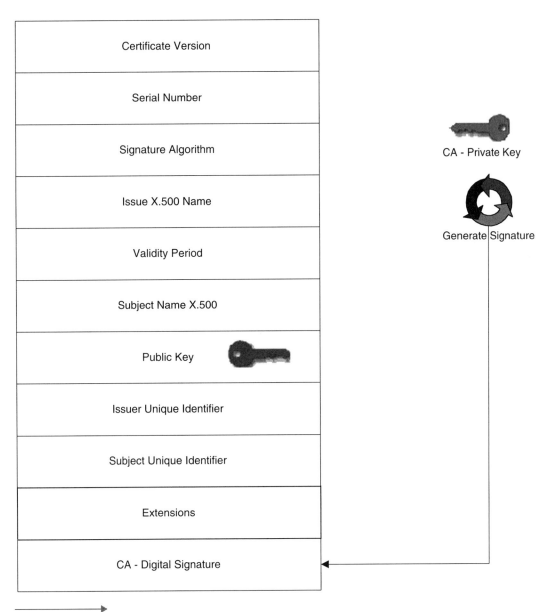

Figure 7.3

Certificate policies

X.509v3 gives the CA the function to include with the certificate a list of policies that were followed in creating the certificate. These policies are intended to help users decide if a certificate is usable for a particular application.

Alternative names

This field contains one or more alternative, unambiguous names.

Certification path constraints

These extensions help different organizations link their PKI infrastructures together. These fields include (1) basic constraints (2) name constraints, and (3) policy constraints. The basic constraints indicate whether the certificate may act as a certification authority or is an end-entity certificate. The name constraints can be used to restrict a name space that will be considered acceptable in subsequent certificates via this certificate. The policy constraints will specify a set of constraints with respect to explicit certificate policy identification and policy mapping.

7.3   Certificate authority

For the most part, there are two basic systems in current use for issuing certificates: a closed system (private hierarchy) and an open system (public hierarchy).

7.3.1   Closed system

The closed system will have a certificate authority as part of one entity. In theory, you could have several organizations and organizational units. Also, in theory, you could distribute the responsibility of supporting and maintaining those organization certifiers. With a closed system, your company is in the business of being a CA. There are many reasons to do this. One situation might be that you have several bank branches and you want to encrypt data between each branch; in that case, you would be the CA and issue the certificates. In reality, you would place the certifier under lock and key and may even put a guard (an actual person) in charge of handing out the key via a very controlled mechanism. You might have a multinational company with several CAs, or in the same example, you might have a multinational company with only one CA.

Advantages

- You are the CA, so you control the certificates.

- You also control the binding of the user to the certificate; in theory, you could physically look at each person and then issue the certificate.

- You manage the certificate structure, naming, validation, and expiration.

- You have control of your own destiny.

- No one else can use certificates or impersonate yours (hang on for a second on this one).

Disadvantages

- You are the CA, so you control the certificates. Why is this a disadvantage? Now you need a support structure to accommodate this mess.

- You will need the proper software and/or hardware to implement the solution.

- You will need to have a support staff to manage the certificates. Remember that certificates expire. Guess what? People may need to change their name (such as in the case of marriages). You will need to figure that out too.

- How will you handle issues about people quitting? (CRL—later)

- Now, in theory, if you are your own CA, then you control that CA and no one else will have it. This is true, but it can also be very false. The issue is that in order to create a certificate, someone or something will need to "touch" the CA—i.e., act as a certifier. The CA certifier is a physical entity that exists somewhere (in a document, file, hard drive, floppy, etc.). As a result, you can lose control of the CA. Even if the CA file has a password, you can still lose control of it. Administrators do quit and move on to other companies. If you do become your own CA, then work with your software vendor and determine methods to protect the CA certificate.

7.3.2 Open system

Now let's talk about open public systems. A public system is one in which an individual or a company can go for certificates. The public CA is typically an independent entity that issues certificates. In some cases, this CA is known as a third-party CA.

Advantages

- Even though you are not the CA, you can set up a service via a public CA to provide certificates on your behalf. You still control the certificates, but you do not control the root certificate.

- Again, you can control the binding of the user to the certificate; in theory, you could physically look at each person and then issue the certificate. (This does not scale very well.) Many vendors have automated systems that can register users and issue certificates. (The automated systems scale very well.)

- By using a service from a public CA, you manage the certificate structure, naming, validation, and expiration, but as we mentioned, you cannot control the root certificate.

- Overall, the cost of an open public system can be less expensive than an open system, because an existing infrastructure and people support the system.

- Reliability of infrastructure is a benefit. Most "known" public systems have a proven track record. We have never heard of a case where a public infrastructure had an outage.

Disadvantages

- In this case, you would not be able to own the root of the certificate. So in theory, someone at the service could create an unauthorized certificate. Here we need to balance some of these issues. We would hope that if your company does any business with any type of service provider, you would look at the following: service levels; legal liability; legal responsibility; and code of ethics.

Each of these issues will need to be reviewed and agreed on. Also, define the consequences for breaches of any of these issues. In the end, you should have a service provider agreement. These agreements define the rights and obligations of the service provider and the company requesting or purchasing the services. The moral of the story: Consult your legal department before using a public CA.

Which is better, a closed private system or a public system? The "consulting" answer is, "It depends." You know the saying, "Ready, aim, fire"? Please don't select the technology before understanding the business problem that you are trying to solve. Following are the issues that you will need to review before making your decision:

- What are the business requirements? (As always, what is the need, what is being supported?)

- What are the user requirements?

- What is the cost?

- What is the cost of doing nothing? (This is very important.)

- Are there other options? Is PKI really the answer?

- What are the support requirements?

- What user issues must be addressed (for example, number of users, location of users, user types—office, roaming, remote—and bandwidth)?

- Based on the business requirements, can you use a public service provider?

- What options do they provide to manage your users?

- What are the training requirements (for example, users, administrators, and help desk)?

- Who owns this project? Is there a person who can make decisions if the project gets stalled?

- What is the cost if you need to be your own CA?

- What happens if the root certificate CA is compromised? (This question needs to be asked for both public and private systems.)

- Based on your decision, what is the per-user cost?

- Can the technology be used on other applications or business services?

- Will this be offered to the general public? What services are available for the general public from a public CA?

- What service levels are required? (This question is for both public and private CAs.)

- Depending on the solution, what process will be used to bind the user to the certificate?

Now you have an idea of how important the CA is. If the CA certificates fall into the hands of the "bad dudes," then they can create certificates that can impersonate a valid member of your organization. With that said, let's delve into what it really means to you and what the true risks are.

Let's start with an example, Figure 7.4, which shows an extract of a certificate taken from a browser. (Note: Serial numbers are 128 bits in length. The serial number shown in Figure 7.4 is not 128 bits.)

In Figure 7.4, the CA is "The Big Cert CA for BUBBA." Let's assume that a "bad dude" has obtained a copy of this cert. What can he do with it?

Figure 7.4

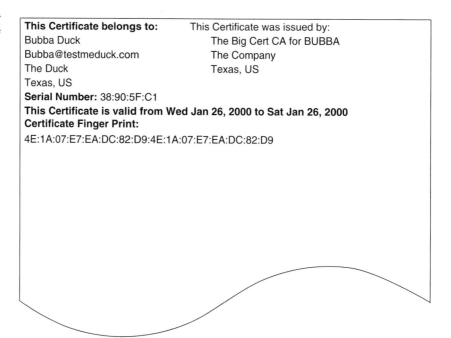

This Certificate belongs to: This Certificate was issued by:
Bubba Duck   The Big Cert CA for BUBBA
Bubba@testmeduck.com   The Company
The Duck   Texas, US
Texas, US
Serial Number: 38:90:5F:C1
This Certificate is valid from Wed Jan 26, 2000 to Sat Jan 26, 2000
Certificate Finger Print:
4E:1A:07:E7:EA:DC:82:D9:4E:1A:07:E7:EA:DC:82:D9

One big issue is access to a directory source that would house public keys.
Let's also make the assumption that it is available in read mode. Following
are some things the bad dude could do:

- First, he could create a bogus user with the stolen CA.

- Then, with access to the public directory, he could send encrypted
  messages to those users, requesting certain actions, or that items be
  returned to him via e-mail.

- He could also sign messages. There is a hitch in this one: If the targeted user's software validates the signature via the public directory,
  this could generate an alert condition to the targeted user. Therefore,
  signing may not work. But guess what? You could send a message to a
  remote user that may not have direct access to the public directory.
  Again, if the user were trained, he or she would know to check the
  fingerprint. Using the fingerprint, you can check for a signed message
  from the "real" Bubba instead of the "fake" Bubba. The targeted user
  could just call the real Bubba and say, "I just got this request from
  you for a billion dollars that you want sent to Cuba. Please read me
  your fingerprint for validation of this transaction."

- The bad dude could possibly authenticate into your web servers with
  illegally obtained certificates. This is easily done if all you do is check

for a root certificate in common, because then the bad dude can access your servers. The bad dude can then access any resource or database that does not have any restrictions (aka "anonymous"). If you have access restrictions, the bad dude will not be able to access those resources for the following reasons: the bogus name is Bad Boy Jim; the access list is David Smith and Maria Jones; and authorization to the resource is controlled via the public keys of each user name. Remember that in this example, the bad dude did not have write access to the directory source, so he or she cannot get the needed public keys into the directory to gain access to an authorized resource. Get it? If not, read it again.

Now let's modify the scenario. What if the bad dude has write access to your directory? In that case, you will need to do the following: update your resume; place it on www.monster.com; start to interview; and consider a job flipping burgers.

We are teasing a bit, but having write access is even worse; now the user can modify the public keys, he or she can intercept encrypted mail, and can, for the most part, grant access to any resource. Get it? If not, reread this section until your head hurts. This is important!

So what are the rules? (This is clearly a "man-in-the-middle attack"— public key substitution. It is not practical for an outsider to pull this off but more likely for an insider or former insider who has had access into critical systems such as PKI and/or e-mail.)

1.   Don't lose control of your CA(s).

2.   Don't grant write access to your directory resource, or, at least, control it and audit it.

7.4   Certification practice statement

We have seen the importance of a CA; now we need to discuss the services that the CA provides, which apply to both open and closed systems. We need to look at the practices of the CA, including the actual services, the legality of the CA, and the trustworthiness of the CA. The concept that drives this is the "Certification Practice Statement," or CPS.[1]

---

1.   This term originated in the American Bar Association Digital Signature Guidelines (http://www.abanet.org/scitech/home.html). Another source of information is RFC 2527.

This document presents a framework to assist the writers of certificate policies or certification practice statements for certification authorities and public key infrastructures. In particular, the framework provides a comprehensive list of topics that potentially (at the writer's discretion) need to be covered in a certificate policy definition or a certification practice statement.[2]

A CPS is valuable for most CAs. You can see the importance of having one for a public CA. Using the CPS from a public CA, your company could review the practices and then determine if you "trust" the CA to manage your PKI. The CPS should also dictate legal responsibilities, roles, policies, and procedures. Following is a list of what should be covered in most any CPS:

1. Introduction

2. What is a certification practice statement? (or, What is a CPS in our organization?)

3. Legal obligations (the company and CAs)

4. Detailed practice specifications

5. Privacy

6. Confidence and reliability (including nonrepudiation)

7. Statement regarding trustworthiness

8. Statement regarding audits

9. Statement regarding root key certificate

10. Statement regarding identification and authentication practices

11. Statement regarding certificate revocation

12. Management of the certificate life cycle

Let's look at each item.

Introduction

The introduction should include the scope and basic responsibilities of the document.

What is a certification practice statement? (or, What is a CPS in our organization?)

Overall, we have described it here in this book. What this section needs is a definition of what it means to your organization. Or, if you are using a service provider, make sure that they have documented this definition.

Legal obligations (the company and CAs)

This section needs to define the rights, duties, and expectations of each party.

Detailed practice specifications

This refers to various actions taken by the CA to validate the certificate applicants' identities and confirm the information they provide during the application process. The type, scope, and extent of confirmation depends on the class of certificate, the type of applicant, and other factors. This also includes processes to manage expired certificates.

Privacy

This section determines the privacy information and how to deal with each customer or user, and which directories public keys are placed in.

Confidence and reliability (including nonrepudiation)

One of the most important factors of PKI is nonrepudiation. This can be used in various applications, including but not limited to messaging. The recipient of an electronic message needs to be confident of a sender's integrity. Nonrepudiation is concerned with binding the sender to the message. The sender should not be able to deny having sent the communication if in fact it was sent.

Statement regarding trustworthiness

The reliability of any PKI system has much to do with the security and authentication practices of each party involved. These practices establish the "trustworthiness" of the system, which is based on good security practices. A very important factor in the trustworthiness of any public key infrastructure is the trust in a "trusted third party," or, the CA. The CA will need to provide a trustworthy infrastructure. This definition of trustworthiness should include (1) administrative personnel (2) employees, and (3) systems and networks.

Statement regarding audits

Audits should be defined and scheduled. Also, the systems for reporting the audits should be defined. (Note: Keep in mind that your CPS may become a public document. In that case, you cannot provide details about the internal workings of the organization. Most CPS statements are not this granular regarding auditing, so be careful about providing too much information, which could be used in security penetration.)

Statement regarding root key certificate

The following items should be considered for this section:

1. Root certificate and public-private key pair creation. (the procedure for root certificate and public-private keys.)

2. Private key security. Describe how the CA will protect access to the private keys after they have been generated.

3. Physical security. Describe the security of the environment and access to the environment, including (1) card key access, if any (2) network firewalls, and (3) physical access audit logs.

4. Backup and storage facilities. Describe the mechanism that will provide backup and recovery of the root keys.

5. Root key compromise. Describe the steps taken to keep the root keys from being compromised and include the plan in the event a compromise does occur.

Statement regarding identification and authentication practices

The identification and authentication process requires that the certificate applicant provide specific information in order to receive certificates. This could include the following (or be a combination of several identifications):

- PIN assigned by an external entity
- Driver's license
- Passport
- Employee ID
- Other type of recognized ID

Statement regarding certificate revocation

This is the process of publishing and managing a Certificate Revocation List (CRL). We will be discussing the CRL in the next section.

Management of the certificate life cycle

The life cycle of a certificate will in most cases follow the diagram in Figure 7.5.

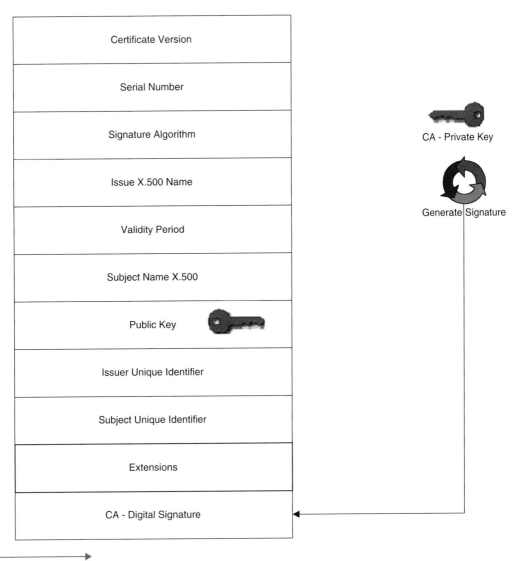

Figure 7.5

7.5   **Certificate revocation list**

At long last, we finally get to the CRL. So what is this magical thing called the CRL?[3] Figure 7.6 shows an example of a CRL, or certificate revocation list. When a certificate is issued to an end user or systems, it is expected to

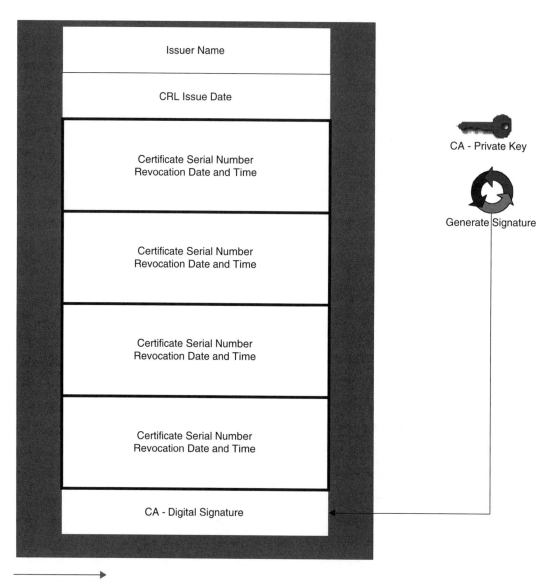

Figure 7.6

be in use for the period that it is valid. So far, so good. Following, however, are circumstances in which you may want to revoke that certificate:

- An employee quits. If an employee leaves your organization, you will want to invalidate the certificates he or she has been using. The CRL will accomplish this step.

- You suspect that the certificate has been compromised. This is actually an old problem, notably with passwords: "Here, use my password while I am gone. It's okay but don't tell anyone." In many browsers, you can export a certificate and import it into another browser. Next thing you know, someone has submitted a purchase order for a billion dollars in chewing tobacco. In this example, you place the old certificate into the CRL and issue a new one.

- A person changes his or her name. In this case, the old certificate is placed into the CRL and a new one is issued. There are some PKI systems that accommodate for new names without issuing a new certificate (such as Lotus Notes).

Overall, the CRL is a list of revoked certificates that is signed by a CA. One of the biggest issues with a CRL is the time difference between when a certificate has been identified as required to be in the CRL and when it actually gets put into the CRL. PKIs have actually been around for several years, and, as a result, many bad habits have been noticed by most organizations, such as:

- Days or even weeks pass before a certificate is placed into the CRL (in some implementations, this is also known as the termination list).

- The certificate is not put into the CRL at all.

- A CRL does not exist!

Make sure you put processes in place to manage certificates that need to be removed from your organization. Another concern is the huge size that the CRL can become. In the case of a large enterprise organization, the CA can be expected to certify thousands, or even hundreds of thousands of entities. Over time, the CRL can get really big. In itself, this could be a problem. Some PKI systems have software that can help manage this. Check with your vendor.

7.6   Key recovery

There are a variety of "key recovery," "key escrow," and "trusted third party" encryption requirements that have been suggested in recent years by government agencies. All key recovery systems require the existence of a highly sensitive and highly available secure secret key system.

Key recovery is sometimes called "key escrow." Key recovery is used as a generic term for these systems, encompassing the various key escrows, trusted third party, and key recovery encryption systems introduced in recent years. Although there are some differences between these systems, the distinctions are not critical for our purposes. A CA can exist without any form of key recovery and a key recovery infrastructure can exist completely independently of any CA infrastructure. More and more businesses understand the importance of key backup because they must be able to retrieve encrypted data when users lose their decryption keys, forget their passwords, or leave the organization.

Why do we need a key recovery mechanism? Users can lose the keys, in which case you may need to declare the keys "compromised." If a user loses a certificate, he or she will not be able to read any encrypted mail, which could result in lost data. Having a key escrowed (or in a backup) will allow you to access that data. But this is also a problem. Another big problem, and one that each company must deal with, is, who will have access to the backups (aka "escrows")? We cannot recommend that all companies have an escrow; in some cases, this could be a violation of the policies and procedures of that company. What we do recommend is that you review the business needs in relation to the security requirements, then make your own decision. Also, you may issue two keys, one for encryption and one for signatures. The encryption key will be escrowed, and the signature certificate will not be escrowed. Why do this? The reason is nonrepudiation: If you back up the signature keys, someone could access the keys and use them illicitly. Following are considerations for having one or more keys and using escrows:

- Business requirements

- Support requirements

- Nonrepudiation requirements

- Encryption requirements

- Roaming users (in some cases, the certificate with the private key is stored in some type of encrypted directory—don't lose control of this!)

- Cost

- Protection requirements if an escrow is implemented in your company

7.7   Lightweight directory access protocol

The Lightweight Directory Access Protocol, or LDAP, is a directory protocol.[4] LDAP defines a simple mechanism for directory clients to query and manage a database of hierarchical entries. Overall, LDAP is a simplification of the X.500 directory access protocol that we discussed in the first part of this chapter. If you delve into the LDAP protocol, you will see that it is a subset of the X.500 access protocol. As a result, LDAP can access X.500 directories, and LDAP and X.500 servers can interoperate within the same environment. LDAP runs directly over TCP, eliminating the need for the complicated OSI (Open Systems Interconnection) stack.

The LDAP directory service model is based on specific and unique entries. An entry is a single collection of attributes with a single key ("key," in this case, is a parameter that can be used to look up something, and not a key for encryption). Each entry will have a name. As you may recall, we have discussed DNs, or distinguished names. The DN is used as a unique value that represents each collection, or entry. Much like the X.500, each of the entry's attributes has a type and one or more values. Again, like the X.500 example that we have shown before, the LDAP directory entries are arranged in a hierarchical, treelike structure. This structure can reflect political, geographic, or organizational boundaries.

The LDAP directory service is based on a client-server model. An LDAP server will offer the directory data via TCP/IP port 389 and SSL encrypted port 636. Clients will access the LDAP server via a set of queries. The results of the queries can be used in messaging, applications, and authentication. One feature that is built into the protocol is that of a referral. If, in the process of a query, an answer is not available on the local server, then, if configured to do so, the LDAP server will attempt to connect to another server. If that server can service the request, then the result of the query will be returned to the client. One example of this could be name resolution; you may have a person's name but not his or her RFC 821 Internet address (this is an address like Bubba@myemailserver. com).

In Figure 7.7, the client sends a request for "Bubba Duck"; the first server performs a lookup and does not find the entry in its local database. The server then sends a referral to the X.500 server and the entry is found. A lookup is performed for "Bubba Duck," the RFC 821 address is returned to the LDAP server, and then sent from the LDAP server back to the client.

LDAP servers are also capable of managing transaction logs, which is a process for chronicling adds and changes, and for deleting entries. Using this system, an LDAP server propagates these changes to other LDAP servers. This way, you can have one LDAP server send the same data to several other LDAP servers.

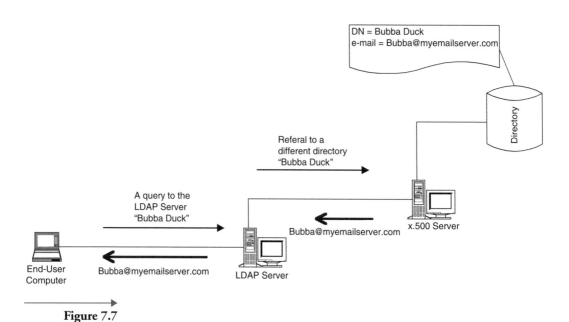

Figure 7.7

There is also a method to access LDAP information via a URL.[5] A pre-defined format is listed in RFC 1959.[6] This format is described as an LDAP search operation to retrieve information from an LDAP directory.

Following is an extract of the RFC 1959 that describes the URL syntax:

2. URL Definition

An LDAP URL begins with the protocol prefix "ldap" and is defined by the following grammar.

```
<ldapurl> ::= "ldap://" [<hostport>] "/" <dn> ["/" <attributes>

            ["?" <scope> "?" <filter>]]

<hostport> ::= <hostname> [":" <portnumber>]

<dn> ::= a string as defined in RFC 1485

<attributes> ::= NULL | <attributelist>

<attributelist> ::= <attributetype>

            |<attributetype> ["," <attributelist>]

<attributetype> ""= a string as defined in RFC 1777
```

5.   http://www.ietf.org/rfc/rfc1738.txt
6.   http://www.ietf.org/rfc/rfc1959.txt

```
<scope> ::= "base" | "one" | "sub"

     <filter> ::= a string as defined in RFC 1558
```

Example:

```
ldap://ldap.itd.umich.edu/o=University%20of%20Michigan,c=

     US??sub?(cn=smith)
```

LDAP can be used to store X.509 certificates for authentication. The certificates are placed into the directory and then accessed via a web server. In Figure 7.8, a user attempts to access a secure page. The web server returns a status code of 401. Then the users send the query back with their credentials (the user logs in). The web server looks to see if the information is local; if the information is not local, it performs a bind operation on the LDAP server and connects to it. Then the web server sends over a query checking for validity of the credentials. If the credentials are valid, a DN is returned back to the web server. The web server then checks to see if that DN has access to the resource being requested; if the request is valid, the page is returned to the browser.

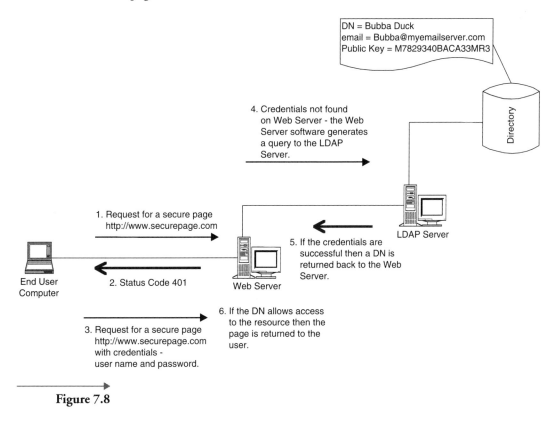

Figure 7.8

7.8   Public key cryptography standards

We are now going to review the Public Key Cryptography Standards, or PKCS. These are specifications that have been produced by RSA. They were first published in 1991 from various groups and early adopters of PKI technology. Currently, there are 15 standards (though some listed here have been combined) defined by RSA:

PKCS #1: RSA Cryptography Standard   Describes rsaEncryption and syntax for RSA public keys and private keys. Also defines three signature algorithms.

PKCS #2   Has been incorporated into PKCS #1.

PKCS #3: Diffie-Hellman Key Agreement Standard   Describes a method for implementing Diffie-Hellman key agreement.

PKCS #4   Has been incorporated into PKCS #1.

PKCS #5: Password-Based Cryptography Standard   Describes a method for encryption with a secret key derived from a password.

PKCS #6: Extended-Certificate Syntax Standard   Describes syntax for extended certificates.

PKCS #7: Cryptographic Message Syntax Standard   Describes syntax for data that may have cryptography applied to it. PKCS #7 is compatible with Privacy-Enhanced Mail (PEM).[7]

PKCS #8: Private-Key Information Syntax Standard   Describes syntax for private-key information. Private-key information includes a private key and public-key algorithm.

PKCS #9: Selected Attribute Types   Defines attribute types for use in PKCS #6 extended certificates, also PKCS #7 digitally signed messages, and PKCS #8 private-key information.

PKCS #10: Certification Request Syntax Standard   Describes syntax for certification requests. A certification request consists of a distinguished name, a public key, and optionally, a set of attributes.

PKCS #11: Cryptographic Token Interface Standard   Specifies an API to devices, which hold cryptographic information and implement cryptographic functions.

---

7.   See RFCs 1421–1424.

PKCS #12: Personal Information Exchange Syntax Standard Specifies a portable format for storing and/or transporting a user's private keys and certificates.

PKCS #13: Elliptic Curve Cryptography Standard This standard is still under development.

PKCS #14: Pseudorandom Number Generation Standard This standard is still under development.

PKCS #15: Cryptographic Token Information Format Standard This standard is targeted at establishing a standard that ensures that users will be able to use cryptographic tokens to identify themselves to multiple standards-aware applications.

Abstract Syntax Notation number one, or ASN.1, is a standard that defines a formal notation for the specification of abstract data types. ASN.1 is a formal notation used for describing data transmitted by telecommunications protocols. Also, ASN.1 covers the structural aspects of information. A main reason for the success of ASN.1 is that this notation is linked with several standardized encoding rules, such as the BER (Basic Encoding Rules) and the PER (Packed Encoding Rules). ASN.1 has been used in PKCS documents, including PKCS #5 v2.0, PKCS #12 v1.0, and PKCS #15 v1.0.

7.9   Public key infrastructure (X.509) standards

One topic not covered is where X.509 comes from and what organizations support it. The "International Telecommunication Union" (ITU) is an organization formerly known as "Consultative Committee on International Telephone and Telegraphy" (CCITT). The ITU provides telecommunications standards as well as the "X." standards, such as X.500 (directory services) and X.509 (secure directory services).[8]

The "Internet Engineering Task Force" (IETF) is an open international community of network designers, vendors, and researchers focused on the evolution of the Internet architecture and the operation of the Internet.[9] The IETF has recognized the X.509 standards to be used in the Internet technologies. To understand the IETF, you need to look at a document that they created:

---

8.   http://www.itu.int/
9.   http://www.ietf.org

The Internet Engineering Task Force is a loosely self-organized group of people who make technical and other contributions to the engineering and evolution of the Internet and its technologies. It is the principal body engaged in the development of new Internet standard specifications. Its mission includes: identifying and proposing solutions to pressing operational and technical problems in the Internet; specifying the development or usage of protocols and the near-term architecture to solve such technical problems for the Internet; making recommendations to the Internet Engineering Steering Group (IESG) regarding the standardization of protocols and protocol usage in the Internet; facilitating technology transfer from the Internet Research Task Force (IRTF) to the wider Internet community; and providing a forum for the exchange of information within the Internet community between vendors, users, researchers, agency contractors, and network managers.

The IETF meeting is not a conference, although there are technical presentations. The IETF is also not a traditional standards organization, although many specifications are produced that become standards. The IETF is made up of volunteers who meet three times a year to fulfill the IETF mission.

There is no membership in the IETF. Anyone may register for and attend any meeting. The closest thing there is to being an IETF member is being on the IETF or working group mailing lists (see the IETF Mailing Lists section). This is where the best information about current IETF activities and focus can be found.[10]

In order to generate some methods and standards to deal with encryption, the IETF formed the Public Key Infrastructure (X.509) (PKIX)[11] working group. The main drive of this working group was to develop the Internet standards needed to support an X.509-based PKI. One of the goals of this PKI is to facilitate the use of X.509 certificates in various applications that reside on the Internet. As part of this process, the working group was looking to promote interoperability between many vendor implementations. The result of this work was to provide a PKI framework based on X.509.[12]

So how do we get a working group to generate a standard? Following is a high-level overview[13]: Overall, we start with a description that will solve some type of technological problem. A team of "smart dudes" will get together and generate a draft document of their solution. We call these draft documents "Internet-drafts."

When submitted to the IETF, the draft documents are then valid for six months. These drafts then go through a process of review and development,

10.   http://www.ietf.org/tao.html
11.   http://www.ietf.org
12.   http://www.ietf.org/html.charters/pkix-charter.html
13.   For a more detailed understanding of this, go to http://www.ietf.org/tao.html

which can consist of several revisions, each of which would be reviewed by the Internet community. If all goes well, and the draft is accepted, it will become a Request for Comments (RFC) document. If a specification has been adopted as an Internet standard, it is given the additional label STD, but it does keep its RFC number.

For more information about the new standard adoption process, PKIX standards, and LDAP standards, check out the references section at the back of this book.

PKS, RC2, and RSA Laboratories are trademarks of RSA Data Security, Inc. All other trademarks belong to their respective companies.

Messaging Security

I shot the sheriff, but not the deputy, and now I have the credit card information from the web site.

8.1   Safe communication: Messaging

Two lovers stand in the bedroom gazing into each other's longing eyes. They move toward the bed, their bodies pulling closer like a magnet and a piece of iron. Their hearts thump like loudspeakers at a rock concert. Closer they move to the point of serious communiqué. Now, with lust in their hearts, they exchange their x.509 certificates and send an encrypted message of love.

Whew—that was hot! What intense communication! Fortunately, our lovers practiced "safe communication." First they exchanged certificates and then consummated their communication. In this case, they set up a secure channel between themselves and established end-to-end privacy. This process involved using the certificates to identify themselves, after which they enabled SSL. And the data flowed in both directions. They lived happily ever after and were totally safe from all bugs and viruses—that is, until one of them said, "I love you." Oops. I just crashed my partner and wiped out his/her hard drive. How can this be? All I did was forward the simple message "I love you." What happened?

The moral of our story is ... love hurts. No, wait, that's not it. The real lesson is that secure messaging is a battle against the elements, which include the following:

- Uninformed users

- Foolhardy administrators

- Premeditated attacks

- Bad use of messaging resources

- Limited implementation of messaging—that is, not enough resources

Messaging is one of the most important mission-critical applications of the network era. For anyone who is not convinced, imagine shutting down the messaging servers in your company for five days. What would happen? The CIO would be inundated with complaints from the company's employees—and even from customers and vendors—that the business was inoperable without messaging capability. As we can see, messaging is critical to doing good business.

Following are some of the components that comprise a messaging system:

- E-mail systems

- The ability to send a messages to multiple recipients

- The ability to send attachments

- The ability to send encrypted messages (S/MIME, PGP, and others)

- The ability to enable an application with messaging components, such as an approval notification

- Calendars and scheduling

- Typically, some type of system to address recipients (an address book)

- Instant messaging integrated with traditional messaging

- Ability to access standards-based e-mail from many different clients, including a browser

Messaging can have many different components and hundreds of features, depending on the vendor. With this power comes a significant security risk. Messaging is an integral part of most of the enterprise businesses in the world. As evidence, you can check out the statistics on the "I Love You" virus. As of mid-May 2000, the "I Love You" virus had caused $8 billion worth of damage to businesses worldwide. This bug impacted more than 600,000 computers.[1]

Billions of e-mail messages are sent over the Internet every day, and one day in May 2000, a few million messages were sent, all with a subject line of "I Love You." A computer science student in the Philippines created this program, thinking it would be contained within his realm of influence. Suddenly, it had replicated itself all over the world. Basically, it worked like this: If a user opened the attachment that was in the message, the virus would send itself to all the contacts in the recipient's e-mail address book. This may not sound too bad on its own, but here is the problem: This virus attempted to send the message to all of the contacts in an address book. In most companies, this could be several dozen to several thousand addresses. Once it hit one business, it was sent on to others. As an example, say the virus arrived at a somewhat small company. The message went into the company, where it parsed itself through the company directory and sent a message out to everyone in the company's directory, including employees, vendors, and customers. This scenario repeated itself in one company after another. Business after business had thousands of e-mail messages running through both the Internet as well as their internal mail systems. In a typical corporate address book, with hundreds and even thousands of users listed, each user opening the attachment would cause it to resend the message to everyone over and over again.

---

1.   For a full report on the Love Bug, check out the CERT Advisory (CERT®) at http://www.cert.org/advisories/CA-2000-04.html.

This made for a vicious cycle, with so many messages that the messaging servers overloaded and crashed to the ground. The virus also overwrote files that use the extensions JPG, JPEG, and MP3. The "From" field, in many cases, showed the message as coming from someone the recipient knew. So the new target would see the message and say, "Oh, that is nice. My sweet snookums says "I love you." Let's see what is in this attachment" (attachment name—LOVE-LETTER-FOR-YOU.TXT.VBS).

Think about the articles that you have read in newspapers and magazines regarding viruses, worms, Trojan horses, logic bombs, and password grabbers. These are all known as malicious software tools. All of these tools can be enabled using messaging as a transport. Most of the major attacks that have crippled computers worldwide have used messaging as the mechanism to deliver their payload. Messaging is powerful, but it is also very vulnerable to attack and it is easy to use as a method of attacking other subsystems. Remember the Chernobyl, Melissa, and Worm viruses? Guess what—they were all spread via e-mail. The end result of these attacks was denial-of-service. These attacks brought major e-commerce web sites to their knees and many web administrators to prayer.

Many of these tools create problems because they do the following:

1.   Attach (delivered)

2.   Copy (effectively replicate themselves)

3.   Resend a copy

4.   Attack—delete some files on the local drive

The technology that recent viruses are using is built into the mailer program or operating system itself. One example is application programs. These use macros that are built into a program, such as word processing. These macro viruses are triggered automatically by tasks within these programs, such as Microsoft Word.

Figure 8.1 shows how the Love Bug took advantage of a scripting language that was built into a mailer program.

1.   A message would arrive in a user e-mail client.

2.   The user would open the message and launch the attachment.

3.   The virus (or agent or tool) would start to run and scan the user's address book.

4.   The virus would start to send messages out to the users listed in the address book, both to the Internet and/or the user company mail system.

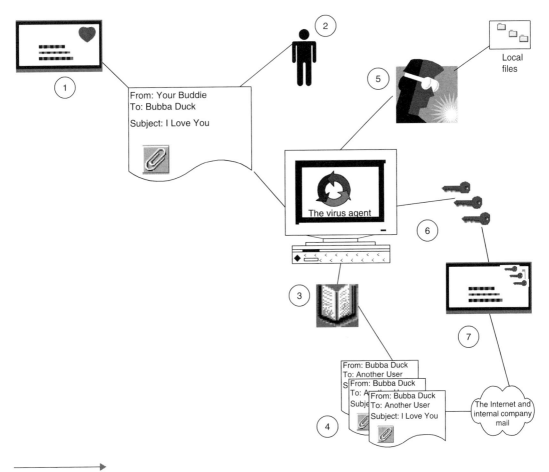

From: Your Buddie
To: Bubba Duck

Subject: I Love You

Local files

The virus agent

From: Bubba Duck
To: Another User
S From: Bubba Duck
To: A...
Subj From: Bubba Duck
To: Another User
Subject: I Love You

The Internet and internal company mail

Figure 8.1

5.   The agent would start to overwrite local files on the workstation. This would include JPEG, MP2, and others.

6.   The agent would then attempt to redirect the user's browser to a web site that would download a program to steal passwords.

7.   If any passwords were captured, the program would send them to a preset address on the Internet.

And the cycle would be repeated over and over.

The sad part of this problem is that these really "bad dudes" are able to mess with our minds and our computers because they are taking advantage of product features. Yes, that is correct—*features*! The macros and scripts that are built into the product are features that enable the product to do many different things. Think of it this way: You have a car, and one of the features is a radio. Someone on your block starts to pirate broadcast some really lousy music on your favorite station frequency. A feature that you use in your car (the radio) has now been used against you. The car still runs, but you cannot listen to your favorite station on the radio. In the case of the virus, not only is it analogous to goofing up your radio station, but it also resets all the other stations that you had programmed. So being a good software citizen, Microsoft issued a fix for many of its products, but at the same time, some of the features were impacted. This is a no-win situation for both the consumer and the software manufacture. In May 2000, Microsoft issued the following URL, which shows some features that may have been impacted by a fix implemented by Microsoft to combat the Love Bug.

Impacts to Love Bug Fix for Outlook 98/2000:

1. *In Word, routing documents through e-mail does not work.*

2. *Palm, Windows CE devices (PDAs) have synchronization issues. These include: Synchronizing with the Inbox displays a prompt and then fails. This is under investigation.*

3. *Due to the programmatic access limits of the update, the SQL SendMail feature is affected and restricted.*

Also check out the CIAC advisory on the bug itself: http://www.ciac.org/ciac/bulletins/k-039.shtml.[2]

Software companies are being held hostage by their own software. Many will argue the point that "the software was developed with holes, poorly written." For the most part that argument is worthless. Why? Following are steps to prove it:

1.   Create some software. Be sure to make it very complex, make it something that does useful work, and that is needed by the general public.

2.   Make the software as secure as you can.

3.   Then tell the world, via a press release, television, newspapers, and the Internet that your software cannot be hacked or misused by the features that are in the program. In essence, your claim is that the software is totally secure.

---

2.   Please check out www.microsoft.com for any updates, and to determine if this URL is still valid.

Do you know what will happen? Over 10,000 hackers from all over the world will make it their "mission" to hack into your software and prove you wrong!

Let's flip the coin to the other side. A poorly written code has been released to the public early. Yes, this does happen! With that said, the following steps must be taken:

1. If you find a bug in a piece of code that would cause some type of harm, damage, or anything bad, it is your responsibility to contact the vendor and alert them to what you have found. Do not, repeat, *do not* post it on a discussion database or forum on the Internet.

2. All software vendors must come clean and fix these bugs (okay, exposures) with best effort. If they don't, the general public will lose confidence in them and eventually stop purchasing their products.

3. Finally, don't become a hacker. (That would make a good song: "Mamas, Don't Let Your Babies Grow Up to Be Hackers.")

As you can see, we are in this together.

The Love Bug is only one of many types of e-mail viruses that exist. Actually the Love Bug combines many different types: virus, worm, Trojan horse, and hoaxes. We will examine each of these.

8.1.1   Virus

A computer virus is a program that spreads by making copies of itself and sending them from computer to computer, wreaking havoc on each computer it visits. The term "virus" is used loosely to cover any sort of program that tries to hide its possibly malicious function while it spreads onto as many computers as possible. A virus can spread itself via a number of mechanisms: a floppy disk, a CD, an e-mail message, and even an application. Viruses can even use your computer's internal clock to trigger the actual program on a certain date.

8.1.2   Worm

A worm gestates in a networked environment and then spreads by spawning copies of itself onto other computers on the network. Worms eat up computer resources such as memory and even network bandwidth. Also, worms sometimes delete data and then spread themselves via e-mail. Here we are again: The transport of choice is e-mail. One of the earliest worms that caused great disruption on the Internet was the Morris worm in 1988. This worm was a harbinger of things to come. The Morris Internet worm burrowed through the Internet of 1988. It only impacted 6,000 out of a possible 60,000 computers. Stop and think about that—only 60,000 computers were on the Internet at that time. That may not sound like much, but that worm hit 10% of the existing community. The Love Bug hit 100 times as many computers. As technology has been growing, so have the worms.

8.1.3   Trojan horse

A Trojan horse is a program that appears legitimate but contains secondary hidden functions that can (and many times do) cause damage. E-mail with the aim of stealing passwords from a victim's computer and then e-mailing the stolen data to a targeted recipient often distributes one of the most common types of Trojan horse.

There are many vendors with information and tools to combat viruses. Following are a few: http://www.symantec.com; http://www.mcafee.com; and http://www.drsolomon.com. For more information about viruses check out http://www.bocklabs.wisc.edu/~janda/virl_faq.html#B01.

8.1.4   Hoax

One of the most irritating e-mail messages one can receive is one that has been broadcasted to everyone in the company warning about a new virus. Why should this make us mad? Because some Good Samaritan is trying to keep us from reading some e-mail that may mess up our computer. Before we go any further, we must say thanks to all of you nice people who are trying to protect us. Second, we'd like to say, "Don't ever do that again!" Out of all the warning messages received in this manner, 99% of them are hoaxes. Here is our advice: Before you forward a message about a virus, do the following:

1.   Check with your company's web site and read the e-mail policy about sending out broadcasts and alerts. You may find a phone number or e-mail address of whom to contact about any potential alerts or viruses.

2.   Go to http://ciac.llnl.gov/ciac/CIACHoaxes.html and check out the latest hoaxes (also check out http://kumite.com/myths/—one of our favorites).

Hoaxes themselves are nothing new. Remember cold fusion: The great breakthrough in 1989 that was going to solve the world's energy problems? When all was said and done, it was discovered that the data has been adjusted to match the wanted results. In other words, it did not work. Things haven't changed much since that famous hoax. People still fall for hoaxes, most notably via the Internet and messaging. For some foolish reason, we trust what our computer tells us. One of the best examples of Internet hoaxes is "The Good Times Virus Hoax." Several messages began circulating via the Internet in 1994. Over time the text of the original Good Times message has been rewritten. This hoax warns you to delete any message with the subject heading "PENPAL GREETINGS" because if you open it, a Trojan horse virus will supposedly remove all the data on your hard drive. Despite the fact that many prominent antiviral authorities and the CIAC Virus Bulletin quickly debunked Good Times as a hoax, the myth refused to die, popping up again several months and even years later.

8.2   Junk mail

At this point in our discussions about messaging security, we are going to talk about two types of mail: junk mail and spam mail. It is appropriate to discuss each separately. The difference is in the premeditation of the type of mail. Junk mail is just that—junk. Spam mail is typically from someone who has added you to some type of mailing list (automatic in most cases) that is sending you messages without your permission. In many cases, but not all, the junk mail comes to you with your permission.

8.2.1   The junk

Let's start with junk mail. This type of mail can actually arrive in your e-mail box due to some action on your part. There was the time you went out on a site and registered to access some information about the site, or when you filled out an information card to receive a free magazine. Now you are receiving e-mail. Some of it you actually want, known as "stuff"—the stuff you want to read. So far, so good. After a while, however, that "stuff" adds up, and the next thing you know, you have junk mail. You have added yourself to hundreds of e-mailing lists. Now, most of these companies that you have been doing business with will typically include a URL with the junk mail. This URL will allow you to remove your address from their distribution system, and reputable companies will then remove you from the list. At this point you say, "I don't see the problem." Well, hold your horses for a minute and keep reading.

Now you are receiving a little bit of junk mail. You asked for it—a subscription here, a catalog update there, a job posting. Let's say that adds up to 20 pieces of junk mail a day—still not much for some. Now let's add on a bit more, and to magnify our problem, let's start this about the end of November. It's the holiday season. We are all happy. We will be taking some time off to eat, drink, be merry, check out the travel and sports pages on the Internet, and then send our colleagues down the hall an electronic season's greetings card. Here is what we do: We go to some great URL, find that e-card, and send it to our buddies. That card may have an attachment, maybe an animated snowman that smiles. When we look at that attachment, we see it is only about 500 kilobytes. That is not very big, so we send the card to our buddies down the hall, who receive it and enjoy it. Our new best friends now forward it to their good buddies, who forward it to others. Finally, someone forwards it outside of the company, and it eventually it is forwarded back into our company to another person. Let's add some of this up: two messages at a meg each plus all that junk mail we are getting. Then multiply it by two factors: 10,000 employees at our company and the holiday season. This adds up to a lot of messages, and many of these messages are bigger than 500 K, especially if some of these geniuses encrypted the message when they sent it out. The end result is that we have a clogged e-mail system with messages to and from known users or companies. This is junk mail, and to our company, this should be classified as nonbusiness use of the messaging environment. (Later in this chapter, we will be discussing acceptable use policies and what should be in them.)

8.2.2   The spam

First off, let's provide a tribute to a wonderful meat product. The name "SPAM" is a registered trademark of Hormel Foods Corporation. Per the request of the Spam web site, we will be following the guidelines as specified in their URL, http://www.spam.com/ci/ci_in.htm.

The guidelines include use of the word "spam" in lowercase when discussing the delivery of unsolicited commercial e-mail, or UCE. The word "SPAM" is owned and trademarked by Hormel Foods. Go to your local grocer and purchase some. It's very good and can be prepared in many different ways.

With that said, let's continue. Here is what we all have experienced: We happily log on to check our e-mail, and there are new messages waiting for us. This is exhilarating. You have mail! Someone likes you. They really like you! With mounting anticipation you look at the subject lines, and you see the following: "Make money now"; "Investment tips that no one else knows"; "Yes, these are the bodies that you dream about"; "Are you over 18 and would you like to be a model?"; "Remember me? We met at ... ."

Of course, these are all valid, genuine messages ... *not*! So after a while you start to see these messages pile up in your in-box, and you may try to reply to some of these messages. You may even request to be removed from the senders' mailing lists. This request does not always work, and in many cases, you will probably receive even more UCE.

Following are several methods that spammers use to get to you:

- Purchase a list of names from various sources. Most reputable e-commerce companies that have your e-mail address will place some type of banner or disclaimer stating that they will not sell your address to an external vendor. But not all companies will offer this disclaimer.

- Get a list right off the Internet itself from anonymous sources, such as:

    1.   If you post an entry on an on-line service or Internet bulletin board

    2.   Spend time in chat rooms on an on-line service

    3.   Have a listing in an on-line service's directory (Remember LDAP? Go to your favorite LDAP site and type in your last name.)

- Create a list of addresses based on a common suffix and a computed local part.

The following example is one of the most clever spam attacks that we have ever seen.

Several years ago, at a public utility, the systems manager reported that there was a problem with the SMTP server. (Remember, SMTP is the standards-based e-mail protocol.) A review of the message queue turned up thousands of messages, all the same size. Extracting one of the messages and opening it revealed an invitation to a pornographic site. Launching the URL and opening the site produced a banner with the message that the site was not in the United States, so there was nothing the public utility could do. At this point you might ask, "What did the 'From' field say?" The "From" field gave the name of a legitimate company in Texas, which, when called, said, "Sorry, these messages are not from us." The spammer had just modified the "From" field to be from a legitimate company, which is very easily done. Let's define some terms before we go further.

Suffix: The part of the Internet address after the @ symbol

Local part: The actual name that you use to make the user unique in that mail server

In BubbaDuck@thisisamailserver.com., BubbaDuck is the local part, and thisisamailserver.com is the suffix.

Now, let's continue.

The spammer creates a program to open a list (even a directory) of words—a very long list of words—and then mixes and matches those words with numbers—for example, Dog, Cat, DogCat, CatDog, Dog1, Dog2, Cat1, Cat2, DogCat1, and so on. Then the spammer's program mixes the computed local part with a preset suffix. This creates thousands of addresses that, in our example, were used to send out the invitation to the pornographic site.

But we are not done. The spammer in this case performed a simple trick—he or she found a site that had the SMTP relay turned on. This is a relatively simple feature that allows messages to be related from one server to another. The spammer found this public utility mail server name via a number of different mechanisms. (For an example, check out http://www.samspade.org/.) Now the spammer has one more step: purchase an account on a local ISP. Then he or she will follow these steps:

1.   Create the target addresses via the automated program

2.   Launch the message toward the target via a local ISP

3.   Relay the message to the target site

The target site may accept the message if the address matches the "Send to" name. If the message is accepted, it will be delivered to the computer user's mailbox. If the message is not accepted, it can be bounced back to the "From" address. In our case, it was a legitimate address, and the poor, innocent company was spammed with rejection into their mail system or even a legitimate user. Not good.

How can you tell if you have the relay turned on? Following is a simple test:

Most operating systems have a program called "Telnet." (The commands are shown in Bold.)

```
Telnet DomainName.com SMTP
HELO fake.domain
MAIL FROM: bogus@fake.domain
RCPT TO: arealaddress@arealsuffix.domain
DATA
end with a .
QUIT
```

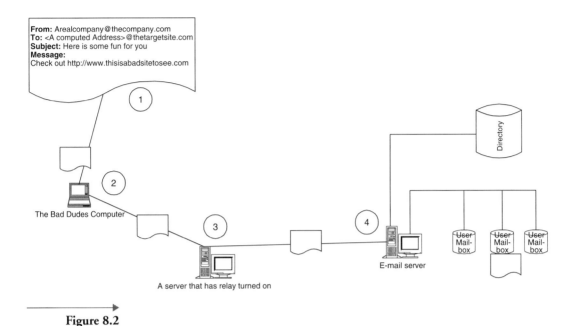

From: Arealcompany@thecompany.com
To: <A computed Address>@thetargetsite.com
Subject: Here is some fun for you
Message:
Check out http://www.thisisabadsitetosee.com

Figure 8.2

This easy trick will tell you if you have the relay turned on (see Figure 8.2). You are probably wondering what was done in the case of the pornographic site relay spammer. Well, the relay setting was turned off. That was it—very easy and back to business as usual. The target server administrator was also contacted, informed of the situation, and asked not to put the public utility site on its blockout list.

So far we have been talking about problems with messaging. We could spend the rest of this book just on messaging problems, but let's talk about solutions. Figure 8.3 shows another way to look at the actual flow of a message. In each case, the large groups are "virtual." Cases can exist where a message will need to be returned to a source mailbox, such as:

- A reply to the message being sent

- A reply from an automated agent—"Out of Office Profile"

- A reply from the router, stating that the message cannot be delivered because the server is down, mailbox is not found, and so on

A return mailbox should be created with the same name that will be in the "From" field. This mailbox can then capture any of these "Replied" messages.

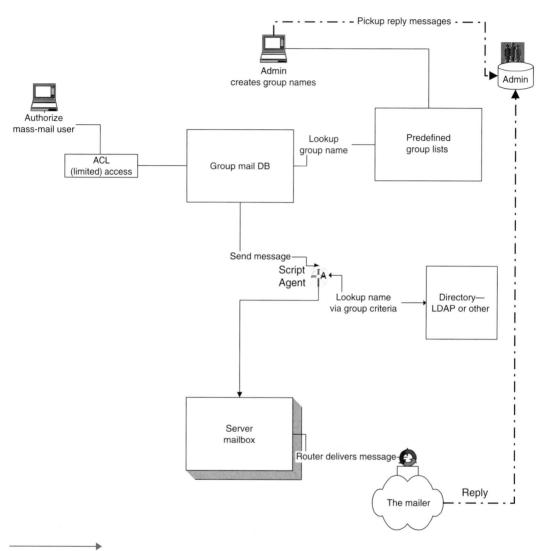

Figure 8.3

Following are the required components of the return mailbox:

1. Method to notify an administration group that a new mass-mail "group" is needed

2. Mail database (logical database)

3. Process to create and/or maintain mass-mail groups, e.g., a database with a group name and criteria listing (logical database)

4.   Custom memo form (with custom "From" field, custom "Send" button, and custom "Form" properties)

5.   Ownership of the process

6.   Ownership of the ACL to the database

7.   Definition of ACL access to all databases

8.   Definition of an administrator to create the mass-mail groups (names and coding criteria)

9.   Definition of access to use the database

10.   Agent to parse a directory source

11.   Authoritative data source to keep the personnel records updated with current employee information

12.   Mail-in mailbox for "Reply" messages

Companywide and location specific "groups" (virtual groups) could be maintained centrally and with only one update. The distribution agents could generate the list based on information from the directory source. This would ensure that an up-to-date list of addresses used would comprehend recent additions and deletions to the directory source. In other words, the directory source *must* be up to date with correct information.

Following are some benefits of a current directory:

- Up-to-date list of addresses would be used

- Large groups would not have to be created/maintained

- Allows for rapid deployment of important messages

- Will address very large distributions (no limits to group sizes)

- Provides centrally located ownership of the entire process, including security and access

- Dimwitted users would not be able to send out large messages with pictures of their dogs

Okay, let's get real—this is a very complex solution. Our example is provided to help you understand the issues and problems. If you really need a mass-mail solution, we recommend that you use a consulting organization to help you out.

8.3   Keep it running

Let's set the scenario—you have a company of 10,000 to 15,000 users. Messaging is mission critical. If the messaging servers are down for more than four business hours, you could lose business. With that said, what are some of the issues and problems that you must deal with, and, more important, what are the solutions?

As you can probably guess, you must start with policies and then go to procedures. What policies does your company have in place? Following are a few possible examples:

- Acceptable use
- Mass-mail
- E-mail virus scanning
- Content scanning
- Message retention

We will discuss each of these and look at the issue, impact, and potential solution. It is important to understand that no one solution will fit every case. When you build the solution for your business, you will need to look at the following factors: service levels (SLAs), the business needs and the cost of security, the corporate culture, and the actual risk and benefits of your selected solutions.

8.3.1   Acceptable use

The messaging acceptable use policies should be part of an overall policy document that covers computing resources. At this time we will focus on messaging.

Every company should review the following two issues that may need to be part of its acceptable use policies: an initial discussion about the use of e-mail, and why e-mail is important to the company. Describe the business environment that involves e-mail. Discuss how company proprietary information will need to be managed if sent via e-mail. Each acceptable use document should include specifics about the responsibility of the employee (or user). Also, the document should show examples of unacceptable behavior. In many companies, a document will be published that is entitled "Messaging Policies, Procedures, and Guidelines."

Following is an example of an acceptable use document:

The Company

Messaging Acceptable Use

Policy and Procedure Document Number 234567

Introduction

The Company provides e-mail as an import asset for the day-to-day operations between both employees and our customers. The Company considers all e-mail sent by the Company employees on the Company's computing and network environment to be the Company's property.

Requirements

Employees cannot expect that e-mail is private or confidential. Due to the retention policies of the Company (see the Company retention policy document #12345), there is a legal risk posed by stored and archived e-mail messages. Messaging, also known as e-mail, should not be used in any way that is harmful to the Company. Examples of such harmful messaging usage can include the following:

- Using messaging resources you have not been specifically authorized to use

- Using someone else's account and password, or sharing your account and password with someone else

- Sending forged e-mail

- Sending bomb threats or "hoax messages"

- Sending chain letters

- Releasing a virus or worm that damages or harms a system or network

- Using the Company's messaging environment as a "test bed" for a new application

- Using the Company's mass-mail systems to send personal notes

- Sending e-mail bombs that may cause problems and disrupt service for other users

- Disclosing the Company proprietary data or information

- Transmitting abusive, sexually explicit, or defamatory materials

- Sending alerts about a virus or a problem with the messaging system. If you have discovered a virus or a problem with the messaging systems, contact the IS support help desk at 1-800-xxx-xxxx, or the Company's help desk URL at http://internal.thecompany.support.get-help.

User Responsibilities

Use only those computing and information technology resources for which you have authorization. Use computing and information technology resources only for their intended purpose. Protect the access and integrity of computing and information technology resources. Check e-mail daily and remain within your limited disk quota. Delete unwanted messages immediately, because they take up disk storage. Keep messages remaining in your electronic mailbox to a minimum. Use good net e-mail etiquette. See the Company document #12345-12 for more information about net etiquette. Also, any employees using a laptop will encrypt e-mail when traveling.

One problem that is very common in the business world is the "flame" letter. This is basically the same as calling the coworker in the next cubical a moron. The court system routinely treats e-mail messages the same way it has always treated any written letters and memos; an e-mail that is spontaneously written and then sent (signed is even worse) may provide evidence against an individual or a company. Think before you send off that message. Yes, we may agree that the dude in the next cubicle is a moron, but don't put that in an e-mail message! After you create your acceptable use policies, make sure you put a good plan in place to communicate the contents of the documents to your employees.

8.3.2   Mass-mail

Mass-mail is another area that many companies overlook. Mass-mail is the ability to send a message to large groups of users within the company. In smaller companies, this may not be a problem, but in larger companies it can be. Following is a real-life example. A woman—we'll call her Mabel— had a picture of her dog. Now most people like dogs, but not everyone appreciates pictures of dogs wearing cute outfits, hats, and the like. Mabel had had this picture of her dog taken by a professional photographer, and because this picture looked so cute, Mabel decided to scan in the picture with a very high-resolution scanner. She then e-mailed it to herself at work. This picture of Fifi was then put into a mail message and sent to 10,000 users. The picture was only about four meg, so it wasn't too bad, but the problem was that the user community got really mad, really fuming mad. This message was forwarded, replied to, and copied. About 20 more variations of this message were sent into discussion databases. If you do the math, 10,000 users times four meg is not very good but still not really bad. The servers could have handled this volume if it stopped there. The problem was in the response from the user community; this is what really multiplied the message. It took a week to stop these messages from flowing and to purge them out of the system. What is the lesson? (Do not send pictures of your dog via e-mail, but there's more.) The answer is in the mass-mail system that is part of your e-mail system. Following are several solutions:

- Add mass-mail procedures to your acceptable use policy documents.

- Train users on the use of mass-mail and when to use it.

- Create a solution in which you can control the mass-mail features in your mail system and limit access to the mass-mail system.

The first two solutions actually work. But the bad news is, they only work in small companies. The larger the company, the harder it is to control the mass-mail system if it is open to the general e-mail user population. Also, there is another potential problem. Spammers have been known to discover the name of an e-mail group that exists in a company's e-mail system. When this happens, they can then bounce a message into the company's corporate messaging environment and invite its employees to a pornographic site. Now that is really bad. Why? Because some of the users in the company may do the following:

- Try to dual with the spammer

- Actually launch the URL sent to them

- Possibly launch an attachment, if it is included, which can spread viruses.

Again, if you have a small company, you may not need a mass-mail solution. Also, check with your e-mail vendor to see if it has solutions that can manage mass-mail. We'll look at an example of a creative solution, but first, review the following goals for our solution:

Goals

- Create a corporate communication system that will allow for sending mail to a large group of users in a large organization.

- Keep the general population from sending messages to the "mass-mail groups."

- Keep external users from bouncing messages into a large group (spam mail).

- Control when mass-mail messages are being sent.

- Have large virtual groups without actually creating groups (maintaining groups can take up a lot of time).

- Use existing groups, if needed.

- Use various directory sources to send messages.

- Send messages to internal, external, and Internet destinations.

- Send via a browser.

1. Identify the directory sources: These can be X.500, LDAP, or any consistent authorities source. The main issue is having an authoritative data source for the directory information. The following information is needed:

   User name (required)

   Some type of unique key (required)

   E-mail address (required)

   Information about location, job title, and so forth (optional)

   Public keys (if needed)

2. The "pseudocode" is the instruction that will actually perform the lookup in the directory source. The user that has access to send corporate communication will see a title name for the code. The end user will never see the exposed code. An administrator will create pseudocode entries, such as the following:

   Title—South Region Users (what the user sees)

   Code—Select all users where region = South

   Title—All Users in France (what the user sees)

   Code—Select all users where country = France

   Title—All Users (what the user sees)

   Code—Select all users

3. Engine profile settings will include references to the data sources, messaging, or any settings related to internal processing.

4. The mail engine will actually send the message, process the pseudocode, and place the message in the mailbox. Using this mechanism, you can hide all of the recipients and control the "From" and "Send to" fields. As part of this process, the engine will attempt to group recipients by servers so that when the message is sent, it will cut down on the network traffic.

5. The "Corp Comm" database is what the users access in order to send a message. Only users with the appropriate access will be able to send messages. Workflow approval can be added as

needed (that is, document placed in draft, approved, the schedule to be sent). The user will be able to create, schedule, and send documents from this database. Minor modifications to a standard mail file will be needed. Authorized users will be able to select a target "group" (virtual group) from a drop-down list, which is driven by the pseudocode. If needed, a simple "Create a group on the fly" can be added. If workflow is not needed, then messages can be mailed in. If authorized users sign the mail, then those messages will be automatically sent to the mail engine after some type of validation.

6. The profile document is what controls the workflow to the "Corp Comm" database and references the pseudocode (see Figure 8.4).

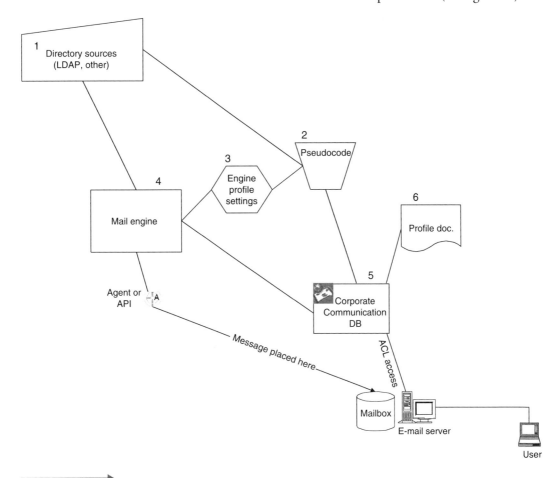

Figure 8.4

8.3.3   E-mail virus scanning

Virus scanning seems simple. The question you need to answer is, "Do we really need to scan e-mail messages?" The answer may not be so simple. Following are some of the options:

- Do not scan any messages.
- Scan all messages sent and received by an end user.
- Scan messages going to the Internet.
- Scan messages received from the Internet.

Do not scan any messages

Many companies will have a desktop virus scanning policy. (Actually all companies should have some type of virus scanning policy, but we are focusing on messaging in this chapter.) If your company does not send messages to the Internet, then you may not want to scan messages. We have a difficult time recommending this option, as very few companies do not send messages to the Internet. Overall, this option is not a good one.

Scan all messages sent and received by an end user

Absolutes don't necessarily fit. The time and cost of scanning all messages may not make sense. In order to implement this solution, you will need to scan messages before they leave each client. Some cases exist in which a company wants to scan all messages, such as a company that has clients scattered all over the trusted network, and there are many different access points to the Internet.

Scan messages going to the Internet

This option is not a common practice; not many companies will scan messages going to the Internet. Why would you want to do that? Again, we use the example of a public utility, which would not want to be sending or forwarding messages with viruses to the Internet.

Scan messages received from the Internet

This option is a very common, proactive practice. Now the question is, "Where do you scan the messages?" You scan the messages at the DMZ or at the firewall, or you can scan the messages at each server that allows messages into the Internet. Many times, there will be an SMTP relay that will filter messages going in and out of the corporate environment.

Combination approach

1.   This approach will scan messages before they are sent into the Internet, and then scan messages at each messaging server.

2.   The message will start at the user's computer outside the DMZ. The message will be sent into the DMZ.

3.   The relay will accept the message, and then scan and clean it. Depending on how you want to configure your relay, it may clean the message and then send it on to the targeted user, or it may just delete the message.

4.   If the message passes the virus scanning (or is cleaned), it will be sent to the messaging server. The message will also be scanned there. This is not so important at this time, but it *is* important that all internal messages between all messaging internal servers be scanned (see Figure 8.5).

There is also a method of scanning known as "policy-based scanning." This type of scanning not only controls scanning but also has access to sent or received messages from the Internet. Many different network vendors and suppliers offer this type of system. Check with your vendors to see if they offer this service or software/hardware.

8.3.4   **Content scanning**

To some people, this option looks like Big Brother. Scanning messages for content really gets people upset, but there are companies that need to do this. Again, it is better to use employee training than to use tools, although this does not always work. In a large company, you may need to implement tools that perform content scanning. Typically, content scanning can determine the following:

- Content of a message based on words (like profanity)

- Size in Kbytes or megabytes of a message sent to/from other users and/or the Internet

- Whether or not a message is encrypted (some companies may require that all messages be encrypted)

- Where messages are sent and/or what domains messages can be received from

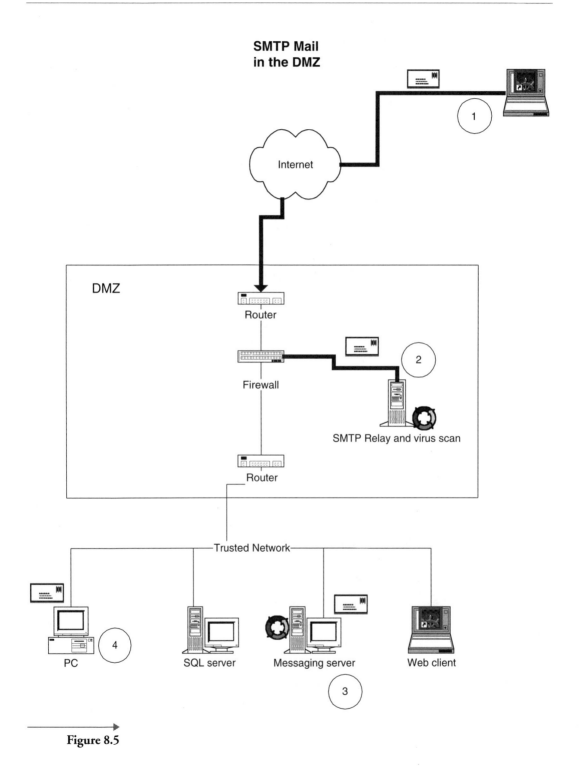

Figure 8.5

8.3.5   Message retention

Message retention covers several areas:

- Legal
- System Design
- System Management

Legal

You have probably seen, just by reading the newspaper, cases when message retention can be a problem. A CEO of a company says, "I never said that our competition was ugly and stupid." Then, thanks to computer forensics or just a backup tape from a server, a message is found that said just that, and it was digitally signed by the CEO. Not good.

System design

When you design your e-mail system, you will take into account how much disk space will be allocated to each user. Even at 10 meg per user, it does not take very long to get to a gig. Also, you need to decide if you will allow users to archive messages and if you will back up the mail system. How many days will you back up the system? Who will have access to the backups?

System management

If you have a quota system on your messaging software, how much quota will you allow? You may need to have custom software built that will manage quotas, archives, and backups. See if your vendors offer these features.

Following is an example of a message retention policy:

Storage Policies for the Company

The implementation of the Company's e-mail infrastructure includes the ability to store messages on the server. In order to maintain message store integrity, sufficient storage availability, and ensure message integrity, controls have been implemented. These controls will affect the message storage area of our server with emphasis on message retention. Messaging system users need to remember to follow these policies when sending or receiving messages.

Message Retention

The following specifics are currently implemented on all messaging servers.

Description

Length in Days Messages Are Held

In-Box

30

Unread Messages

30

Read Messages

60

On-Server Archive

60

Automated tools have been implemented to maintain the message store retention. These tools will remove messages from the various message stores based on the preceding policies described. This process will be implemented starting at 22:59 hours every night.

Server-Based Storage Limitations

All users will be assigned a limited amount of space on each server. Once the user reaches 100% of space quota, the user will be unable to place any additional messages on the server. In that case, new e-mail will be returned as undeliverable. If the user reaches or exceeds his or her quota, he or she must e-mail from the server to restore normal delivery.

The following specifics are currently implemented on all messaging servers.

Description

Storage Limits

User Mail File

20 Meg

On-Server Archive

10 Meg

Read Messages

60

On-Server Archive

60

Message Restrictions

Please recall the following restrictions when sending messages:

1. 0 to 2.9 meg can be sent or received at any time.

2. 3+ meg will be blocked at each messaging server.

The larger the message, the greater the impact on delivery of all messages within the infrastructure. If the user needs to send a large file that is over 3 meg, the user must place the file on the "file distribution" web site. (See http://www.thisisthefiledistsetifortheCompany.com.)

Temporary Exceptions

If for any reason an exception is necessary, contact your manager.

Permanent Exceptions

Each user has the option of purchasing additional e-mail storage space. See your manager for approval.

Out of Office

If someone is to be out of the office for vacation or leave of absence, they must fill out an "Out-of-Office Profile" document and enable the document. This step will keep mail from being bounced when the user is away.

Account Abandonment

In order to maintain disk cost and space, abandoned (inactive) accounts will be managed as follows (Accounts are "abandoned" when not logged into for over 180 days, unless an Out-of-Office Profile has been set.):

1. Each account will be removed on the 181st day.

2. Out-of-Office Profile set greater than 200 days will be deleted (unless approved by your manager).

Areas of Responsibility

It is the responsibility of each user to maintain his or her e-mail storage area. As each user approaches the mail file quota, decisions on message retention will be the user's responsibility. In-box, out-box, and trash areas will be cleaned daily, requiring users to make decisions on messages in a timely manner. The user may archive mail file to his or her local computer. The user is then responsible for backup of that data.

8.3.6   SMTP configuration settings

Most SMTP servers will have configuration settings that you should review
before placing your SMTP server on-line. These settings include the following:

- Verifying user names (VRFY)
- Verifying a mailing list (EXPN)
- Enabling requests for deferred queue processing (ETRN)
- Limiting message size (SIZE)

Verifying user names (VRFY)

The VRFY command enables SMTP clients to send a request to your server
to verify that mail for a specific user name resides on the server. The server
sends a response indicating whether the user is local and whether mail will
be forwarded. A response of "250" indicates that the user name is local,
"251," that the user name is not local, but the server can forward the message. The VRFY command is defined in RFC 821.

Verifying a mailing list (EXPN)

If both the SMTP client and the server support the SMTP EXPN command, SMTP clients can ask your server to verify that a particular mailing
list resides on the server. The EXPN command is defined in RFC 821.

Enabling requests for deferred queue processing (ETRN)

If both the SMTP client and the server support the ETRN command, the
client can initiate processing of the deferred queue for the client server. In
essence, the client can pull messages from the target server. If any messages
await delivery to the domain suffix given in the ETRN command, the
server will then attempt to send those messages. The ETRN command is
defined in RFC 1985.

Limiting message size (SIZE)

If both the SMTP client and the server support the SIZE command, clients
can list the size of a particular message to the server, and the server can
accept or reject the message based on its size. Any attempts to send a message larger than the specified size will automatically fail, and the server will
return an error message indicating that the message has exceeded the maximum size allowed. The SMTP SIZE extension is also supported on a per-
message basis. In this example, the SMTP client tells the server how big a
message is going to be. At that time, before the message gets transferred, the

server can tell the client if the message is too big. SIZE is a good way not only to save a lot of bandwidth, but also to increase the reliability of the mail system. Rather than waiting days to discover that the message hasn't been delivered, the sending mail system would receive immediate feedback. The SIZE command is defined in RFC 1870.

Following is an extract from RFC 821 on SMTP commands:

The SMTP Specifications

4.1 SMTP Commands

4.1.1 Command Semantics

The SMTP commands define the mail transfer or the mail system Function requested by the user. SMTP commands are character Strings terminated by <CRLF>. The command codes themselves are alphabetic characters terminated by <SP> if parameters follow and <CRLF> otherwise. The syntax of mailboxes must conform to receiver site conventions. The SMTP commands are discussed below.

A mail transaction involves several data objects that are communicated as "arguments" to different commands. The reverse-path is the argument of the MAIL command, the forward-path is the argument of the RCPT command, and the mail data is the argument of the DATA command. These arguments, or data objects, must be transmitted and held pending the confirmation communicated by the end of mail data indication, which finalizes the transaction. Distinct buffers are provided to hold the types of data objects; that is, there is a reverse-path buffer, a forward-path buffer, and a mail data buffer. Specific commands cause information to be appended to a specific buffer, or cause one or more buffers to be cleared.

HELLO (HELO)

This command is used to identify the sender-SMTP to the receiver-SMTP. The argument field contains the host name of the sender-SMTP.

The receiver-SMTP identifies itself to the sender-SMTP both in the connection greeting reply and in the response to this command.

This command, and an "OK" reply to it, confirm that both the sender-SMTP and the receiver-SMTP are in the initial state—that is, there is no transaction in progress and all state tables and buffers are cleared.

MAIL (MAIL)

This command is used to initiate a mail transaction in which the mail data is delivered to one or more mailboxes. The argument field contains a reverse-path.

The reverse-path consists of an optional list of hosts and the sender mailbox. When the list of hosts is present, it is a "reverse" source route and indicates that the mail was relayed through each host on the list (the first host in the list was the most recent relay). This list is used as a source route to return nondelivery notices to the sender. As each relay host adds itself to the beginning of the list, it must use its name as known in the IPCE to which it is relaying the mail, rather than the IPCE from which the mail came (if they are different). In some types of error reporting messages (for example, undeliverable mail notifications), the reverse-path may be null (see Example 7).

This command clears the reverse-path buffer, the forward-path buffer, and the mail data buffer, and inserts the reverse-path information from this command into the reverse-path buffer.

continued

RECIPIENT (RCPT)

This command is used to identify an individual recipient of the mail data; multiple recipients are specified by multiple use of this command.

The forward-path consists of an optional list of hosts and a required destination mailbox. When the list of hosts is present, it is a source route and indicates that the mail must be relayed to the next host on the list. If the receiver-SMTP does not implement the relay function, it may use the same reply it would for an unknown local user (550).

When mail is relayed, the relay host must remove itself from the beginning forward-path and put itself at the beginning of the reverse-path. When mail reaches its ultimate destination (the forward-path contains only a destination mailbox), the receiver-SMTP inserts it into the destination mailbox in accordance with its host mail conventions.

For example, mail received at relay host A with arguments

FROM:<USERX@HOSTY.ARPA>

TO:<@HOSTA.ARPA,@HOSTB.ARPA:USERC@HOSTD.ARPA>

will be relayed on to host B with arguments

FROM:<@HOSTA.ARPA:USERX@HOSTY.ARPA>

TO:<@HOSTB.ARPA:USERC@HOSTD.ARPA>.

This command causes its forward-path argument to be appended to the forward-path buffer.

DATA (DATA)

The receiver treats the lines following the command as mail data from the sender. This command causes the mail data from this command to be appended to the mail data buffer. The mail data may contain any of the 128 ASCII character codes.

The mail data is terminated by a line containing only a period, that is the character sequence "<CRLF>.<CRLF>." This is the end of mail data indication.

The end of mail data indication requires that the receiver must now process the stored mail transaction information. This processing consumes the information in the reverse-path buffer, the forward-path buffer, the mail data buffer, and on the completion of this command, these buffers are cleared. If the processing is successful, the receiver must send an "OK" reply. If the processing fails completely, the receiver must send a "failure" reply.

When the receiver-SMTP accepts a message either for relaying or for final delivery, it inserts at the beginning of the mail data a time stamp line. The time stamp line indicates the identity of the host that sent the message, and the identity of the host that received the message (and is inserting this time stamp), and the date and time the message was received. Relayed messages will have multiple time stamp lines.

When the receiver-SMTP makes the "final delivery" of a message, it inserts at the beginning of the mail data a return path line. The return path line preserves the information in the <reverse-path> from the MAIL command. Here, final delivery means the message leaves the SMTP world. Normally, this would mean it has been delivered to the destination user, but in some cases it may be further processed and transmitted by another mail system.

It is possible for the mailbox in the return path to be different from the actual sender's mailbox; for example, if error responses are to be delivered a special error handling mailbox, rather than the message senders.

The preceding two paragraphs imply that the final mail data will begin with a return path line, followed by one or more time stamp lines. These lines will be followed by the mail data header and body [2]. See Example 8.

Special mention is made of the response, and further action is required when the processing following the end of mail data indication is partially successful. This could arise if, after accepting several recipients and the mail data, the receiver-SMTP finds that the mail data can be successfully delivered to some of the recipients, but it cannot be to others (for example, due to mailbox space allocation problems). In such a situation, the response to the DATA command must be an "OK" reply. But, the receiver-SMTP must compose and send an "undeliverable mail" notification message to the originator of the message. Either a single notification, which lists all of the recipients that failed to get the message, or separate notification messages must be sent for each failed recipient. All undeliverable mail notification messages are sent using the MAIL command (even if they result from processing a SEND, SOML, or SAML command).

Example of Return Path and

Received Time Stamps

Return-Path: <@GHI.ARPA,@DEF.ARPA,@ABC.ARPA:JOE@ABC.ARPA>

Received: from GHI.ARPA by JKL.ARPA; 27 Oct 81 15:27:39 PST

Received: from DEF.ARPA by GHI.ARPA; 27 Oct 81 15:15:13 PST

Received: from ABC.ARPA by DEF.ARPA; 27 Oct 81 15:01:59 PST

Date: 27 Oct 81 15:01:01 PST

From: JOE@ABC.ARPA

Subject: Improved Mailing System Installed

To: SAM@JKL.ARPA

This is to inform you that …

Example 8

SEND (SEND)

   This command is used to initiate a mail transaction in which the mail data is delivered to one or more terminals. The argument field contains a reverse-path. This command is successful if the message is delivered to a terminal.

   The reverse-path consists of an optional list of hosts and the sender mailbox. When the list of hosts is present, it is a "reverse" source route and indicates that the mail was relayed through each host on the list (the first host in the list was the most recent relay). This list is used as a source route to return nondelivery notices to the sender. As each relay host adds itself to the beginning of the list, it must use its name as known in the IPCE to which it is relaying the mail, rather than the IPCE from which the mail came (if they are different).

   This command clears the reverse-path buffer, the forward-path buffer, and the mail data buffer, and inserts the reverse-path information from this command into the reverse-path buffer.

SEND OR MAIL (SOML)

This command is also used to initiate a mail transaction in which the mail data is delivered to one or more terminals as well as mailboxes. For each recipient, the mail data is delivered to the recipient's terminal if the recipient is active on the host (and accepting terminal messages), otherwise to the recipient's mailbox. The argument field contains a reverse-path. This command is successful if the message is delivered to a terminal or the mailbox.

   The reverse-path consists of an optional list of hosts and the sender mailbox. When the list of hosts is present, it is a "reverse" source route and indicates that the mail was relayed through each host on the list (the first host in the list was the most recent relay). This list is used as a source route to return nondelivery notices to the sender. As each relay host adds itself to the beginning of the list, it must use its name as known in the IPCE to which it is relaying the mail, rather than the IPCE from which the mail came (if they are different).

   This command clears the reverse-path buffer, the forward-path buffer, and the mail data buffer, and inserts the reverse-path information from this command into the reverse-path buffer.[3]

---

3.   http://www.ietf.org/rfc/rfc0821.txt

9

What Are We Doing Here?

Hay, Earl! "What is a Trojan horse virus?"

9.1   **Risk analysis**

Risk analysis is the process of determining where you most need to focus your time, efforts, and financial resources to develop a security implementation. This process will include the analysis of the threats, the impacts of those threats, and the corresponding risks. Once you have executed this process, significant business risks and weaknesses will be more evident, and this will help you develop counterstrategies.

The formula to determine risk is: Risk = Impact + Threats + Likelihood

As you perform your risk analysis, you will determine what is most important to the business in terms of security. You will also review the potential impacts to the business, which will be business-specific results of a particular attack. One significant part of the analysis is to understand the service level agreements (SLAs). If you cannot support your business requirements—say, due to a service outage—then you may suffer a significant loss of revenue.

As you walk through the risk analysis process, you will be introduced to the following tools: the technology security review (TSR), the control directory (CD), and the environment risk table (ERT). These tools will help you develop a strategy to accomplish the following goals:

1.   Eliminate risk

2.   Reduce risk to an acceptable level

3.   Minimize the damage from an incident

4.   Create the countermeasures needed for each incident type.

You should include at least the following factors when you perform your risk analysis.

- Physical network architecture

- Firewalls

- Routers

- Messaging servers

- Web servers

- Operating systems

- Application services

- Application servers

- Server level protocols and data flow
- Authentication and authorization infrastructures
- Nonrepudiation
- Application implementation

We will focus on five steps for risk analysis:

1. Asset identification
2. Threat identification
3. Estimation of likelihood of occurrence (this is the TSR document)
4. Analysis of applicable controls and their costs (this is the CD document)
5. Implementation of countermeasures (this is the ERT document)

9.1.1   Asset identification

The first step of risk assessment is to take inventory of all the components of your computing infrastructure, including hardware, software, data, information, and knowledge. Understand the value of what you are protecting before you try to protect it.

9.1.2   Threat identification

Next, review the inventory from step one and determine how and to what extent each component is vulnerable. See the next section of this chapter for details.

9.1.3   Estimation of likelihood of occurrence (TSR)

The TSR document will guide you through the process of documenting the likelihood of an incident. We devote a complete section to the TSR in this chapter.

9.1.4   Analysis of applicable controls and their costs (CD)

This step is where you assign the control to each potential incident and estimate the cost of each control.

9.1.5   Implementation of countermeasures (ERT)

Finally, we have arrived. This step is where the rubber hits the road. The ERT will combine the data from the TSR and the CD. This is when you decide which controls are most cost-effective and/or required.

9.2   The threats

We have spent several chapters talking about technology, SSL, X.509, SMTP, messaging, and the "bad dudes." The next question we need to ask is, "How do we keep a business running in this crazy, open Internet environment?" We will work on finding the answer together.

We will discuss the factors that you need to know to keep your business running—in other words, the continuity of operations. Before we go further, however, a simple exercise needs to be completed. First, you must fill in Table 9.1 and determine the service levels of the various functions of your business. The table has three categories (more can be added if needed):

1.   Business function

2.   Critical definition

3.   Service level

9.2.1   Business function

This is the function for which you are trying to set a service level. Again, this is one of those functions that we are doing backward. You may have this service level defined already; if not, it needs to be defined. The backward part is that you may be defining a service level now. This should actually have been done when you first built your business case and model. An example of this would be the web server that houses the order form for customer orders.

Table 9.1

Business Function	Critical Definition	Service Level

9.2.2   Critical definition

This provides details about the function. For example, why is it important? What is the impact if the function or service is down?

9.2.3   Service level

If this has not been done previously, define a scale that will reflect each of your functions—for example, 100% uptime.

However, if you really decide on 100% uptime, understand that uptime of 100% is typically very difficult and costly. This table cannot replace a complete SLA analysis. The point of this exercise is to illustrate that you cannot implement security without integrating your SLA and security requirements together.

Security, SLAs, and risk management are tightly related to quality management. Security measures must be implemented based on these factors, and always using the business goals and objectives as the guiding light. You are in business to generate a profit or to increase your market share, not to implement security requirements. Security provides protection of the business against incidents, mistakes, and premeditated manipulation, so that the impact of security incidents is minimal and the business remains viable and continues.

9.2.4   Threats

A threat is a danger that could impact the security of business assets, which could lead to a potential dollar loss, capital damage, or loss of customer confidence. In the Internet age, most companies use both an internal network and the Internet to support their daily business processes. Information, knowledge, and data are managed by complex hardware and software. This infrastructure manages customers' contact data, inventory (SKUs), accounting information, and more. This electronic business infrastructure must be controlled and kept within the business community that owns it. This infrastructure cannot be compromised, stolen, corrupted, or destroyed. This infrastructure is what the business runs on. We talked about data categorization before and will not repeat it here, but you must understand how valuable the data is and how it can be accessed.

Threats to your business can come from many different sources:

- Human error
- External attacks (hackers)

- Dishonest people

- Technical sabotage

- Fire, flooding, acts of God

- Current or former disgruntled employees

    What are the steps required to determine the specific threats?

1. Define basic security objectives (in relation to your SLAs)—for example, availability, confidentiality, and integrity.

2. Define the various potential system threats and safeguards, such as external users, Internet employees, hackers, or CERT advisories based on the technological solutions that you have for your business.

3. Generate a business impact analysis. What is the impact on the business if a threat is realized? (The impact is a business consequence, not a technical one.)

4. Utilize a scale that will assess the impact to the business. Following are some examples:

    - Low impact—No or very minor effect; major business operations are not affected.

    - Minor impact—Business operations are unavailable for a certain amount of time; some revenue is lost, but customer confidence is not impacted.

    - Moderate impact—Intermediate loss to business operations occurs, with some loss in customer confidence.

    - Significant impact—Customer confidence has been significantly impacted; some customers will be lost permanently.

    - High impact—The impact is high, but the company may survive at a considerable loss of revenue.

    - Disaster—The effect is catastrophic; the company cannot survive. Start looking for a new job.

5. Determine the likelihood of a threat. Following is an example scale:

    - The threat is highly unlikely to ever occur.

    - The threat is likely to occur only once in the lifetime of the service or product.

- The threat is likely to occur once per year.

- The threat is likely to occur once per month.

- The threat is likely to occur once per week.

- The threat is likely to occur daily.

6. List the threats. You must create a technology security review (TSR) for each process. The TSR will list the threats and the suggested controls.

7. Create a control directory (CD). The control directory will list the items in the TSR in relation to the impact and the likelihood of a threat. Also, the suggested controls will be added to this directory.

8. Create an environment risk table (ERT), which is a document that shows the financial cost of security in relation to the value of what is being secured.

9.3 Technology security review

The technology security review is a process that reviews each technology or service within the organization. We will be talking about exposures and controls. An "exposure" is anything that can make your system vulnerable to an incident, including any of the attacks listed in the preceding section. The "control" is what can be put in place to keep the attack from being successful. The following template demonstrates the various items that will need to be reviewed.

Technology Security Review

Name of technology or service reviewed _____

Expected or current user of the technology or service _____

Exposures _____

Exposure # _____

Exposure summary _____

Exposure source (testing, CERT) _____

Suggested control # _____

Detail suggested control _____

Cost or impact to the business of this control _____

# of required controls _____

Detail required control _____

Cost or impact to the business of this control _____

Comments _____

This is actually a simple form, but the information recorded on it can be very helpful. You will fill out this form for every approved software product and/or service that could be impacted by security. For example, under "Name of technology or service reviewed," the following might be indicated.

- A web site

- The OS that is used on the web site

- The web server

- The applications on the web server

- The routers used

- The firewall

- The architecture of the DMZ

"Expected or current user of the technology or service" determines the scope of where this software or service will be used. Potential answers could be:

- External customers

- Employees

- Vendors

- Internal customers (employees resulting in a charge back to a cost center)

The next step is to list the exposures, which is interesting, because you cannot identify all exposures. Here is a suggestion: If you are using a vendor for software, contact the vendor to discover what known exposures exist. Also, check out some of the known hacking sites, such as http://www. l0pht.com/, and the CERT listing for your software, http://www.cert.org. Table 9.2 shows some examples of exposures.

Then, for each potential exposure, list any suggested controls that could counteract the attack listed.

Table 9.2   *Exposures*

# (Any Tracking #)	Exposure Summary	Exposure Source (Testing, Cert)
1001	OS can crash due to a DDoS	Cert advisory XXX.xx.V3
2023	Users can send sensitive mail outside of the company	Mail encryption is available but it cannot be forced on the users
3011	Hacking tool can grant administrator access for any user	From a hacker site
4067	Ninjas break into the 30th floor and force people to reveal their passwords	No known occurrences of this type of attack

Table 9.3   *Suggested Controls*

#	Detail Suggested Control	Cost or Impact to the Business of this Control
1001	Upgrade firewall to Version 3.1	Upgrade is free from vendor
4067	Train an army of Ninjas	$100,000

Table 9.4   *Required Controls*

#	Detail Required Control	Cost or Impact to the Business of this Control
2023	Train users on S/MIME	Added cost of training—extra cost will be $10 per user
3011	Upgrade O/S to service pack 9	Upgrade is free from vendor

Then, for each potential exposure, list any required controls that could counteract the attack listed.

As with any form, you will need a section for comments. Comments could be used to point out any specific issues or controls that should be considered.

The following issues should be considered when reviewing any service or software:

- Accidental destruction, modification, disclosure of information
- Too many or too few system administrators
- Incorrect system configuration
- Fraud, theft, embezzlement
- Attacks by social engineering
- Inadequate security awareness, lack of security guidelines
- Lack of documentation
- Abuse of privileges/trust
- Selling of confidential corporate information
- Mixing of test and production data or environments
- No change control
- Operating system design errors
- DNS spoofing
- Introduction of unauthorized software or hardware
- Mixing of test and production data networks
- DoS and DDoS
- Trojan horses
- Spoof messages
- External attackers masquerading as valid users or customers
- Equipment failure due to defective hardware
- E-mail bombing
- Physical destruction of computing devices or media
- Poor backups
- Backups of data that should not be backed up
- Unauthorized physical access to system
- Disclosure of company secrets
- Subversion of DNS to redirect e-mail or other traffic
- Malicious and/or deliberate damage of information
- Modification of business data—for example, customer or accounting data
- Password cracking

The preceding examples comprise just a small list of the issues that you would be concerned with.

Before we can go any further, you must define the impacts to the business. An "impact" is the result of an incident that causes some type of loss to the business. The following are some examples, with financial impact assumed to be part of each:

- Data disclosure—This can be as simple as someone sending information out of the trusted environment to someone who should not have this information.

- Data integrity compromised—The best example of this is credit card information that has been stolen from various web sites.

- Loss of customer confidence—The credit card issue would also apply here, but this could also be a situation in which someone hacks your web site and places pornography on it.

- Network impact—This is when someone attacks the network, making it unusable for the customer or employee.

- Messaging impacts—This is when messaging is impacted and you cannot communicate via your messaging infrastructure.

9.4   Control directory and environment risk table

The control directory is a summary of each technology security review document. Now, however, we start to add the risk and probability of the exposure actually occurring in your environment.

Following are some examples for messaging related issues:

Once you have the control directory filled out, you will need to chart the data in an environment risk table, which is actually composed of two tables: the impact table and the cost table, which is driven by the impact table.

After filling out the charts, you will analyze the results. In our example, you would do the following:

In Tables 9.5 and 9.6, look at the Recommend columns. Extract the information for each column that shows a YES. This is the data that you will use to determine a total security plan and a budget. The other items listed may provide some level of security, but may not be practical to implement.

Table 9.5   *Threat Examples (1)*

Threat	Control	Potential of Occurrence	Cost	Recommend
2023—Data sent to external users	Train users	High	$10,000	Yes
4067—Ninjas break in on the 30th floor and force people to reveal their passwords	Army of Ninjas	Very Low	$1,000,000	No
3011—Hacking tool can grant admin access for any user	Upgrade O/S to service pack 9	Medium	Under $1,000 (labor cost)	Yes

Table 9.6   *Threat Examples (2)*

Threat	Control	Potential of Occurrence	Cost	Recommend
A virus can damage messages	Install virus scanning software	High	$35,000	Yes—Includes hardware and software
Messaging administrator can access and manipulate data content with owner of any mailbox	Administrator training and auditing	Medium	$3,000	Yes
Messages received from SMTP message systems may not reflect the true sender	Difficult to manage—best control is to train users on how to receive encrypted and signed messages	High	Cost covered in other initiatives	Yes
Mail Bomb—Script—e.g., Love Bug	Use virus scanning software, and incident handling and user training	High	Cost covered in other initiatives	Yes

→

Table 9.7

		Impact Area			
	Data Disclosure	Data Integrity Compromised	Loss of Customer Confidence	Network Impact	Messaging Impacts
High	Employees send sensitive messages to external customers without encryption	Hackers access and modify data on Server in DMZ	Credit card data stolen from site	DoS or DDoS attacks	Love Bug type script Bomb
Medium	Employees give out password to other employees	Hackers are able to access and modify business data on the trusted network	Web site down for X% of SLA	Router is compromised by hacker	Mass Mail system not implemented
Low	Backup tapes stolen and used externally	System backups are not tested, so restores are not valid	Web site down for Y% of SLA	Hacker is able to access trusted network	Non-business use of messaging resources

→

Table 9.8 *Cost of Impact Table*

		Impact Area			
	Data Disclosure	Data Integrity Compromised	Loss of Customer Confidence	Network Impact	Messaging Impacts
High	$$$	$$$	$$$	$$	$$
Medium	$$	$$$	$$$	$$	$
Low	$$	$$	$	$	$

9.5   Competitive asset

"Quality control" is defined by *Merriam Webster's Collegiate Dictionary* as "an aggregate of activities (as design analysis and inspection for defects) designed to ensure adequate quality especially in manufactured products."[1]

1.   *Merriam Webster's Collegiate Dictionary, 10th Ediition.*

Quality control can also be defined as a system for ensuring quality of output involving inspection, analysis, and the actions to make required changes. Implementing a security process for an Internet-facing enterprise business is like initiating a quality control program. As your enterprise provides service to your customers, you will need to make it safe from the outside world. As a factory incurs expenses to ensure consistent product quality, so must an Internet business incur security expenses. If the service fails to live up to the expectations of the customer, the business can fail. Customers expect consistency, accuracy, and responsiveness when they purchase a service or a product. If the business fails to meet one or more of these expectations, repeat business from these customers can be lost. In the same way, a customer who cannot safely conduct business via the Internet loses confidence. Today's business environment relies on the use of the Internet and the safety it is expected to provide. Quality and consistency cannot be overlooked by the Internet business. The value of the company is affected by the way customers view the quality or safety of transactions. Quality control cannot be viewed just as a necessary expense; it must be considered a competitive asset. The company who has truly done its homework will have a reliable security system in place so it can provide a service that is competitive. A secure transaction is a quality transaction. Customers will be willing to use your services if they feel safe.

Today, many stories abound about credit card numbers being stolen and used. Conducting business transactions on the Internet can be a scary experience. Fears of privacy violation are prevalent. The Internet is a place where we, the consumers, place confidential financial information on the line. The information we enter can be very personal and it can be quite distressing to worry that it is available to anybody. The customer needs to be reassured, or he or she will either decide not to do business over the Internet or go to a competitor who he or she may feel provides a secure environment.

A balance needs to be struck here. Let's look at an example: You have a business on 101 Main Street. You open the doors for business at 9 A.M. and close at 7 P.M. every day. This morning, when you went to open the business, you found 10,000 pounds of horse manure at the front door. With all of this stuff in front of the door, you cannot get into the building to do business and your customers can't either. This is known as a denial-of-service attack. (We have discussed denial-of-service attacks at length in other chapters, so we will stick with the analogy here.) Getting rid of all this excrement and reopening the business will take about two days. Having done that, you plan to hire security guards to monitor the door at all times and make sure that it never happens again. You will need to consider the same for your Internet business.

But be warned: Be careful how you choose to promote the safety of your site. Do not paint a bull's-eye on your door. The dilemma in our story is this: The security guard can protect you since you are facing Main Street, but with the Internet-facing enterprise, you will be facing the Internet. Please do not take out an advertisement in the *Wall Street Journal* that says, "We are a secure Internet enterprise and cannot be hacked!" This action would invite every hacker from the 12-year-old down the street to the catatonic geek at the library web terminal to attack your site. We *do* want you to market your security as a competitive advantage, but not as a dare for hackers to try to break through your security wall.

Many important decisions in a business boil down to the effects they will have on revenues and, expenses, and, subsequently, on the profits of the company. Security costs money like everything else, and if you needlessly spend too much on security, you may not be able to generate a profit. This process involves capital expenditures for the hardware and the software used as security assets. In many cases, a consulting firm must be hired to perform the work, and to be available for future upgrades and problems. Personnel must be trained to use the system, and there will be some expenses involved in the constant monitoring such a system requires.

It may be expensive, but if we were talking about a factory producing Widgets and the necessity of producing a quality product, we can agree on the necessity of the expense. The quality product being produced here is a secure transaction. The quality of the transaction and the value of the transaction to the customer revolve around the safety of the transaction. A quality Internet transaction is a secure transaction.

If we agree that the expense is a necessary one, what costs to do we need to look at? Quality costs involve four main items:

1.   Prevention—here, the prevention of a security breach

2.   Appraisal—these are recurring costs

3.   Internal—problem identified and resolved before customer is involved

4.   External—customer is involved, now must make amends

Prevention costs

This cost begins with the decision to do something about security. The costs involve planning, information gathering, designing the security system, training, and analyzing the system for problems. The planning stage depends on an extensive analysis of the business and its needs.

Appraisal costs

These are the costs of constant monitoring and surveillance that the company practices on itself. Reports should be created and maintained that list how many security glitches have occurred, and where and how they were handled. A security program is not a one-time cure-all; in fact, it requires frequent updates to stay ahead of the "bad dudes." It must always be a continual process.

Internal costs

These are the costs of repairing a security incident before a customer realizes it has occurred. This can include the cost of incident handling.

External costs

These costs can be the most severe. A customer (or several) is involved. It could be that his information was compromised, or she did not get what she requested because the order was deleted by an error somewhere along the system. Your site may have been down for an extensive time period due to something from the outside entering your system and tying it up. At this point, the customer can try again to buy from you because you have always been reliable in the past, or the customer can choose to go elsewhere. If the latter happens, you have most likely permanently lost that customer. That customer will no longer trust your site to be secure and reliable. If the Internet is the only place you conduct business, you could end up being forced to close down. This is the largest cost of maintaining a quality service.

The biggest problem associated with tracking the cost of quality is quantifying the numbers themselves. How do you account for lost revenue and how do you apply a cost to customer complaints? If they have security-related problems, many customers will not come to your site again. It is difficult to ascertain what they would have spent. Probably the best numbers you can estimate involve personnel and keeping track of how many problems they handle in a day, and assigning a time to each.

Another method may be recording the number of hits on a site. The customer may have never gotten into the site, but you will have records of the total tries and the completed transactions. This method involves estimating again, but it will allow you to better assess the true value of those external costs.

Let's look at costs using the following example:

Prevention costs	$100,000
Appraisal costs	$50,000
Internal costs	$50,000
External costs	$35,000
Total quality costs	$235,000
Sales for the same period	$450,000
Quality index = Total quality costs * (100%)	Sales base
Quality index = $235,000 * (100%) =	52%
	$450,000

Now, this may appear to be a rather high ratio, but what would have been the cost of closing down the business had a security program not been implemented, and a security breach had occurred? Let's look at the numbers if nothing had been spent on security:

Prevention costs	$0
Appraisal costs	$0
Internal costs	$25,000 (let's assume that some monitoring is being done)
External costs	$400,000
Total quality costs	$425,000
Sales for the same period	$450,000
Quality index = Total quality costs * (100%)	Sales base
Quality index = $425,000 * (100%) =	97%
	$450,000
Quality index =	97%

Now the quality index ratio has risen drastically, even with the assumption we have made that the sales base has remained at the same level. If a security breach occurred, customers either could not access the site, or they heard from any number of sources how unreliable your connection was, so they stayed away altogether. You will not be able to remain competitive in the marketplace, and another firm that maintains a secure site will get all the sales. At this juncture, your choices are either to spend a lot of capital on playing catch-up (if the capital is available) or to sell the business (or what remains of it).

The bad news is that the cost of maintaining a secure environment may not decrease much over time. Conditions will constantly change and so will your security needs. If you are providing quality transactions, customers will come to rely and depend on them, and thus increase your sales. Over the course of time, the increase in sales may cause your quality cost index to decrease. Forecasting is an integral part of decision making regarding the security process. Expense forecasting was considered, but how about forecasting what the consumer will expect from a firm with an Internet presence? The days of the brick-and-mortar structure are rapidly changing. A customer buying on the Internet does not interact one-on-one with an individual. The transaction is conducted on the computer screen without any paperwork changing hands.

If a company wants to conduct business in this environment, future, as well as present, requirements of the consumer must be considered. Forecasting must take into account daily, weekly, or monthly sales targets. Long-range forecasts that extend three years or more must also be factored into the decision being made about the security requirements for a company. If a company manufactures Widgets and sells them over the Internet, there may not be a building where the customer deals face-to-face with a service rep. A customer is a demanding entity, someone who demands fast, efficient, and safe transactions. These expectations will never change, but the customer's standards of what meets or exceeds these expectations are constantly changing.

Let's go back to our Chapter 2 example of the Company. The Company has a reputation for producing the best Widgets available. When transactions were mailed or telephoned in, the customer knew to allow extra time for the transaction to be processed and completed. Over the Internet, however, the customer enters an order and expects it to be sent out that very day, or the next day, at the latest. The effort required to place the order was minimal, little time was used up, and the customer is free to go on to something else. After the order has been placed, the Company is expected to fill it safely and with little delay. If the Company does not have up-to-date security processes in place, this transaction may not flow as expected. The Company has been smart, however, and has forecast these customer expectations, and is able to meet them.

But it does not stop there. Let's suppose the same customer wants to place a new order next month, or even next week. In that small passage of time, conditions have changed. Circumstances that compromise security, or that the customer assumes have compromised security, have occurred. The Internet environment is shifting constantly, and therefore, appraisal expenses must be ongoing. Installing a security process is not like installing a hot-water heater. We do not allow it to function without maintenance until it breaks down, at which time we replace it with a newer, better model. The security process is just that—a process—and it must be a continual one, lest there be problems that can be very costly to fix later on.

What about the customer's perception? Let's assume the customer has been reading stories in the media about unsecured sites and transactions being lost, or payment information being intercepted and stolen. The customer may be apprehensive, and when he or she accesses the Company's web site, he or she may expect to see certain screens or information that indicates a secure environment. The customer has read that the Other Guy's Company, which produces comparable Widgets, has installed a highly secure system and is therefore the safest site on the Internet. The Company has to foresee this concern and needs to either have planned for a change or already have implemented it. Reassurances must be made to the customer, or a sale could be lost, including any future ones. Constant vigilance will be required by the Company in order to compete effectively. Security is an extension of the quality of the service provided. It cannot be ignored.

One approach for forecasting future expenses is through the "moving average method." The results of past periods are used to estimate future expenses. Following is the formula:

Moving average = Number of incidents

 Period of time

The time period can be days, months, or even years. This flexibility allows you to plan for these security expenses using the number of incidents as a point of comparison. Table 9.9 shows some examples.

By plotting the three sets of numbers on a line graph, we can see that the five-month moving average has a smoother run. This may misdirect your forecast because it looks like everything is going along pretty consistently. Errors are occurring, but they appear to not be deviating as much. The three-month moving average plot, however, is closer to the current number

Table 9.9

Month	Number of Incidents	Three-Month Moving Average	Five-Month Moving Average
January	220		
February	190		
March	200		
April	175	203.3	
May	210	188.3	
June	150	195.0	199.0
July	175	178.3	185.0
August	230	178.3	182.0
September	310	185.0	188.0
October	290	238.3	215.0
November		276.7	231.0

of incidents occurring, since it is tracking data in a tighter time period. It does not provide an exact match, but it is suitable for forecasting purposes.

The three-month moving average has provided an estimate of how many instances we can expect to occur, but decisions must be made as to what to do with this information, and how to handle the expenses that will be required to keep the situation under control. We say "keep the situation under control" rather than "solve the situation" because, remember, the Internet environment is always changing. The possibility of security breaches will never really go away. It can be maintained, however, within acceptable limits. What is acceptable? Using the information such as in table 9.9, we know the frequency of these incidents occurring over several time periods, and, coupled with sales transactions data, we can compute the ratio of number of incidents to number of successful sales transactions on a per-month, three-month moving average and five-month moving average basis. If the ratio is high—say, 50% or more—we can safely say that the Company is losing half of all possible sales per month to security incidents. Where are these sales going? They are going to the competition, of course—the majority of them, anyway. The industry as a whole will face the problem of dealing with security incidents. What level will be acceptable to you and your customers? This is where surveys of your employees and customers can help you find the answer.

As you decide, remember that you are in business to make money and to ensure the viability of your company. Viability requires that you be competitive. If an investor were to evaluate an Internet business, what would he or she want to see? Such an evaluation would very likely include an evaluation of the company's financial standing. The income statement of a company lists the sales figures less expenses for a given time period, which results in the net income for the company. The list of expenses should include the cost of security. If an investor were to compare your company to other possible investments, how would it stack up? Today's investor is savvy enough to know that without a good security process in place, your company will not survive all the possible pitfalls that can occur due to the interconnectivity of the Internet. Also, one of the contingency listings in the financial statements should acknowledge the possibility of a security breach and the possible related costs. Insurance for security can be purchased and should also be included in the list of expenses. There should also be evidence of a continuing relationship with an external firm that specializes in security, which is the equivalent of an accounting firm that comes in to audit the financial records. There should be a security team that comes in periodically to audit the firm's security and advises the company on updates in order to help keep the company truly secure. The capital expenditures breakdown should list security hardware and software purchased as security assets. In the future, we can expect audit statements to be issued by the security firms that perform the periodic audits of the Internet enterprise. The statements will attest to the fact that the company audited is following accepted security practices. The statements will reflect that due diligence is being practiced by the company. The security firm will be performing the same function as that currently being performed on a company's financial records by accounting audit teams.

The security audit statement will become as important as the accounting audit statement. Potential investors will be provided some assurance as to the computing security capability of a firm. Customers will also be provided some assurance that their transactions will be handled securely, consistently, accurately, and in a timely manner. After the security system has been successfully audited, the customer will feel that he or she can safely access a company's web site and make purchases. The investor may feel compelled to invest in the company.

A company does not exist in a vacuum. It depends on customers and, if it plans to grow, on investors. The perceptions that these individuals hold can be responsible for the rise or fall of a company. Security firms that perform the auditing will be accountable for being intimately knowledgeable with the regulations that govern how they perform the audits and what they are looking for. Security firms will be required to have their auditors receive continuous training in order to stay current. How can someone audit a process and attest that it is up-to-date on all the regulations for security if this individual is not aware of the current regulations? The Internet's future existence depends on it providing a secure environment in which individuals can conduct private transactions without fear. If this problem is not addressed in a regulatory format, like accounting practices, investors will lose faith and move back to the brick-and-mortar businesses.

The traditional businesses will have accounting auditors attesting to their reliability, and investors will feel more secure about investing their money in these firms. Internet businesses cannot let this happen. Security must become another competitive asset, just like the practice of having unbiased external auditors come in each year to audit financial statements. Security audits will be an expense that a firm is obligated to incur. The absence of a security audit report ought to become a red flag to possible investors, indicating that a company may be subject to security problems. This is the way of the future. This is what Internet firms must undergo in order to remain viable in this highly competitive world.

10

Disaster Recovery

"This is not a bank robbery—I am hacking your web site."

10.1   Introduction

Jesse James rides into town to rob your bank. He walks in and blows up the safe. In the process the bank is destroyed. Your situation is now very bad: no money, no safe and no bank. Now what do you do?

You, the information technology (IT) manager, may face the same situation, in which the infrastructure is damaged beyond use. Now what do you do? One answer is to scramble and quickly try to repair the damage from the disaster, or try to find another site. Suppose your data center burns to the ground—let's look at minimum steps needed to get the enterprise back on-line. Let's assume that you have a central data center and all servers and mission-critical applications are at this data center. Let's also assume that you have off-site backups. Following are the steps:

1.   Assess the damage. Is there any thing left that can be reused? Probably not. If the fire and smoke did not do enough damage, then water from the fire trucks finished the job.

2.   Notify internal and external business partners about the incident. Why? What if one of your partners were trying to send you an order. Your warehouse may not have been damaged and you could possibly take the order over the phone.

3.   Obtain necessary office supplies and workspace.

4.   Build and/or rebuild business processes via stand-alone systems and/or manual processes.

5.   Obtain and install necessary hardware components, such as:

   - Wan, LAN, routers, servers, printers, and coffee machines

   - Software, backup tapes

   - Phone lines

   - Network circuits

6.   Execute pilot and system tests before going back on-line, including testing system functionality and security controls.

7.   Obtain a facility. (This can take several days.)

The preceding steps represent just a small subset of the issues that will need to be addressed in a very short time. In reality, without proper planning, this process could take weeks and/or months. Can your business afford to be without IT infrastructure for this length of time?

Not all interruptions to an IT infrastructure come in the form of a disaster. A business will need basic security practices to keep the business up and running. Consider the following example to help reinforce the point: You have just purchased a new car. It is a very nice car—a $45,000 sticker and loaded with cool features that everyone wants. What will you do to protect your new car?

- Purchase insurance.

- Install an antitheft alarm system.

- Have a set of unique keys.

- Have a deluxe locking gas cap.

- Have a wireless system to ask for navigation and/or to open the car.

- Have locking lugs on the wheels.

Not bad. You have taken all the correct precautions, and now your car is 100% protected from being stolen. I'm afraid not. There are many ways to steal that car. In fact, with some social engineering, you could even get the door opened for you via the new "wireless" feature.

So now what can you do?

You must make a "best effort" to protect your business within the scope and budget needed to support the business. It is the same as with auto insurance. You would not want to pay more for the insurance than the value of the car, and the same logic must be followed with your business as well. It is important to keep this in mind when determining the level of security to be implemented along with the associated costs. Your number-one goal should be to implement security such that continuity of operations is achieved and the business remains a viable entity.

The next step is "incident handling." Incident handling is a process that deals with an event that is unplanned and unexpected—a situation that requires immediate action to prevent a loss of business, assets, or public confidence. Incident handling has several goals:

- Handle a security incident

- Keep the business running

- If needed, make a temporary fix to the incursion

- Facilitate the process to make a permanent fix to the incursion

Incident handling includes several components:

- A policy that outlines the strategy for the incident handling requirements
- A plan that details the processes needed to support incident handling
- Procedures that make up each step for each process
- A team that will implement the procedures

It would be nice if a company never needed an incident response strategy. With today's attacks on web sites, however, you will need one. The key is to be prepared for these attacks. With that said, let's look at each step to create a workable incident response strategy.

10.2 Incident handling requirements

As with all of our policies, we need to look at the business drivers. Before you make any decisions on incident handling, you need to look at the service level requirements of what you are protecting. Your service level agreement (SLA) will work hand in hand with incident handling and disaster recovery. If you have an SLA that your web server will be up from 8 A.M. to 5 P.M. on weekdays, do you really need to have an incident response team ready to pounce on a problem 24 hours a day, seven days a week? Balance the needs and definitions of your incident response team to that of your SLA's. (If you want to learn more on SLAs, check out this article in *CEO Magazine*. It is old but good: http://www.cio.com/archive/111598_sla.html.) Also, if you run a business that truly needs 100% up time, you may need to have several sites worldwide as "hot sites." This would be linked into an automated system that pushes your users over to a "working" site. Again, the strategy needs to match the needs of the business and the SLA's.

The incident handling policy should also have some high-level definition of monitoring requirements. There are several different methods that you can use to monitor your security. This information should be fed back into the process that identifies the countermeasures for your site. You can have a real-time system that launches some type of automatic response based on a particular attack. Or you can have low-tech systems that beep when a certain threshold is reached. Or—really low-tech—someone notices that the server is down. The policy should not dictate which tool to use, but instead, define the requirements needed to meet the strategy. For example, "In the event that a server is down, an out-of-band alert will notify an administrator within 15 minutes."

In this example, you may select some simple system that checks the server every five minutes looking for an HTTP status code of "200." If that code is not returned after two tries, the server is considered "down." In that case, the administrator is alerted. A generic incident handling policy should have the following components (not in any particular order):

1. A reporting system: This system will provide updates and support for the number of incidents. Based on the severity of the incidents, this information will be sent to the Security Officer, then to the CIO, and then to the CEO. This reporting will provide awareness for security incidents within the company.

2. An analysis system: This system will "handle" each incident. The components of the analysis system include the following:

   - Evaluation: What is the scope of the incident?

   - Initial response and notification: What should be done and who is to be notified?

   - Legal: What are the legal ramifications involved?

   - Communication: This is different from notification. Communication is updating the employees or general public. In some cases, due to customer confidence issues, you cannot report the incident to the general public. (This is a real issue with banks.)

   - Reporting: If the incident has a significant financial impact, then you will need to report the incident to local law enforcement and to the FBI. Also report/check with CERT.

   - Documentation: Keep track of the incident through logs and reports. Documentation should also be used to generate feedback into the corporate security policies, which can generate a permanent fix or a change in policy.

10.3   Incident handling processes

An incident handling plan is basically being prepared to deal with an incident before it actually occurs. Part of this process is trying to forecast what type of responses you may encounter. Again, see your service levels for the level of responses that may be required. It is critical to document these steps. Documentation will eliminate some of the ambiguity that occurs during an incident. The following processes should be defined in your plan:

1. Identify the monitoring systems that will be used, such as alerts, trip wires, and so on.

2. Have a process that defines high-level steps of the corporate incident handling strategy (such as a flowchart). This should be distributed to every member of the incident handling team.

3. Establish a process that will notify the correct team members.

4. Create a process to test the incident handling system.

5. Forecast the costs of implementing and maintaining the incident response system.

6. Forecast the potential costs of not having an incident response system.

7. Create some initial communication documentation for dealing with the incident and/or outage.

8. Create communication documents that will be distributed to all personnel who need to know about an incident response team. For example, the Web Master will need to know about the team and its responsibilities. (The Web Master may even be on the team.)

9. A member from the incident response team must be a member of the security committee.

10. Maintain a list of phone numbers of personnel who will support the incident response team.

11. Define severity levels for the incident response process. Following are some examples:

    - Critical: The site may fail over to a backup, such as in the case of a fire or flood.

    - Severe: The site may be required to shut down for repair or restore (e.g., DDoS attack, Love Bug attack).

    - Moderate: The site may be required to block traffic from a particular IP address or domain name. This level may impact a future blacklist of URLs or IP addresses. This level could also be due to an internal procedure error: Someone may not have followed the change control processes.

    - Low: This level should be reported as a minor incident and may not involve the incident response team.

10.4   **Incident handling procedures**

The flowchart in Figures 10.1–10.3 show the basic steps you should take to build your incident handling response system.

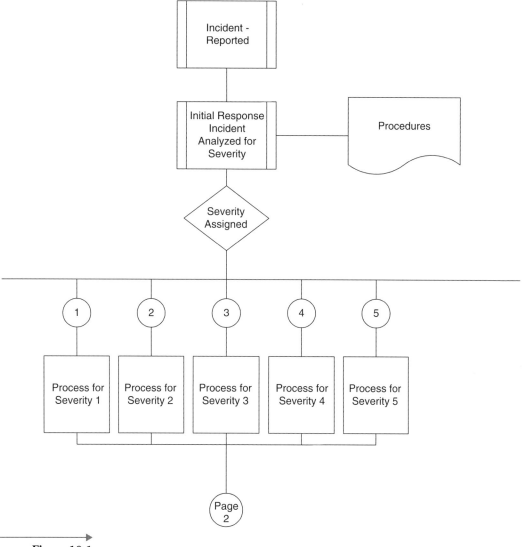

Figure 10.1

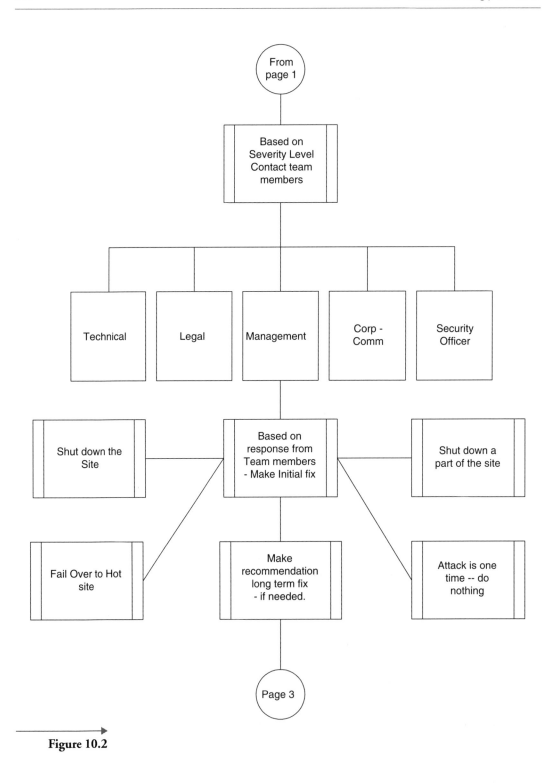

Figure 10.2

Figure 10.3

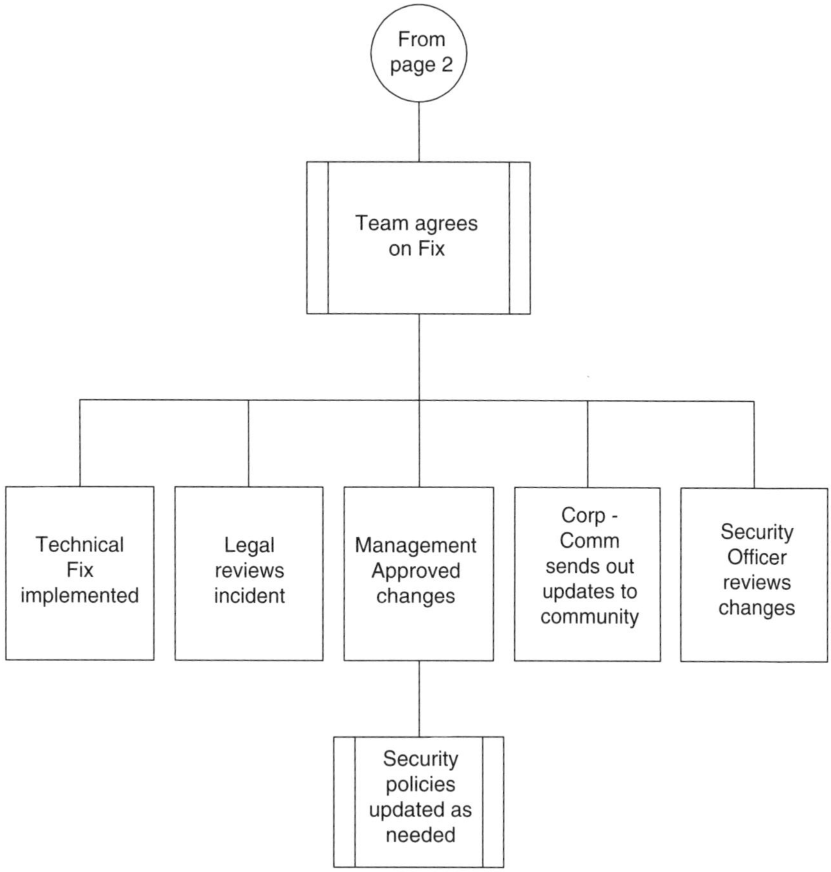

```
                                    ┌──────────┐
                                    │   From   │
                                    │  page 2  │
                                    └──────────┘
                             ┌──╥─────────────────╥──┐
                             │  ║   Team agrees    ║  │
                             │  ║     on Fix       ║  │
                             │  ║                  ║  │
                             └──╨─────────────────╨──┘

   ┌────────────┬────────────┬────────────┬────────────┬────────────┐

┌──────────┐ ┌──────────┐ ┌──────────┐ ┌──────────┐ ┌──────────┐
│ Technical│ │  Legal   │ │Management│ │  Corp -  │ │ Security │
│   Fix    │ │ reviews  │ │ Approved │ │   Comm   │ │ Officer  │
│implemented│ │ incident │ │ changes  │ │sends out │ │ reviews  │
│          │ │          │ │          │ │updates to│ │ changes  │
│          │ │          │ │          │ │community │ │          │
└──────────┘ └──────────┘ └──────────┘ └──────────┘ └──────────┘
                          ┌──╥──────────╥──┐
                          │  ║ Security ║  │
                          │  ║ policies ║  │
                          │  ║updated as║  │
                          │  ║  needed  ║  │
                          └──╨──────────╨──┘
```

1.   We start out with an incident. The incident is detected or
     reported into the system.

2.   A focal point contact will review the incident and decide on the
     severity of the incident (may consult with other members on the
     needed course of action).

3.   A severity will be assigned. The level of response will reflect the
     severity of the incident.

4.   The required team members will be contacted and the needed
     action will be implemented.

5.   An initial fix may be required. If so, the fix will be attempted. If
     not, a permanent solution will be developed and implemented.

6.   One step that is missing is the analysis of the cost impact to the company. This will need to be considered and reported. The cost analysis can impact the "lessons learned" part of the process.

7.   Finally, the security policies need to be updated from what was learned from the incident.

10.5 Incident handling team implementation

The incident response team is the heart and soul of the incident response system and must have a clearly defined scope of responsibilities. The members of the business as a whole must know that they have an incident response system in place and a team that supports it. An incident response team is composed of a cross section of various business groups, made up of professionals who come to the rescue when an emergency arises. This team, by default, will have authority to make command decisions based on the best interests of the business. A successful team will include technical personnel, management personnel, and legal and communication experts. The team will have various ownership roles within the confines of the incident response system. When you compile your team, you will need to look at the following roles and assign people to fill them:

1.   Management

2.   Technical lead

3.   Legal support

4.   Communications

5.   Interface to the security committee

6.   Security officer

The incident response team must be ready to respond to an incident the moment it occurs. In order to facilitate this, you must create a high-level decision matrix. The following categories make up that decision matrix:

1.   Owner: makes the decisions and owns the process

2.   Helpers: team members who help out on a process

3.   Advisors: team members who advise on a process

4.   Implementers: person or persons doing the work

5.   Updaters: part of the team that is updated with the status and actions from other team members

Table 10.1 shows some examples.

Table 10.1

Activities/Roles	Technical Lead	Technical	Legal	Communications	Management
Initial Response	Owner	Implements	Updated	Updated	Updated
Implements temporary fix	Implementer	Owner	Updated	Updated	Advises
Sends communications	Advisor	Advises	Advises	Implements	Owner
Check with local law enforcement on incident (or FBI)	Updater	Updated	Owner	Updated	Implements
Implements permanent fix	Implementer	Owner	Updated	Updated	Updated
Financial impact to business	Updater	Updated	Advises	Updated	Owner

The team compiled by the business must meet the requirements of the business being protected. The most important step is to include all the departments affected by the incident in the loop. There may be some steps each department will need to perform in response to the event by which they have been affected. The team membership will also need to be reevaluated periodically as needs change or as new components are added to the Internet system. Team membership should always be an ongoing process.

10.6   Disaster recovery and business continuity

Disaster Recovery (D/R) is the process that many organizations utilize for high availability solutions. Backup and restore methods are designed and implemented to allow secure storage of critical data to be used in the event of a catastrophic failure within the environment. A catastrophic failure includes such disasters as the collapse of the supporting infrastructure (such as an earthquake) or a "routine" failure in a piece of equipment. Sites prepare elaborate schemas to move critical data to removable media backup (such as tapes), which are then stored in an off-site facility. In the event of a catastrophic failure, new equipment can be commissioned to replace that equipment affected by the failure. This might take the form of hot sites where servers run mostly idle but contain current data for immediate recommissioning, warm sites where servers run in a powered-down state but are available for quick commission to replace failed equipment, or cold sites where servers have to potentially be procured, installed/configured, and then have the critical data restored prior to commission.

10.6.1 Business continuity

Business continuity (B/C) provides for servers to remain operational in the event of a catastrophic failure. Duplicate equipment exists to provide for the availability of either the "primary" or "fail-over" equipment to be utilized by the end-user community. B/C solutions are designed such that end users are oblivious of a catastrophic failure. Many times these solutions will include application based solutions; i.e. operating system solutions like NT Wolfpack, Linux, or Beowulf, or hardware solutions like HACMP or Mirroring. Business continuity is of course a vital activity. However, prior to the creation of a business continuity plan, it is essential to consider the potential impacts of disaster and to understand the underlying risks. These are the foundations upon which a sound business continuity plan should be built.

The following describes some of the basic steps that any company should review as part of their disaster recovery and/or business continuity plans:

- **Policy**—Develop and create a policy on disasters and business continuity
- Remember the risk analysis—now you need to conduct a **Business impact analysis**
- Develop and create **recovery strategies and action plans**
- Develop and create a **contingency plan**
- Develop **pilots and testing plans**

Policy

As with any important process and/or program you will need to have support from senior management. This will also include a budget. When you build the policy be sure and include the following items:

Service Level requirements, mean time between failure statistics, mean time to recovery expectations.

Roles and responsibilities—who, what, when, and where.

Areas of impact. Example:

- Hot sites for the data center
- Fail over sites for order processing
- Vendor support in the event of a disaster

Business impact analysis

Business impact analysis (BIA) is an important part of any organization's business continuity plan; it includes an analysis process to reveal any vulnerability, and a planning component to develop strategies for minimizing risk. One of the basic assumptions behind BIA is that every component of the organization is reliant upon the continued functioning of every other component, but that some are more crucial than others and require a greater allocation of funds in the wake of a disaster. For example, a business may be able to continue more or less normally if the company bookstore has to close, but would come to a complete halt if the server room burns to the ground. The business impact analysis will identify costs linked to failures, like:

- Loss of messaging components (e-mail, instant messaging, ...)

- Inability to pay employees (payroll systems down)

- Order systems down (transaction cannot be realized from customers and/or vendor)

Each company should create a business impact report. This document will quantify the importance of business components and suggests appropriate budgets needed to implement required measures.

Recovery strategies and action plans

As part of your planning process you will need to determine and define your enterprise recovery strategies—some of these should include the following:

- Roles and responsibilities

- Backup methods

- Site definitions

Roles and responsibilities

The size and definition of the disaster recovery team will vary with each enterprise. The large enterprises will need larger more diverse teams.

Earlier in this chapter we defined the basic team that you will need to incident handling. Overall the same team can be used. The difference is in the implementation of the solution. The table above shows where the team determines the problem, the scope of the problem, and the solution. This is where the team determines the action needed to keep the business running; or get the business running as soon as possible.

It is important for an enterprise to develop the top five or ten scenarios that may impact the business—these "example problems" will help guide the plan and cost needed to build the disaster recovery team. Level one could be a simple virus or e-mail that is not in the virus definition file. At first you may think that this hardly needs a team to jump in and save the day. The authors have seen large enterprises shut down due to a simple macro virus invading the corporate mail system. In some cases it was made worse by a single administrator trying to fix the problem while the virus was spreading from user to user—think of the vaudevillian trying to keep 20,000 plates spinning. Not possible—this is where the incident response team comes to the rescue with processes and procedures (and experience). Now a Level 5 type of incident could be a fire in the data center—in this case all is lost. Fire, water, confusion, and in the end—no data center. Again the team will need to be called into action to execute the plan. In the case of a worst case scenario, the team should include the following members:

- The incident response team as listed above

- Damage assessment team

- Alternate site fail over team

- Hardware team

- Operating system administration team

- Application team

- Network and telecommunication team

- Emergency communication help desk (cell phones, pagers, home number access…)

In most cases the disaster recovery team would be part-time—like the volunteer fire department. Also in some companies vendor specialists will be on-call for an emergency. Take the time up-front to develop SLAs and contracts with your vendors so they can help you get back on-line quickly.

Also be sure to run system 'tests' to see if your team is ready for a disaster. Include the vendors in the exercise.

Backup methods

System backups can be key in any type of incident and/or disaster. Enterprise data should be backed up based on a predefined schedule. Scheduled test restores should be conducted at least once a month; some companies will execute a restore daily to make sure the data from the day before is properly backed up.

There are many different types of backup:

- External storage media backups

- Hierarchical backup

- Journaling

- Off-site backup or clustering

- Hot site mirroring

External storage media backups   This is your old standard backup—Full, incremental, and differential. Data is copied from the hard disk to another device, tape, floppy (not very efficient), CD, another hard disk, and more. Note: make sure your applications and your backup software are compatible—some applications may keep a file open and confuse the backup software.

Hierarchical backup   This is basically the same as external storage media backup, but with a big difference. The data is managed by a set of rules—one common rule is the age of the data. As the data is aged (or accessed), it is transferred to slower media. Example: Let's say you have daily transactions, and as each transaction is completed, you store it on the live disk. Eventually the disk will run out of space, so you now move the data to another disk so you can mine the data—like a monthly report. This data is also put on a backup tape. As the data gets older you may now move it to an optical storage media, a larger but slower storage. A backup may also be made on a duplicate disk and moved to another site. The message here is to try and understand how much live data you need on your active systems and how much archive data you need for data mining. Then you will understand how often you need to archive that data out from the live site.

Journaling   There are many different types of journaling—one example is where an enterprise actually journals the transaction logs to another site. In the event of a disaster, a full backup is executed and the transaction logs are executed against the backup. In this case the amount of data lost is normally zero.

Off-site backup or clustering   Off-site backups are straightforward—take the data and move it off-site. (Duh!). Clustering is one form of that—this is where the data is network (wan) clustered live to another site. If a file is changed on the primary site, then it is automatically duplicated on the clustered site. The difference between journaling and clustering is the amount of data. Journaling is moving just the delta of each transaction and clustering is moving complete files or volumes.

When selecting an offsite storage facility and vendor, consider the following:

Cost—this is always important.

Geographic area—the distance from the organization and the probability of the storage site being affected by the same disaster event as the organization

Accessibility—the length of time necessary to retrieve the data from storage and the storage facility's operating hours

Security—the security capabilities of the storage facility and employee confidentiality, which must meet the data's sensitivity and security requirements

Environment—the structural and environmental conditions of the storage facility (i.e., temperature, humidity, fire prevention, and power management controls)

Site definition

Why is a fail-over site needed? The basic answer is—in the event of a primary site outage, then the business can continue.

Overall you would hope that a primary site outage would be rare. But the determination that a primary site is at risk is based on the following criteria.

- Business impact
- Location

Business impact   What is the SLA for your business? Can your business be down for several days due to a fire, flood, or loss of facility? The answers will help you determine what type of site that you will need for a fail-over. Lets say you are a credit-card company that has transactions every minute or every second. If you go down for a few minutes, then you could be open to credit card fraud and, of course, lost business. What if you lose your building for several days? It's the same with an airline company or a bank with several offices. In any of these examples, a company would lose business and possibly go out of business if they cannot move to a working site quickly. On the other end of the spectrum is the Small-to-Medium business. In the smallest case, the owner could keep a backup over at his partner's house, purchase a computer from a local vendor, and be on-line in about 4–6 hours. Overall, little to no impact on the business.

Location   Due to your business and other factors you may have your business and data center in the middle of a hurricane and/or tornado zone. In this case you can lose your IT facility. Also you may have a business in a part of town that has a high crime rate. In either case you can lose your computers and/or facilities. Take the time to understand the impact of where you house your business in relation to localized impacts. Check with your insurance company and see if they have any data for your area— example: if you live in the 100 year flood plain.

Let's look at a few example of backup sites:

Billy Jo-Bob's House   You won't find this one listed in any other books on disaster recovery. OK, this is not a well-known-site type; this is the simplest of recovery mechanisms. Keep a copy of a daily backup at someone's house, like your business partner, or a trusted employee. Remember, be sure to test your recovery capability at least once a month.

Hot Sites   This is the best of the best, and normally the most expensive. The hot site can perform not only as a hot site, but also as a load balancing site, or even an overload site. The hot site is normally built with necessary system hardware, supporting infrastructure, and support personnel and the sites are staffed 24 hours a day, 7 days a week.

Mirrored Site   This is a redundant facility that contains duplicated data from the primary site. Some type of system clustering is normally used. Mirrored sites must be identical to the primary site in all technical respects. These sites provide the highest degree of availability because the data is processed and stored at the primary and alternate site simultaneously. These sites typically are designed, built, operated, and maintained by the organization. The mirrored site is the hot site plus all of the active data.

A Warm Site   This is a dedicate facility that contains some or all of the IT infrastructure needed to get back on-line. The warm site will typically include:

- Servers
- Some clients

- Software
- Network and telecommunications
- Backup power systems

The site may need to be "enabled" before it can be used. This enabling process would include:

1. DNS updates

2. Backup take loads

3. Network routing for business traffic

4. Movement of IT staff to the site for setup and business operations.

A Cold Site   will consist of a facility with enough space and infrastructure to support some temporary IT operations. Typically you might have:

- Spare computers—not configured
- Power—but may not have a UPS system
- Some telecommunication equipment
- Basic environmental controls

You may not have active telecommunication circuits, but in place of that you may have SLA's from the local provider to get you service in a short period of time. Regardless of the type of alternate site chosen, the type of site needed must be able to support system operations as defined in the contingency plan.

Contingency plans

In preparation for Year 2000, many organizations developed some contingency plans for their mission critical IT systems. However, these plans were designed to a specific event, program failure, and are not comprehensive enough. Companies must go beyond their information systems and develop comprehensive contingency plans for all mission critical systems. After the tragic events of September 11, 2001, many organizations initiated a systemic review of their internal support systems. Companies that had some type of plan were able to get back on-line quickly, while others contacted their hardware and software vendors for help. Organizations must review their current plans and update them on a regular basis. Organizations must ensure they can rapidly provide a minimally acceptable level of critical services during an outage and/or a disaster. The following is an example of the steps needed in a contingency plan.

1. Establish organizational planning guidelines

2. Develop detailed contingency plans (specific steps)

3. Validate the plans

4. Communicate the plans

Pilots and testing plans

Once all of the plans are developed, they should then be tested. A pilot is a device that a company can use to test a basic assumption and to then determine if the plan and technology can provide the needed solution. There are basically two types of pilots:

- Technical

- Process

The technical pilot will include all of the hardware and software components. The process pilot will include the actual steps to implement the solution. Pilots are normally timed into nonproduction pilots and production pilots. The nonproduction pilots are conducted in the LAB. Production pilots are executed on production equipment—but normally scheduled to holidays and/or off-hours.

Appendix I

Security Tools

AI.I Tools

There are many tools that you can use to test and/or monitor your computing environment. The following is a small sample of what you can find available from many different vendors. Check the URL for each tool for ownership, copyright, or trademark considerations.

Tool Name: TCP/IP wrapper program

Category: Unix Security

Description: The TCP/IP wrapper program provides network-logging information about TCP/IP access. The wrapper program can also provide an administrator with the ability to deny or allow access from certain systems or domains.

URL: ftp://ftp.porcupine.org/pub/security

Tool Name: ZoneAlarm

Category: Monitoring

Description: ZoneAlarm is used to protect your Internet-connected PC from hackers, crackers, and bears. ZoneAlarm includes several different services including firewall, application control, and an Internet lock.

URL: http://www.zonelabs.com

Tool Name: Crack

Category: Unix Password Cracking

Description: Crack is a free program designed to identify UNIX passwords that can be found in available dictionaries.

URL: ftp://coast.cs.purdue.edu/pub/tools/unix/crack

Tool Name: NetBus Detective 5.2

Category: Monitoring Tools

Description: NetBus is a hacking tool that many hackers use for accessing another computer. The program is actually two parts: One tool is used by the hacker, and the other is started (placed) on the computer that the hacker wants to visit. NetBus Detective 5.2 will search for all NetBus programs and other hacking programs on your computer and remove them.

URL: http://www.microsoft.com

Tool Name: Argus

Category: Monitoring Tool

Description: Argus is a network monitoring tool that implements a client-server model to capture data and associate it into "transactions." Argus provides network-level auditing, and it can verify compliance to a router configuration file.

URL: ftp://ftp.andrew.cmu.edu/pub/argus

Tool Name: BlackICE Defender

Category: Internet Monitoring

Description: BlackICE Defender delivers intrusion detection and personal firewall protection to your Internet-connected computer. BlackICE can scan cable, DSL, and dial-up Internet connections.

URL: http://www.networkice.com

Tool Name: ISS (Internet Security Scanner)

Category: Scanner

Description: The ISS tool is a program that will interrogate all computers within a specified IP address range and determine the security status of each system in relation to several common system vulnerabilities.

URL: ftp://coast.cs.purdue.edu/pub/tools/unix/iss

Tool Name: Exchange Plus

Category: E-Mail Scanner

Description: Exchange Plus scans for content and attachments. Automatic attachment compression can help save bandwidth.

URL: http://www.aspeonsoftware.com

Tool Name: ScanMail

Category: E-Mail Scanner

Description: ScanMail scans for content, viruses, and attachments.

URL: http://www.antivirus.com

Tool Name: Tripwire

Category: Monitoring tool

Description: Tripwire is a security utility that compares a designated set of files and directories to information stored in a previously generated information store. Any differences are flagged and logged, including added or deleted entries.

URL: ftp://coast.cs.purdue.edu/pub/tools/unix/Tripwire

Tool Name: HostScan

Category: Monitoring Tool

Description: HostScan allows you to scan any or all TCP/IP services running on a computer.

URL: http://www.savant-software.com

Tool Name: 4-Net

Category: Monitoring Tool

Description: 4-Net is an Internet tools package. It allows you to indefinitely maintain your Internet connection by simulating Internet activity. Use 4-Net to monitor your Internet connection's latency or your file download speeds.

URL: http://www.cartoonlogic.com/4net

Tool Name: COPS

Category: Unix Security—Reporting Tool

Description: COPS is a publicly available collection of programs that attempts to identify security issues in a UNIX system.

URL: ftp://coast.cs.purdue.edu/pub/tools/unix/cops

Tool Name: Attacker 2.1

Category: Port Listener

Description: Attacker 2.1 is a TCP/UDP port listener. The PC owner will provide a list of ports to listen on, and the program will notify them when a connection or data arrives at the port.

URL: http://members.home.com/rkeir/attacker.html

Tool Name: Big Brother 1.3

Category: Network Testing

Description: Big Brother 1.3 consists of local clients that test system conditions and the availability of network services and sends status reports to one or more DISPLAY servers, where these reports appear as little dots on a web page.

URL: http://bb4.com/features.html

Tool Name: SATAN

Category: Network Testing

Description: SATAN is a testing and reporting tool that collects a variety of information about networked hosts.

URL: ftp://ftp.porcupine.org/pub/security

Tool Name: CommView 1.0

Category: Network Monitoring tool

Description: CommView 1.0 is an application for capturing and analyzing network packets.

URL: http://www.tamos.com/cv.htm

Tool Name: NoBackDoors

Category: Monitoring Tool

Description: NoBackDoors is an antihacker program that searches a computer and detects back door programs like NetBus and Back Orifice. This program can be set to run in the background and continually scan for "bad dudes."

URL: http://home.swipnet.se/technotel

Tool Name: ESMonitor

Category: Monitoring Tool

Description: ESMonitor is a networked systems monitoring package that will periodically check the status of systems and notify the appropriate users in the event that a system is down.

URL: http://www.eronsoft.com/products.html

Tool Name: Internet Anywhere Toolkit

Category: Generic Tools

Description: The Internet Anywhere Toolkit is a set of diagnostic tools, including Ping, Finger, WhoIs, TraceRoute, Name Server LookUp, Time, and Quote of the Day.

URL: http://www.tnsoft.com/toolkit.htm

Tool Name: MailMarshal

Category: E-mail Scanner

Description: MailMarshal scans for content, viruses, and attachments and can help prevent e-mail spoofing.

URL: http://www.marshalsoftware.com

Tool Name: Net-Commando 2000

Category: Virus and Trojan Detection

Description: Net-Commando 2000 is an Internet security package designed to detect and remove all known and unknown Trojan horse viruses.

URL: http://www.deltadesignuk.com

Tool Name: WorldSecure Mail

Category: E-mail Scanner

Description: This tool scans for content, viruses, and attachments. It can automatically encrypt messages at the server.

URL: http://www.tumbleweed.com

Tool Name: ProtectX

Category: Monitoring Tools

Description: ProtectX is a hacker protection program for a PC. It monitors a system on the specified ports, notifies a user if someone tries to connect, and logs the IP number of the intruder.

URL: http://www.plasmateksoftware.com

Tool Name: Elron CommandView Message Inspector

Category: Scanner

Description: Elron scans for content and attachments.

URL: http://www.elronsoftware.com

Tool Name: NetHound

Category: Monitoring Tool

Description: NetHound will notify an assigned person in case of server malfunction by sending alerts via pager, e-mail, and pop-up windows to any number of alert recipients.

URL: http://www.people-network.com/nethound.htm

Tool Name: MailSweeper

Category: E-Mail Scanner

Description: This tool scans for content, viruses, and attachments, and also helps prevent e-mail spoofing.

URL: http:// www.mimesweeper.com

Tool Name: OstroSoft Internet Tools

Category: Network Monitoring Tool

Description: OstroSoft Internet Tools is an integrated set of network (Internet) information utilities that is intended for use by network, domain and systems administrators, network security professionals, and Internet users.

URL: http://www.ostrosoft.com/ostronet.html

Tool Name: PrivacyMaker

Category: Utility

Description: This program makes computer activities private. It securely cleans, hides, or encrypts cookies, cache, history, files, and folders. It clears the document menu. It includes the antihacker feature of a desktop alarm.

URL: http://www.privacymaker.com

Tool Name: PortWatch

Category: Port Monitor

Description: PortWatch is an application that watches a user-specified TCP port for a connection, data, and close events. When these events occur, the user is alerted and information about the event is logged.

URL: http://www.isd.net/jturgeon/portwatch

Tool Name: Share finder

Category: Network Scanner/Server Scanner

Description: Share finder is a tool for administrators to examine what is being shared on their networks.

URL: http://nfisher.campus.vt.edu/ogre%20electronics

Tool Name: The VirusMD Personal Firewall

Category: Personal Firewall

Description: The VirusMD Personal Firewall program will monitor up to 12 user-selected ports at a time, including some ports that most modern firewalls miss. It will sound an alarm Klaxon when an intruder is detected.

URL: http://www.virusmd.com

Tool Name: Webtrends for Firewalls and VPNs

Category: Network Reporting Tool

Description: Webtrends for Firewalls and VPNs is a comprehensive security and network traffic reporting solution. It analyzes firewall and proxy-server log files and allows the user to generate customized graphs and detailed tables on bandwidth consumption and security issues.

URL: http://www.webtrends.com/products/firewall

A1.2   Other tool URLs

Dr Solomon's Computer Virus Information—http://www.drsolomon.com

Internet Security Firewalls—http://www.greatcircle.com/tutorials

Linux Security—http://bach.cis.temple.edu/linux/linux-security

McAfee—ttp://www.mcafee.com

NCSA—http://www.ncsa.uiuc.edu

NT Security Issues—http://www.somarsoft.com

Packet Filtering in Internet Firewalls—http://www.willamette.edu/~dlabar/firewall.html

Paranoia's Home Page—http://www.paranoia.com

RSA Data Security—http://www.rsa.com

Security Monitoring Programs—http://www.alw.nih.gov/Security/prog-monitor.html

Security Related RFCs—http://www.cert.dfn.de/eng/resource/rfc/

SSH (Secure Shells) Home Page—http://www.cs.hut.fi/ssh

Symantec Virus Information—http://www.symantec.com/avcenter/index.html

Trusted Information Systems—http://www.tis.com

Unix Network Security Tools—http://ciac.llnl.gov/ciac/ToolsUnix-NetSec.html

Unix System Security—http://stimpy.cac.washington.edu/~dittrich/R870/security-checklist.html

Appendix 2

The CERT Report

The Computer Emergency Response Team (CERT) is one of the main agencies for Internet security. The Defense Advanced Research Projects Agency (DARPA) formed CERT in November 1988. The mission of CERT is to aid the Internet community in responding to computer security events, to raise awareness of computer security issues, and research aimed at improving security systems.

CERT provides 24-hour technical assistance in responding to computer security breaches, product vulnerability assistance, technical documents, and seminars.

Following are steps recommended by CERT for reporting security incidents.

The authors and editors of this book would like to thank CERT® for the reference material provided in this chapter.

Special permission to reproduce "CERT® Coordinate Center Incident Reporting Guidelines" at URL http://www.cert.org/tech_tips/incident_reporting.html and "CERT® Coordination Center Windows NT Intruder Detection Checklist" at URL http://www.cert.org/tech_tips/win_intruder_detection_checklist.html, © 2000 by Carnegie Mellon University, in The Internet Security Guidebook: From Planning to Deployment is granted by the Software Engineering Institute.

The "CERT® Coordination Center incident Reporting Guidelines" and "CERT® Coordination Center Windows NT Intruder Detection Checklist" are available on the Internet (http://www.cert.org).

Readers may learn about the latest updates to these documents at http://www.cert.org. CERT® and CERT Coordination Center® are registered in the U.S. Patent and Trademark Office.

CERT® Coordination Center

A2.1 Incident reporting guidelines

This document outlines suggested steps for reporting incidents to the CERT Coordination Center (CERT/CC). System administrators can use this information to report incidents effectively to the CERT/CC, other computer security incident response teams (CSIRT's), or other sites.

Introduction

I. What type of activity should I report?

    A. The CERT/CC's incident definition

    B. The CERT/CC's incident priorities

II. Why should I report an incident?

    A. You may receive technical assistance.

    B. We may be able to associate activity with other incidents.

    C. Your report will allow us to provide better incident statistics.

    D. Contacting others raises security awareness.

    E. Your report helps us to provide you with better documents.

    F. Your organization's policies may require you to report the activity.

    G. Reporting incidents is part of being a responsible site on the Internet.

III. Who should I report an incident to?

    A. Your site security coordinator

    B. Your representative CSIRT

    C. The CERT Coordination Center

    D. Other sites involved in the incident

    E. Law enforcement

IV. What should I include in my incident report?

    A. When reporting an incident to the CERT/CC

    B. When reporting to other sites and CSIRT's

          1.   Incident reference numbers

          2.   Information about how to contact you

          3.   Disclosure information

          4.   A summary of hosts involved

          5.   A description of the activity

          6.   Log extracts showing the activity

          7.   Your timezone and the accuracy of your clock

          8.   Clarify what you would like from the recipient

   V.   How should I report an incident to the CERT/CC?

       A.   Electronic Mail

       B.   Telephone Hotline

       C.   Facsimile (FAX)

       D.   Encrypting Reports to the CERT/CC

          1.   Pretty Good Privacy (PGP)

          2.   Data Encryption Standard (DES)

  VI.   When should I report an incident?

       Document revision history

I. What type of activity should I report?

What type of activity you should report, and the level of detail included in your report, depends on to whom you are reporting. Your local policies and procedures may have detailed information about what types of activity should be reported, and the appropriate person to whom you should report.

A. The CERT/CC's incident definition

The CERT Coordination Center is interested in receiving reports of security incidents involving the Internet. A good but fairly general definition of an incident is: The act of violating an explicit or implied security policy.

Unfortunately, this definition relies on the existence of a security policy that, while generally understood, varies between organizations. We have attempted to characterize below the types of activity we believe are widely recognized as being in violation of a typical security policy. These activities include but are not limited to: attempts (either failed or successful) to gain unauthorized access to a system or its data unwanted disruption or denial of service the unauthorized use of a system for the processing or storage of data changes to system hardware, firmware, or software characteristics without the owner's knowledge, instruction, or consent.

We encourage you to report any activities that you feel meet these criteria for being an incident. Note that our policy is to keep any information specific to your site confidential unless we receive your permission to release that information.

B. The CERT/CC's incident priorities

Due to limited resources and the growing number of incident reports, we may not be able to respond to every incident reported to us. We must prioritize our responses to have the greatest impact on the Internet community. The following type of reports receive the highest priority and are considered emergencies:

possible life-threatening activity

attacks on the Internet infrastructure, such as:

root name servers

domain name servers

major archive sites

network access points (NAPs)

widespread automated attacks against Internet sites

new types of attacks or new vulnerabilities

II. Why should I report an incident?

There are several reasons to report an incident to the CERT Coordination Center. We may be able to provide technical assistance in responding to the incident, or put you in touch with other sites involved in the same activity. Your reports allow us to collect and distribute better information about intruder activity through our statistics and documents. Reporting incidents to the CERT/CC and others helps to promote greater security awareness and improve the security of the Internet. Your organizational policies or local laws may require you to report the activity to us or some other CSIRT. Finally, notifying other sites of possible security intrusions is an important part of being a good Internet citizen.

A. You may receive technical assistance

A primary part of our mission is to provide a reliable, trusted, 24-hour, single point of contact for security emergencies involving the Internet. We facilitate communication among experts working to solve security problems and serve as a central point for identifying and correcting vulnerabilities in computer systems.

When you report an incident to us, we can provide pointers to technical documents, offer suggestions on recovering the security of your systems, and share information about recent intruder activity. In our role as a coordination center, we may have access to information that is not yet widely available to assist in responding to your incident.

Unfortunately, our limited resources and the increasing number of incidents reported to us may prevent us from responding to each report individually. We must prioritize our responses to have the greatest impact on the Internet community.

B. We may be able to associate activity with other incidents

The CERT/CC receives reports of security incidents from all over the world. In many cases, these incidents have similar characteristics or involve the same intruders. By reporting your incident, you allow us to collect information about recent activity in the intruder community as it relates to your incident. We may also be able to put you in touch with other sites who are pursuing legal actions against the intruder.

C. Your report will allow us to provide better incident statistics

The CERT/CC collects statistics on the incidents reported to us. Your reports help identify vulnerabilities that are being actively exploited in the intruder community, provide information about the frequency of these attacks, and identify areas where greater community awareness is needed.

These statistics are made publicly available via our web page, the CERT/CC annual report, and at presentations made at conferences.

D. Contacting others raises security awareness

When you report an incident to the CERT/CC, we suggest that you contact the other sites involved in the activity, and that you include us in those messages. This benefits the other sites by alerting them to possible intruder activity on their systems. In many cases, unsuccessful probes you report may identify more serious security issues at the originating site.

Additionally, contacting other sites may help you respond to your security concerns by providing more information, a different perspective, or even by identifying the intruder.

E. Your report helps us to provide you with better documents

The comments and suggestions that you provide while involved in the handling of an incident allows us to improve our tech tips, advisories, and other computer security publications. Your questions help us to understand what subjects require greater attention in future documents. And taken as a whole, your reports allow us to understand the current state of the computer security practice.

F. Your organization's policies may require you to report the activity

Your organization's policies may require that you report this activity to the CERT/CC or another CSIRT. On the other hand, your policy may require that you not report or discuss this activity with anyone other than your site security coordinator. Before reporting activity to the CERT/CC or anyone else, check your local policies and procedures on how to proceed.

Local and/or federal laws may further dictate your behavior regarding the handling of computer security incidents. If you work for a public agency, you may be required to report the activity to a specific CSIRT. If your systems involve sensitive data, you may not be able to discuss the incident without permission. Before reporting activity to the CERT/CC or anyone else, check with your management and legal counsel.

G. Reporting incidents is part of being a responsible site on the Internet.

There is a strong historical precedent for communicating with other sites about security incidents. The Request for Comments document "Guidelines for the Secure Operation of the Internet" (RFC1281) reads:

The Internet is a cooperative venture. The culture and practice in the Internet is to render assistance in security matters to other sites and networks. Each site is expected to notify other sites if it detects a penetration in progress at the other sites, and all sites are expected to help one another respond to security violations. This assistance may include tracing connections, tracking violators and assisting law enforcement efforts.

III. Who should I report an incident to?

To determine who you should report a security incident to, first consult your local security policies and procedures. If the procedures do not explicitly identify who you should report an activity to, you should discuss the incident with your management and legal counsel before proceeding.

A. Your site security coordinator

Many security procedures identify a site security coordinator who serves as a central resource for handling violations of your security policies. This person may coordinate and handle all communications with other CSIRT's, law enforcement and other sites.

B. Your representative CSIRT

Many companies, universities, and countries have a computer security incident response team (CSIRT) dedicated to handling incidents involving their constituency. The Forum of Incident Response and Security Teams (FIRST) is a coalition of such CSIRT's. FIRST aims to foster cooperation and coordination in incident prevention, to prompt rapid reaction to incidents, and to promote information sharing among members and the community at large.

More information about FIRST can be found on their web page at: http://www.first.org/

To determine if your site is represented by a member of FIRST, you may want to review the list of FIRST teams which includes email addresses, telephone numbers, and brief descriptions of each team's constituency.

C. The CERT Coordination Center

The CERT Coordination Center welcomes reports from any site experiencing a computer security problem involving the Internet. We encourage you to include the CERT/CC on any messages you send to other sites or CSIRT's (within the limits of your site's security policies and procedures). This information will enable us to better meet our incident coordination objectives.

Information about how to contact the CERT/CC is available in section V of this document.

D. Other sites involved in the incident

Since intruders frequently use compromised hosts or accounts to attack other systems, we encourage you to report any intruder activity directly to the registered point of contact(s) of the originating host. They may be unaware of the activity involving their systems, and your note will provide the incentive to check for signs of intrusion.

We would appreciate being included on the "Cc:" line of any messages you may send to other sites regarding intruder activity.

Information about finding contact information for sites involved in incidents is available at: http://www.cert.org/tech_tips/finding_site_contacts.html

E. Law enforcement

The CERT Coordination Center is not an investigative or law enforcement agency. We do not investigate (or maintain or disclose information about) individual intruders, and we do not conduct criminal investigations. Our activities focus on providing technical assistance and facilitating communications in response to computer security incidents involving hosts on the Internet.

If you are interested in contacting law enforcement to conduct a legal investigation, we encourage you to review your local policies and procedures for guidance on how to proceed. We also encourage you to discuss the intruder's activity with your management and legal counsel before contacting law enforcement. Your legal counsel can provide you with legal options and courses of action based on your or your organization's needs. We do not have legal expertise and cannot offer legal advice or opinions.

U.S. sites interested in an investigation of crimes involving the Internet can contact their local Federal Bureau of Investigation (FBI) field office. To find contact information for your local FBI field office, please consult your local telephone directory or see the FBI's contact web page, available at: http://www.fbi.gov/contact.htm

Sites in other countries may want to discuss the activity with their local law enforcement agency to determine the appropriate steps that should be taken with regard to pursuing an investigation.

IV. What should I include in my incident report?

When reporting intruder activity, it is important to ensure that you provide enough information for the other site or CSIRT to be able to understand and respond to your report.

A. When reporting an incident to the CERT/CC

The CERT Coordination Center has developed an Incident Reporting Form (IRF) designed to assist you in reporting an incident. This form is available at: ftp://ftp.cert.org/pub/incident_reporting_form

This form prompts for all of the information discussed below in an organized manner. Completing the form may help you have a more complete understanding of the intruder's activity, even if you do not send it to the CERT/CC.

Many of the questions are optional, but having the answers to all the questions enables us to provide the best assistance. Completing the form can also help avoid delays introduced when we request the additional information needed to assist you.

The CERT/CC IRF is not intended for reporting activity to other sites or CSIRT's. Some of the information requested on the form may be sensitive in nature and is requested for the CERT/CC's internal use only. Note that our policy is to keep any information specific to your site confidential unless we receive your permission to release that information.

Some CSIRT's have adapted the CERT/CC IRF for use within their constituency. Before reporting activity to another CSIRT, we encourage you to see if they provide a similar incident reporting form.

B. When reporting to other sites and CSIRT's

1. Incident reference numbers

The CERT/CC and many other CSIRT's assign incident reference numbers (e.g., CERT#XXXX) to reported activity. These numbers help us to track correspondence and identify related activity. Please be sure to include all incident reference numbers that have been assigned to the incident, either by the CERT/CC or other CSIRT's.

Each CSIRT has their own procedures regarding the assignment of incident tracking numbers. The CERT/CC attempts to assign a single number to all activity involving one intruder. Each number is unique and randomly selected. We encourage you to reference this number when corresponding with other sites or CSIRT's that are involved in the incident.

When reporting activity that may be the work of multiple intruders, we request that you report each incident separately. (A common example would be two probes originating from different sites, with no other indications that the probes are related.)

Most CSIRT's, including the CERT/CC, request that the incident reference number be clearly displayed in the "Subject:" line of any mail messages regarding the incident.

2. Information about how to contact you

When contacting other sites, remember that they may not be able to contact you as easily as you might think. Perhaps they disconnected from the Internet immediately after you alerted them to the intruder's activity, and are now unable to respond to your e-mail message. Also, some companies limit long distance or international dialing from company telephones.

To ensure that others are able to respond, provide as much contact information as you are willing to disclose. In most cases, this should include at least an e-mail address and a telephone number. You may also wish to include a pager number, a fax number, or even a cellular telephone number. A traditional mail address may help the other site understand where you are located geographically.

It is also a good idea to specify an alternate contact at your site in case you are unavailable. Similar contact information should be provided for the alternate contact.

3. Disclosure information

The CERT Coordination Center's policy is to not release any information about a site's involvement in an incident, without the site's explicit permission to do so. While this policy ensures that you can report intruder activity to us in confidence, it also hinders our ability to put you in contact with other sites involved in the incident.

If we are authorized to offer information about your involvement in an incident to the other sites involved, other CSIRT's, or law enforcement, please state this clearly in the incident report.

Most CSIRT's have nondisclosure policies, and many sites will respect your nondisclosure requests as well. In general, a short statement describing your concerns (or lack thereof) should be included in any incident report to help the recipient understand and respect your wishes. Keep in mind however, that there is no way to ensure that other sites involved in the activity will comply with your request.

4. A summary of hosts involved

In many incidents, the most obvious indication of related activity is the hosts involved. For example, several of the hosts used to attack your site may have been used to attack another compromised host last week. For this reason, it is a good idea to include a brief summary of the hostnames and IP addresses known to be involved and their relationship to the incident.

However, you may want to exercise caution in identifying compromised hosts at your site, particularly before recovering the security of these systems. Your policies and procedures for handling computer security incidents may specify how much information you are able to release about the hosts involved at your site.

5. A description of the activity

One of the most important parts of any incident report is a description of the intruder's activity. Mention any vulnerabilities which were exploited, modifications that were made to the system, or software that was installed.

When reporting to a CSIRT, this information will allow the incident handler to provide assistance specific to the activity at your site. When reporting to another site, it helps the recipient understand what kind of intruder activity to look for on their systems.

When describing intruder activity, it is important to remember that other administrators may have more or less experience with computer security. You may want to include references to advisories or other documents which describe the activity in more detail.

6. Log extracts showing the activity

Whenever possible, you should include log entries showing the activity with your report, particularly when the logs provide significantly more detail than your description. Log entries may also be more easily understood by sites that do not speak your language fluently.

Log entries that are not related to the intruder activity should be removed to help avoid confusion. What you immediately recognize as normal entries may appear to be intruder activity to someone else.

If the intruder's activity generated a large number of very similar entries, it is usually sufficient to extract a sample portion of the log, and indicate this in the message. A quick estimate of the number of log entries is useful as well.

A description of the log format may also be helpful to system administrators who are not familiar with the logs provided. This is very important for log entries that do not include descriptive text, or are generated by tools that are not widely distributed.

When sending log entries to other sites, take care to ensure that you do not violate any nondisclosure policies you may have. Sensitive information can be removed by replacing it with X's. You may want to make a note of this in your report to ensure that the other site is aware of the changes.

If you do not have logs showing the intruder's activity (perhaps because they were deleted by the intruder), then state this clearly in your report to help minimize requests for this information.

Even if you do not include log entries showing the activity, we encourage you to describe the date and time when the events occurred. This allows the other site to review their logs when looking for related activity at their site.

7. Your time zone and the accuracy of your clock

Since the recipient may be in a different time zone, you should clearly identify the time zone for your comments and logs. A time-zone reference relative to GMT (or UTC) such as GMT-5 is preferred, since less formal time-zone designations can be misinterpreted. For example, EST (Eastern Standard Time) may have different meanings for people inside and outside the United States.

If the times recorded in the log entries are known to be inaccurate by more than a minute or two, you may want to include a statement warning the recipient of this inaccuracy. On the other hand, if the system was synchronized with a national time server via NTP (Network Time Protocol), then you may want to mention this as well.

Dates, times and time zones are just a few examples of several topics that can be very confusing when used casually in international communications. Danny Smith of the Australian incident response team (AUSCERT) has prepared a document for FIRST, with several suggestions on preventing confusion when communicating with sites or CSIRT's in other countries. This document is available from: http://www.first.org/docs/international_comms.html

8. Clarify what you would like from the recipient

If you are reporting intruder activity solely for the other site's benefit, let them know that you do not expect a response from them regarding your report. If you would like them to take a specific action, such as acknowledging your message, or providing you with additional information regarding the activity, request this politely in your message.

Keep in mind that the other site's incident handling policies and procedures may prevent them from responding as you have requested. Internet service providers frequently have policies protecting the identity of their customers, and will not release this information without a subpoena.

If a site requests information or an action from you that violates your site's security policy, politely explain that you are unable to respond as they requested.

Finally, when requesting assistance from the CERT/CC or another CSIRT, remember that resource limitations may prevent them from responding as you have requested.

V. How should I report an incident to the CERT/CC?

You can report intruder activity to the CERT/CC via electronic mail, telephone hotline, or FAX machine. We encourage you to encrypt your reports to ensure your privacy, and to authenticate your identity.

A. Electronic mail

The CERT Coordination Center's preferred mechanism for receiving incident reports is through electronic mail. Electronic mail allows us to prioritize the incidents reported to us, and to reply to those messages quickly and efficiently.

Electronic mail also provides an accurate and efficient medium for exchanging information too complex to discuss over the telephone, such as packet dumps, or large log files. Finally, e-mail provides a reliable log of communications that we may refer to in the process of responding to an incident.

Our electronic e-mail address is: cert@cert.org.

B. Telephone hotline

If you have disconnected from the Internet to recover from a compromise, or if you are unable to send mail due to a denial of service attack, you can contact the CERT/CC on our telephone hotline.

Our telephone hotline number is: +1 412-268-7090.

Occasionally, a compromised system's electronic mail will be monitored by the intruder. If you are unable to obtain Internet mail access from a secure system, and you do not want to alert the intruder by using e-mail on the compromised system, you may also want to contact us on the telephone.

Please keep in mind that while the CERT hotline is staffed 24 hours a day, outside of normal working hours incident handlers are available only for emergency calls. Normal working hours are from 8:00am to 8:00pm EST(GMT-5)/ EDT(GMT-4), Monday through Friday. Hours may vary on holidays or under other special circumstances.

C. Facsimile (FAX)

When electronic mail is not available or provides inadequate security, and you have logs or other information that is not easily conveyed on the telephone, you may want to send that information to us via FAX.

The CERT/CC FAX machine is checked regularly during normal working hours. Faxes received during the evenings, weekends, and holidays will be reviewed on the next business day.

Our FAX number is: +1 412-268-6989.

D. Encrypting Reports to the CERT/CC

Electronic mail provides little or no privacy for the information you send across the Internet. If you wish to ensure that mail sent to the CERT/CC is not read by unauthorized people while in transit, we encourage you to use a strong encryption algorithm.

The CERT Coordination Center currently supports two encryption mechanisms. The first is a public key based on the Pretty Good Privacy (PGP) product. We also support shared private keys through the Data Encryption Standard (DES).

1. Pretty Good Privacy (PGP)

PGP is the CERT/CC's preferred encryption mechanism. It provides authentication and privacy. No special arrangements have to be made with us in advance in order to communicate securely via PGP.

You can obtain our public key from our web server at: http://www.cert.org/contact_cert/encryptmail.html

This key will allow you to ensure the privacy of messages sent to us, and verify the authenticity of messages you receive from us.

If you encrypt messages you send to the CERT/CC, we will respond with encrypted messages whenever possible. Since it can be difficult for us to confirm the validity of your public PGP key, please be sure to include your public key in the body of any encrypted messages you send to us.

The CERT/CC signs all outgoing mail with our PGP key. If you receive any communication from us without a PGP signature, or with an invalid PGP signature, please consider the message suspect, and let us know. We encourage all sites communicating with us to encrypt and sign their e-mail messages with PGP.

More information about PGP is available from: http://www.pgp.com/

2. Data Encryption Standard (DES)

A shared private DES key must be established over a secure communication channel before messages can be exchanged. Please call our telephone hotline during normal business hours to establish a shared private DES key.

VI. When should I report an incident?

Incident reports that are sent shortly after the incident occurred are the most likely to be valuable to the recipient and to us. This does not imply that an incident report becomes useless after some period of time. We encourage you to report all activity you discover, even if the intruder's activity is quite old by the time you report it.

Other then being extra careful to ensure that the date of the activity is clearly identified, we encourage you to report the incident as you would any other incident, since other sites may not yet be aware of the incident.

This document is available from: http://www.cert.org/tech_tips/incident_ reporting.html

CERT/CC Contact Information

Email: cert@cert.org

Phone: +1 412-268-7090 (24-hour hotline)

Fax: +1 412-268-6989

Postal address:

CERT Coordination Center

Software Engineering Institute

Carnegie Mellon University

Pittsburgh PA 15213-3890

U.S.A.

CERT personnel answer the hotline 08:00–20:00 EST(GMT-5)/EDT(GMT-4) Monday through Friday; they are on call for emergencies during other hours, on U.S. holidays, and on weekends.

Using encryption

We strongly urge you to encrypt sensitive information sent by e-mail. Our public PGP key is available from http://www.cert.org/CERT_PGP.key

If you prefer to use DES, please call the CERT hotline for more information.

Getting security information

CERT publications and other security information are available from our web site http://www.cert.org/

To be added to our mailing list for advisories and bulletins, send email to cert-advisory-request@cert.org and include SUBSCRIBE your-email-address in the subject of your message.

* "CERT" and "CERT Coordination Center" are registered in the U.S. Patent and Trademark Office.

NO WARRANTY

Any material furnished by Carnegie Mellon University and the Software Engineering Institute is furnished on an "as is" basis. Carnegie Mellon University makes no warranties of any kind, either expressed or implied as to any matter including, but not limited to, warranty of fitness for a particular purpose or merchantability, exclusivity or results obtained from use of the material. Carnegie Mellon University does not make any warranty of any kind with respect to freedom from patent, trademark, or copyright infringement.

Copyright 1998, 1999, 2000 Carnegie Mellon University.

CERT® Coordination Center

A2.2 Windows NT intruder detection checklist

This document is being published jointly by the CERT Coordination Center and AusCERT (Australian Computer Emergency Response Team).

Introduction

    A.   Look for Signs That Your System May Have Been Compromised

        1. Examine log files

        2. Check for odd user accounts and groups

        3. Look for incorrect group memberships

        4. Look for incorrect user rights

        5. Check for unauthorized applications from starting

        6. Check system binaries

        7. Check network configuration and activity

        8. Check for unauthorized shares

        9. Examine jobs run by the scheduler service

    10. Check for unauthorized processes

    11. Look everywhere for unusual or hidden files

    12. Check for altered permissions on files or registry keys

    13. Check for changes in user or computer policies

    14. Make sure the system has not been moved to a different Workgroup or Domain

    15. Examine all machines on the local network

B. Review Other AusCERT and CERT Documents

    1. CERT Summaries

    2. "Steps for Recovering from a Windows NT Compromise"

    3. Contacting AusCERT

    4. Contacting CERT®/CC

C. Consider running intrusion detection systems if possible

Document revision history

This document outlines suggested steps for determining whether or not your system has been compromised. System administrators can use this information to look for several types of break-ins. We encourage you to review all sections of this document and modify your systems to address potential weaknesses.

In addition to the information in this document, we provide three companion documents that may help you:

- http://www.cert.org/tech_tips/win_configuration_guidelines.html contains suggestions for avoiding common NT system configuration problems

- http://www.cert.org/tech_tips/win-UNIX-system_compromise.html contains suggested steps for recovering from a compromise on an NT system

- http://www.cert.org/tech_tips/win-resources.html contains descriptions of tools that can be used to help secure a system and deter break-ins

We also encourage you to check regularly with your vendor(s) for any updates or new patches that relate to your systems.

Note: All action taken during the course of an investigation should be in accordance with your organization's policies and procedures.

A. Look for signs that your system may have been compromised

    1. Examine log files for connections from unusual locations or for other unusual activity. You can use the Event Viewer to check for odd log-on

entries, failures of services, or odd system restarts. If your firewall, web server, or router writes logs to a different location than the compromised system, remember to check these logs as well. But remember that this is not foolproof unless you log to append-only media; many intruders edit log files in an attempt to hide their activity.

2. Check for odd user accounts and groups. You can use the User Manager tool or the "net user," "net group," and "net localgroup" commands at the command line. Ensure that the built-in GUEST account is disabled if the system does not require guest access.

3. Check all groups for invalid user membership. Some of the default NT groups give special privileges to the members of those groups. Members of the Administrators group can do anything to the local system. Backup operators can read any file on the system. PowerUsers can create shares.

4. Look for invalid user rights. To examine user rights use the User Manager tool under Policies, User Rights. There are 27 different rights that can be assigned to users or groups. Generally the default configuration for these rights is secure.

5. Check to see if unauthorized applications are starting. There are a number of different methods an intruder could use to start a back door program, so be sure to

■ Check the Startup folders. Check all items in c:\winnt\profiles*\start menu\ programs\startup folders. You can also examine all the shortcuts by selecting Start, Programs, Startup. Note that there are two startup folders, one for the local user and one for all users. When a user logs on, all of the applications in both the "All Users" and in the users startup folder are started. Because of this it is important to check all of the startup folders for suspicious applications.

■ Check the registry. The most common locations for applications to start through the registry are

LISTING 1

http://www.cert.org/tech_tips/win-listings.html#A

Listing #1

```
HKEY_LOCAL_MACHINE\System\CurrentControlSet\Control\
Session Manager\KnownDLLs

HKEY_LOCAL_MACHINE\System\ControlSet001\Control\
Session Manager\KnownDLLs
```

HKEY_LOCAL_MACHINE\Software\Microsoft\Windows\
Current Version\Run

HKEY_LOCAL_MACHINE\Software\Microsoft\Windows\
Current Version\RunOnce

HKEY_LOCAL_MACHINE\Software\Microsoft\Windows\
Current Version\RunOnceEx

HKEY_LOCAL_MACHINE\Software\Microsoft\Windows\
CurrentVersion\RunServices

HKEY_LOCAL_MACHINE\Software\Microsoft\Windows NT\
CurrentVersion\Windows ("run=" line)

HKEY_CURRENT_USER\Software\Microsoft\Windows\
Current Version\Run

HKEY_CURRENT_USER\Software\Microsoft\Windows\
Current Version\RunOnce

HKEY_CURRENT_USER\Software\Microsoft\Windows\
Current Version\RunOnceEx

HKEY_CURRENT_USER\Software\Microsoft\Windows\
CurrentVersion\RunServices

HKEY_CURRENT_USER\Software\Microsoft\
Windows

NT\CurrentVersion\Windows ("run=" value)

Listing #2

```
@echo off

    for /f "tokens=1 delims=[]" %%I in ('reg query HKLM\
    SYSTEM\CurrentControlSet\Services') do call:
    PULLINFO1 %%I

    set START_TYPE=

    goto :EOF:

    PULLINFO1

    for /f "tokens=3 delims=" %%I in ('reg query HKLM\
    SYSTEM\CurrentControlSet\Services\%1 ^| findstr
    "Start" ') do call :PULLINFO2 %1 %%I

    goto :EOF

    :PULLINFO2

    for /f "tokens=3,4 delims=" %%I in ('reg query HKLM\
    SYSTEM\CurrentControlSet\Services\%1 ^| findstr
    "ImagePath" ') do call :SHOWINFO %1 %2 %%I %%J
```

```
goto :EOF

:SHOWINFO

if /i {%2}=={0} set START_TYPE=Boot

if /i {%2}=={1} set START_TYPE=System

if /i {%2}=={2} set START_TYPE=Automatic

if /i {%2}=={3} set START_TYPE=Disabled

if not "%4" == "" (echo %1—%START_TYPE%—%3\%4) else
(echo %1—%START_TYPE%—%3)

goto :EOF
```

Listing #3

```
@echo off

    for /f "tokens=1,2 delims=:" %%I in ( 'netstat—an
    ^| findstr "0.0.0.0:[1-9]"' ) do call :CLEAN %%I
    %%J

goto :EOF

:CLEAN

    set X=0

    for /f "tokens=1,2,3 delims=TAB " %%A in
    ( 'findstr /I "\<%3/%1\>" port-numbers.txt' ) do
    call :SETUP %%A %%C %3 %1

    if %X% == 0 echo %3/%1 ***UNKNOWN***

goto :EOF

:SETUP

    echo %3/%4 %1 %2

    set X=1;

goto :EOF
```

Listing #4

```
@echo off

REM  This script is an example to enforce better NTFS
security on the file system.

REM  Copyright 1998 Carnegie Mellon University

REM  August 1998
```

```
REM

REM  v0.91 Sept 04, 1998

REM Note that the %SystemRoot%\yes.txt is just a text
file at c:\winnt\yes.txt that REM simply contains a 'y'
and then a hard return in it. CACLS asks if you are sure
REM all the time. The piping of the yes.txt will answer
yes to that prompt.

REM

REM xcacls is used for a few items. It is part of the NT
Resource Kit, but not REM in the default install of NT.

REM  Set the files on the Root Directories to read only
for users

REM


C:

cd \

cacls.exe . /G administrators:f system:f users:r
<%SystemRoot%\yes.txt

cacls.exe * /C /G administrators:f system:f users:r
<%SystemRoot%\yes.txt

REM  Prevent general users to access the boot files...

REM


C:

cd \

cacls.exe boot.ini  /G administrators:f system:f
<%SystemRoot%\yes.txt

cacls.exe ntbootdd.sys /G administrators:f system:f
<%SystemRoot%\yes.txt

cacls.exe ntdetect.com /G administrators:f system:f
<%SystemRoot%\yes.txt

cacls.exe ntldr  /G administrators:f system:f
<%SystemRoot%\yes.txt

REM     Program Files directories...

REM
```

REM First recurse through and just give read access to everyone to everything

REM in Program Files on C: and all files on the D:.

C:

cd \

cacls.exe "Program Files" /c /t /g administrators:f system:f users:r <%SystemRoot%\yes.txt

REM   The TEMP directories....

REM

REM change permission on temp directory to allow additions from normal users...

REM

REM It would be best to give dir-rwx and file-none for the everyone group, but cacls.exe

REM isn't that specific. You can use the GUI or xcacls from the resource kit.

xcacls.exe c:\Temp /c /t /g "creator owner":cop administrators:f system:f users:exw /y

REM To prevent non-admins from deleting the temp directories . . . (put a locked file in it)

copy %SystemRoot%\yes.txt c:\Temp\secure.dir

cacls.exe c:\Temp\secure.dir /g administrators:f system:f <%SystemRoot%\yes.txt

attrib +h c:\Temp\secure.dir

REM   The System Directory . . . . (C:\winnt)

REM

C:

cd %SystemRoot%

cacls.exe * /c /g administrators:f system:f users:r <%SystemRoot%\yes.txt

xcacls.exe . /g "creator owner":cop administrators: f system:f users:exw /y

```
cacls.exe config  /t /c /g administrators:f system:
f users:r <%SystemRoot%\yes.txt

cacls.exe cursors  /t /c /g administrators:f system:f
users:r <%SystemRoot%\yes.txt

cacls.exe help  /t /c /g administrators:f system:
f users:r <%SystemRoot%\yes.txt

cacls.exe forms  /t /c /g administrators:f system:
f users:r <%SystemRoot%\yes.txt

cacls.exe inf  /t /c /g administrators:f system:
f users:r <%SystemRoot%\yes.txt

cacls.exe java  /t /c /g administrators:f system:
f users:r <%SystemRoot%\yes.txt

cacls.exe media  /t /c /g administrators:f system:
f users:r <%SystemRoot%\yes.txt

cacls.exe ShellNew /t /c /g administrators:f system:f
users:r <%SystemRoot%\yes.txt

cacls.exe system  /t /c /g administrators:f system:
f users:r <%SystemRoot%\yes.txt

cacls.exe system32 /t /c /g administrators:f system:f
users:r <%SystemRoot%\yes.txt

xcacls.exe SendTo  /c /t /g "creator owner":cop
administrators:f system:f users:exw /y

REM The profiles tree need to stay the same...

cacls.exe profiles /g administrators:f system:
f "creator owner":c everyone:r <%SystemRoot%\yes.txt

REM Give access to .inf files, .exe files and .hlp files
under system . . . consider using REM just X (execute)
for the com and exe files.

cacls.exe *.inf /t /g administrators:f system:f users:r
<%SystemRoot%\yes.txt

cacls.exe *.hlp /t /g administrators:f system:f users:r
<%SystemRoot%\yes.txt

cacls.exe *.txt /t /g administrators:f system:f users:r
<%SystemRoot%\yes.txt

cacls.exe *.com /t /g administrators:f system:f users:r
<%SystemRoot%\yes.txt
```

```
cacls.exe *.cpl /t /g administrators:f system:f users:r
<%SystemRoot%\yes.txt

cacls.exe *.exe /t /g administrators:f system:f users:r
<%SystemRoot%\yes.txt

cacls.exe *.dll /t /g administrators:f system:f users:r
<%SystemRoot%\yes.txt

REM     Exceptions to the rules . . . . Nothing is
simple.

REM


C:

cd %SystemRoot%

xcacls.exe system32 /e /g "creator owner":cop users:exw
/y

xcacls.exe help  /e /g "creator owner":cop users:exw /y

xcacls.exe forms  /e /g "creator owner":cop users:exw /y

cacls.exe cookies /t /c /g administrators:f system:f
"creator owner":c <%SystemRoot%\yes.txt

cacls.exe history /t /c /g administrators:f system:f
"creator owner":c <%SystemRoot%\yes.txt

cacls.exe occache /t /c /g administrators:f system:f
"creator owner":c <%SystemRoot%\yes.txt

cacls.exe repair /t /c /g administrators:f system:f
<%SystemRoot%\yes.txt

cacls.exe system32\viewers /t /c /e /g users:r
<%SystemRoot%\yes.txt

REM do printers

REM cacls.exe system32\spool\printers /t /c /e /g
"creator owner":c <%SystemRoot%\yes.txt

REM cacls.exe system32\spool\drivers /t /c /e /g
"creator owner":c <%SystemRoot%\yes.txt

REM allow write in the "Temporary Internet Files"

cacls.exe "Temporary Internet Files" /t /c /e /g
administrators:f system:f "creator owner":c
<%SystemRoot%\yes.txt
```

Check for invalid services. Some backdoor programs will install themselves as a service that is started when the system boots up. Services can then run as any user with the "Logon as Service" user right. Check services that are started automatically and be sure that they are necessary. Also check that the services executable file is not a Trojan horse or backdoor program.

The following batch file will help gather information about NT Services running on a system from the registry. The output will list the service key, startup value, and the executed file. This batch file uses the REG.EXE command, which is part of the NT Resource Kit. Files and the registry are not modified with this batch file.

LISTING 2

Check your system binaries for alterations. Compare the versions on your systems with copies you know that have not been altered, such as those from your initial installation media. Be cautious of trusting backups; they could also contain Trojan horses.

Trojan horse programs may produce the same file size and time stamp as the legitimate version. Because of this, just checking file properties and time stamps associated with the programs is not sufficient for determining whether or not the programs have been replaced. Instead, use MD5, Tripwire, and other cryptographic checksum tools to detect these Trojan horse programs (provided that the checksum tools themselves are kept secure and are not available for modification by the intruder). You may want to consider using a tool (PGP, for example) to "sign" the output generated by MD5 or Tripwire, for future reference.

Using antivirus software will also help you check for computer viruses, backdoors, and Trojan horse programs. But remember that malicious programs are continuously created, so it is important to keep your antivirus software up to date constantly.

6. Check your system and network configurations for unauthorized entries. Look for invalid entries for settings like WINS, DNS, IP forwarding, etc. These settings can be checked using the Network Properties tool or using the "ipconfig /all" command at the command prompt. Make sure that only the Network Services you want to have running on your system are listed in the Network Services configuration. Check for odd ports listening for connections from other hosts by using the "netstat—an" command. The following batch file parses out ports that are in a listen state and then tries to show what service may be running on that port. This batch file uses the well-known port numbers file which can be retrieved from the following location. http://www.isi.edu/in-notes/iana/assignments/port-numbers

Additional ports used by Microsoft products can be found in the following Microsoft Knowledgebase articles. You may want to build a file in the format of the previous port numbers file that lists various services that are running on your NT systems.

Windows NT, Terminal Server, and Microsoft Exchange Services Use TCP/IP Ports

http://support.microsoft.com/support/kb/articles/q150/5/43.asp

SMS: Network Ports Used by Remote Helpdesk Functions

http://support.microsoft.com/support/kb/articles/q167/1/28.asp

XGEN: TCP Ports and Microsoft Exchange: In-depth Discussion

http://support.microsoft.com/support/kb/articles/q176/4/66.asp

How to Configure a Firewall for Windows NT and Trusts

http://support.microsoft.com/support/kb/articles/q179/4/42.asp

In the batch file make sure you replace the word "TAB" with an actual tab. This file does not modify or write to any files. It does require a file named "port-number.txt." This file lists port numbers as well as possible services listening on that port.

LISTING 3

7. Check for unauthorized shares. You can use the "net share" command at the command prompt or use the Server Manager tool to list all the shares on a system. NT provides a way to show hidden shares by adding a '$' to the end of a share name. There are a few default share names that NT uses (such as PRINT$), but if you are not sharing a printer with other users, check to see why that share was created. If you notice an odd share name the tools will show you the actual location on the system that is being shared. A drive or directory can have multiple share names. Each of these shares can have different permissions associated with them.

8. Check for any jobs scheduled to run. Intruders can leave back doors in files that are scheduled to run at a future time. This technique can let an intruder back on the system (even after you believe you had addressed the original compromise). Also, verify that all files/programs referenced (directly or indirectly) by the scheduler and the job files themselves, are not world-writable. To check for jobs currently pending use the "at" command or the WINAT tool from the NT resource kit.

9. Check for odd processes. You can use the Task Manager tool or the pulist.exe and tlist.exe commands from the NT resource kit at the command prompt to gather information about the processes running on your system. Pulist.exe and tlist.exe are included in the NT resource

kit. A number of shareware/freeware applications also exist to show what files are in use.

With the pulist command, you can see who started each process. Services are usually associated with the SYSTEM account. The tlist command with the—t flag will show you what processes started child processes.

10. Look throughout the system for unusual or hidden files. These can be used to hide tools and information (password cracking programs, password files from other systems, etc.). Hidden files can be seen with the NT Explorer. Select View, Options, Show all Files. To view hidden files at the command prompt type "dir /ah."

11. Check for altered permissions on files or registry keys. Part of properly securing an NT system is to set the proper permissions on files and registry keys so that unauthorized users cannot start unauthorized programs (e.g., backdoors or keyloggers) or change system files. In order to check many files throughout your directory tree you can use the XCACLS.EXE program that is part of the NT Resource Kit. The NT Security Configuration Manager can also be used to analyze your system against a configuration you have defined previously. This would help to determine what may have been modified.

12. Check for changes in user or computer policies. Policies are used on NT systems to define a wide variety of configurations and can be used to control what users can and cannot do. Since a number of items are configured in the policy editor (poledit.exe) it is recommended to keep a current copy of the policies you create in case they are altered and you need to determine what was changed.

13. Make sure the system has not been redefined to a different domain. An intruder may attempt to gain Domain Administrator access to a workstation by changing the current domain to a domain that the intruder has control over.

14. When searching for signs of intrusion, examine all machines on the local network. Most of the time, if one host has been compromised, others on the network have also been compromised.

B. Review other AusCERT and CERT documents

1. For further information about the types of attack that have recently been reported to the CERT Coordination Center and for a list of new or updated files available for anonymous FTP, see our past CERT Summaries at http://www.cert.org/summaries/

2. If you suspect that your system has been compromised, please review "Steps for Recovering from a System Compromise" at http://www.cert.org/tech_tips/win-UNIX-system_compromise.html

You can also review other appropriate files in our tech_tips directory.

3. Incidents involving Australian and New Zealand sites should be reported to AusCERT (Australian Computer Emergency Response Team). To report a computer security incident to AusCERT use the following contact information.

Internet: auscert@auscert.org.au monitored during business hours (GMT+10:00)

Telephone: +61 7 3365 4417 monitored during business hours (GMT+10:00)

Hotline: +61 7 3365 4417 monitored 24 hours, 7 days for emergencies (GMT+10:00)

Facsimile: +61 7 3365 7031

Australian Computer Emergency Response Team

The University of Queensland

Brisbane

Qld 4072

AUSTRALIA

4. To report a computer security incident to the CERT Coordination Center, please complete and return a copy of our Incident Reporting Form, available from http://www.cert.org/ftp/incident_reporting_form

The information on the form helps us provide the best assistance. It enables us to understand the scope of the incident, to determine if your incident may be related to any other incidents that have been reported to us, and to identify trends in intruder activities.

C. Consider running intrusion detection systems if possible

1. Freeware/shareware intrusion detection systems:

The COAST Intrusion Detection System Resources web page has a list of some freeware/shareware intrusion detection systems. It is available at:

http://www.cerias.purdue.edu/coast/ids/

2. Commercial intrusion detection systems:

There are a number of commercial intrusion detection tools available, we only list some herein:

Kane Security Monitor (KSM) http://centauri.ods.com/security/products/ksm.shtml

OmniGuard/ITA (OmniGuard/Intruder Alert) http://www.axent.com/Axent/Products/IntruderAlert

Real Secure http://solutions.iss.net/products/rsecure/rs.php

CyberCop Monitor http://solutions.sun.com/catalogs/all/Internet_and_Intranet/Security/42189.html

Intact http://pedestalsoftware.com/intact/

This document is available from: http://www.cert.org/tech_tips/win_intruder_detection_checklist.html

CERT/CC Contact Information

Email: cert@cert.org

Phone: +1 412-268-7090 (24-hour hotline)

Fax: +1 412-268-6989

Postal address:

CERT® Coordination Center

Software Engineering Institute

Carnegie Mellon University

Pittsburgh PA 15213-3890

U.S.A.

CERT personnel answer the hotline 08:00–20:00 EST(GMT-5)/EDT(GMT-4) Monday through Friday; they are on call for emergencies during other hours, on U.S. holidays, and on weekends.

Using encryption

We strongly urge you to encrypt sensitive information sent by e-mail. Our public PGP key is available from http://www.cert.org/CERT_PGP.key

If you prefer to use DES, please call the CERT hotline for more information.

Getting security information

CERT publications and other security information are available from our web site http://www.cert.org/

To be added to our mailing list for advisories and bulletins, send e-mail to cert-advisory-request@cert.org and include SUBSCRIBE your-email-address in the subject of your message.

Copyright 2000 Carnegie Mellon University.

Conditions for use, disclaimers, and sponsorship information can be found in http://www.cert.org/legal_stuff.html

* "CERT" and "CERT Coordination Center" are registered in the U.S. Patent and Trademark Office.

NO WARRANTY

Any material furnished by Carnegie Mellon University and the Software Engineering Institute is furnished on an "as is" basis. Carnegie Mellon University makes no warranties of any kind, either expressed or implied as to any matter including, but not limited to, warranty of fitness for a particular purpose or merchantability, exclusivity or results obtained from use of the material. Carnegie Mellon University does not make any warranty of any kind with respect to freedom from patent, trademark, or copyright infringement.

Glossary

Application—Part of the OSI reference model (see OSI—Open Systems Interconnection). The application layer is also known as layer seven, the highest layer in the OSI model.

Authentication—Verification of a claimed identity.

Biometric—A unique, measurable characteristic or trait of a human being used for automatically recognizing or verifying an identity.

CA (Certificate Authority)—An authority that issues and manages security credentials for a PKI.

CA Private Root Key—A cryptographic key known only to the CA that is used to certify user or server certificate requests.

CERT (Computer Emergency Response Team)—The CERT Coordination Center is an organization that grew from the Computer Emergency Response Team formed by the Defense Advanced Research Projects Agency (DARPA) in November 1988 in response to the problems generated during the Internet worm incident. (See http://www.cert.org/)

Certificate—A digital identifier linking an entity and a trusted third party with the ability to confirm the entity's identification. Typically stored in a browser or a smart card.

Certificate Owner—A person or system bound to the certificate. The owner is the person that has access to view and manipulate the certificate.

Certificate Policy—A set of rules that indicates the applicability of a certificate to a particular environment or application with common security requirements.

Certification Practice Statement (CPS)—This is a statement of the practices that a certificate authority (CA) employs in issuing certificates.

Cipher—Alternative term for an encryption algorithm.

Ciphertext—Text (or data) that has previously been encrypted.

CRL (Certificate Revocation List)—A database of certificates no longer valid within a given PKI infrastructure.

Cryptography—A discipline that embodies principles, means, and methods for the transformation of data in order to hide its information content, prevent its undetected modification, and prevent its unauthorized use.

CSMA/CD (Carrier Sense Multiple Access/Collision Detect)—The protocol for carrier transmission access in Ethernet networks.

DARPA (Defense Advanced Research Projects Agency)—A research branch of the U.S. Department of Defense that was one of the founder's projects that led to the development of the Internet.

Data Link—Part of the OSI reference model, this layer provides error control and synchronization for the physical level.

DDoS—A distributed denial of service attack. This DoS attack exploits several machines to make the attack.

Decryption—The process of transforming ciphertext back into plaintext.

Denial-of-Service Attacks (DoS Attacks)—Acts intended to cause a service to become unavailable or unusable. In an Internet environment, a service might be an application such as a web or mail server, or a network service.

DES (Data Encryption Standard)—A method of data encryption using a private (secret) key. DES uses a 56-bit key to each 64-bit block of data.

Digital Certificate—A digital certificate is an electronic mechanism that binds a set of credentials to a particular person or system. A CA will issue the certificates.

Digital Signature—Data appended to, or a cryptographic transformation of a data unit, that allows a recipient of the data unit to prove the source and integrity of the data unit and protect against forgery.

DMZ (Demilitarized Zone)—A network inserted as a "buffer zone" between a company's private, or trusted, network and the outside, untrusted network.

DNS (Domain Name System)—A method by which Internet domain names are converted into IP addresses.

Encryption—A process of disguising information so that it cannot be read or interpreted by an unauthorized person.

Ethernet—A network that is specified in a standard IEEE 802.3. Xerox, DEC, and Intel originally developed Ethernet.

Ethical Hackers—Legal hackers who will hack into your system after obtaining legal and company permission. These hacking companies are paid to perform this operation and will provide a report on the findings after hacking into your systems.

Firewall—Hardware and/or software that will protect the trusted resources of a private network and help prevent attacks from untrusted networks.

Foot Printing—The process of obtaining data about a particular individual or company. This information can be obtained from various resources, including public resources (also known as profiling).

FTP (File Transfer Protocol)—Uses TCP/IP ports 21 and 22.

Hacker—A person that wants to get into your computer systems without authority.

HTTP (Hypertext Transfer Protocol)—The protocol used via the World Wide Web.

HTTPS (Secure Hypertext Transfer Protocol)—A protocol developed by Netscape that will encrypt the data at the "network" layer (see SSL).

IETF—Internet Engineering Task Force.

IMAP (Internet Message Access Protocol)—A standard for accessing electronic mail from a server. Typically used on port 143 or, "IMAP for SSL IS ON 993."

IP (Internet Protocol)—A method data sent from one computer to another on any network (public or private).

IPSec (Internet Protocol Security)—An in-development standard for security at the network layer of network communication. This protocol can be used with VPN (Virtual Private Network).

ISO—International Organization of Standards.

ISP (Internet Service Provider)—A company that provides individuals and/or companies with access to the Internet and other related services.

Key—A series of numbers that is used by an encryption algorithm to transform plaintext data into encrypted data.

Key Generation—The process for creating keys in a browser (see <keygen> tag at http://users.knoware.nl/users/schluter/doc/tags/TAG_KEYGEN.html).

Key Management—Systemic processes associated with the secure generation, transport, storage, and destruction of encryption keys.

Key Recovery—A PKI key management process associated with the retrieval of a key lost by the key holder.

Key Ring File—A file that can house the certificate.

Key Serial Number—A 128-bit number associated with a certificate.

L2F (Layer Two Forwarding)—Protocol used in VPNs.

L2TP (Layer Two Tunneling Protocol)—Protocol used in VPNs.

LDAP (Lightweight Directory Access Protocol)—The Internet standard for simple directories used for messaging and similar applications.

LDIF (LDAP Data Interchange Format)—A file format used to import or export data from a Lightweight Directory Access Protocol directory. These files are ASCII text files. In many cases, the files can be exported from one source and imported into another type of software. For example: Export data from an LDAP directory and import it into a private data source to register users.

LRA (Local Registration Authority)—Evaluates and approves or rejects certificate applications on behalf of a CA.

MD2 (Message Digest Two)—An algorithm that takes as input a message of arbitrary length and produces as output a 128-bit "fingerprint" or "message digest" of the input.

MD5 (Message Digest Five)—An algorithm that takes as input a message of arbitrary length and produces as output a 128-bit "fingerprint" or "message digest" of the input.

MIME (Multipurpose Internet Mail Extensions)—A method to exchange different kinds of data files on a network: video, audio, images, and others. MIME is transported via the SMTP protocol.

NNTP (Network News Transfer Protocol)—A protocol used by computers for managing the notes posted on UseNet newsgroups.

Nonrepudiation—Cryptographic assurance that a message sender cannot later deny sending a message, or that the recipient cannot deny receipt.

Nontrusted Network—A network that is defined by a company as not being trusted; in many cases, this can even be the Internet.

OSI (Open Systems Interconnection)—Also known as the OSI reference model. This describes a standard for how messages should be transmitted between any two points in a network. The reference model defines seven layers that take place at each end of a communication (see Application).

PGP (Pretty Good Privacy)—See www.pgp.com for information and product descriptions.

Physical—The first layer of the OSI reference model. This layer connects the bit stream through the network at the electrical and mechanical level.

Physical Access—Can define access to a particular computer or site. Physical access should be controlled in a secure environment.

PIN—Personal Identification Number.

Ping—A program that lets you verify that a particular IP address exists and can accept requests. Ping is typically used as a diagnostic.

Ping of Death—A technique that hackers use to overwhelm a computer with ping requests.

PKCS (Public-Key Cryptography System)—A set of standard protocols developed by RSA for secure information exchange.

PKI—Public Key Infrastructure.

PKIX—A set of standards for PKI from the IETF.

POP (Point-of-Presence)—A location where a network can be accessed.

POP3 (Post Office Protocol Three)—A standard protocol for receiving e-mail. POP3 typically uses TCP/IP port 110.

Port—A mechanism for TCP to communicate with an application.

PPP (Point-to-Point Protocol)—A protocol for communication between two computers.

PPTP (Point-to-Point Tunneling Protocol)—A protocol that allows corporations to extend their own corporate network through encrypted "tunnels" over a nontrusted network (a good example would be via the Internet).

Presentation—Another layer of the OSI reference model. This layer can be part of an operating system that converts incoming and outgoing data from one presentation format to another.

Private Key—A cryptographic key known only to the user, and implemented in public key cryptography in decrypting or signing information.

Protocol—The special set of rules for communications that computers use when sending signals between themselves.

Public Key—A cryptographic key implemented in public key cryptography to encrypt data to the key's owner, or to verify the key owner's signature. The public key can be published, for example, in LDAP, without revealing the owner's corresponding private key.

Public-Private Key Pair—A form of asymmetric encryption in which all parties possess a pair of keys, one private and one public, for use in encryption and/or digital signing of data.

RC2—A block cipher encryption method. Data is encrypted blocks at a time instead of each character (stream cipher/RC4). Block ciphers are slower than stream ciphers, as data is encrypted only when a block is full.

RC4—A stream cipher encryption method. Each plaintext symbol/character is dynamically translated to ciphertext.

Registration Authority—That mechanism or person who, as part of a PKI, is involved in verifying and enrolling users.

RFC (Request for Comments)—An Internet document or standard that is the result of committee drafting and subsequent review by interested parties.

RSA—The encryption algorithm invented by Rivest, Shamir, and Adleman in 1976.

S/MIME (Secure Multipurpose Mail Extensions)—A standard for secure e-mail.

Service Provider—See ISP.

Session—Another layer of the OSI reference model. This layer sets up, coordinates, and terminates conversations, exchanges, and dialogues between the applications at each end.

SLA—Service Level Agreement.

Smart Card—Typically, a small plastic card with a microprocessor that can store information (for example, X.509v3 certificate).

SMTP (Simple Mail Transfer Protocol)—A TCP protocol used in sending and receiving e-mail, normally over TCP port 25.

SSL (Secure Sockets Layer)—Created by Netscape for managing the security of message transmissions in a network (see HTTPS).

TCP—Transmission Control Protocol.

TCP/IP—Transmission Control Protocol and Internet Protocol.

Transport—This OSI layer ensures complete data transfer and manages the end-to-end control and error checking.

Trinoo—A tool used by hackers as a DDoS.

Trip Wires—A mechanism or tool that detects hack attacks and alerts someone, such as an administrator, about the attack.

Trusted Network—A network that has been defined by a company as "trusted."

URL—Uniform Resource Locator.

Vinton Cerf—The father of the Internet.

Virus—A piece of programming code that causes some unexpected and usually undesirable event on a computer.

VPN—Virtual Private Network.

WAP—Wireless Access Protocol.

Worms—Viruses that attack several computers.

WWW—World Wide Web.

X.500—A directory standard (see http://www.itu.int/).

X.509—A certificate standard (see http://www.itu.int/ and http://www.ietf.org).

References

Encryption

Company Name:	CyPost Corporation
Address:	900–1281 West Georgia Vancouver, BC V6E 3J7
Phone Number:	(604) 904-4422
E-mail Address:	info@cypost.com
URLs:	http://www.cypost.com
Category:	Encryption
Product Name:	Navaho Lock with Voice
Product Description:	Encrypted Voice e-mail.

Navaho Lock with Voice allows users to record, compress, and encrypt private voice e-mail for transmission across any digital network, without sacrificing the tone, feeling, or integrity of the message. Navaho Lock with Voice also reduces the time spent typing traditional text-based e-mail messages.

Electronic shredder

Navaho Shredder offers a high level of disk sanitization, allowing users to securely delete files and documents from any computer. Navaho Shredder has been designed to meet and exceed the U.S. Department of Defense standard (DoD 5220.22-M) for data removal. The program is currently capable of overwriting data stored on disk a total of nine times, exceeding the DoD standard for data removal.

Built-in compression

Navaho Lock with Voice automatically compresses all documents and files by as much as 70%—maximizing disk space and dramatically reducing transmission times.

Choice of encryption strength

Navaho Lock with Voice offers the widest selection of encryption standards, including 40-, 56-, 112-, 128-, and 168-bit key-lengths and algorithms to meet the individual security needs of your business. Users are able to customize security settings and select unique pass phrases by contact or group.

New drag-and-drop user interface

Further improving ease of use and increasing user productivity, the new drag-and-drop user interface allows users to encrypt, compress, or shred files by simply dragging and dropping them into the Drop area.

Company Name:	DSEnet
Address:	5201 South Westshore Blvd. Tampa, FL 33611
Phone Number:	(813) 902-9597
E-mail Address:	questions@dsenet.com
URLs:	www.dsenet.com
Category:	Encryption
Product Name:	DSEnet Encryption

Product Description: DSEnet Encryption provides users with the ability to securely encrypt and store their information. There is no better way to keep intruding hackers, nosy coworkers, pesky younger siblings, and cunning competitors from your critical information.

Encrypt documents, spreadsheets, presentations, e-mail attachments, graphs, charts, images, music, and most files residing on your computer with DSEnet Encryption.

DSEnet Encryption is an easy to install, quick to learn, and simple to use software utility that secures data stored on a computer's hard drive.

Keys

- encryption prevents unwanted access
- easy to learn and operate, little training required
- easy to use explorer style interface
- encrypts individual files, groups of files, and folders
- DSEnet Encryption occupies only 4 MB of disk space.
- user key and password combination protects data
- strong 256-bit encryption algorithm

Operating Requirements: Microsoft Windows 95, 98, Me, NT 4.0, 2000 Professional/Advanced Server -32MB RAM

Filters

Company Name:	Charles River Media
Address:	10 Downer Avenue Hingham, MA 02043
Phone Number:	(781) 871-4184
E-mail Address:	info@charlesriver.com
URLs:	www.charlesriver.com
Category:	Filters
Product Name:	Internet Watchdog
Product Description:	Allows the user to record and monitor computer activity.

Company Name:	surfControl, a division of JSB
Address:	100 Enterprise Way, Mod A-1 Scotts Valley, CA 95066
Phone Number:	(831) 431-1400
E-mail Address:	surfsales@surfCONTROL.com
URLs:	www.surfcontrol.com
Category:	Filters

Product Name:	surfCONTROL Family of Products
Product Description:	Control the use of your Internet.
Company Name:	Blue Ocean Software, Inc.
Address:	15310 Amberly Drive, Suite 370 Tampa, FL 33647
Phone Number:	(813) 977-4553
E-mail Address:	info@blueocean.com
URLs:	www.blueocean.com
Category:	Filters
Product Name:	Track-It
Product Description:	Record-keeping system.
Company Name:	SonicWall, Inc.
Address:	1160 Bordeaux Dr. Sunnyvale, CA 94089-1209
Phone Number:	(408) 745-9600
E-mail Address:	sales@sonicwall.com
URLs:	www.sonicwall.com
Category:	Filters
Product Name:	SonicWALL DMZ
Product Description:	Provides protection from hackers and content filters. For larger companies.
Company Name:	Whale Communications
Address:	400 Kelby Street, 15th Floor, Fort Lee, NJ 07024
Phone Number:	(201) 947-9177 or (877) 65-WHALE
E-mail Address:	info@whale-com.com
URLs:	www.whalecommunications.com
Category:	Filters

Whale Communications is the established leader in SSL VPN and web-application security solutions. It offers several products intended to:

Securely grant employees remote access to internal resources such as applications and files, and enable partners, customers, and prospects to interact with important business systems.

At the core of the five e-Gap products is Whale's innovative Air Gap technology, which provides the utmost security by isolating application servers and tightly controlling application layer access to them. The e-Gap suite utilizes an application-centric approach to unite all of the components that protect the application into a single appliance. Encryption, authorization, authentication HTTP payload screening, automatic rule-set generation and a physical air gap all reside within an integrated platform.

Whale's products include:

The e-Gap® Remote Access Appliance enables organizations to rapidly provide employees with browser-based access to corporate Intranet applications and files without jeopardizing security. Also known as a clientless VPN or SSL VPN, e-Gap Remote Access frees the employee from being bound to a particular location, laptop, or device for the purpose of accessing their Intranet resources, while conforming to the strictest policies of network security. e-Gap Remote Access can deliver applications like e-mail, CRM, and Human Resources, as well as network file shares, to locations such as a client site, home offices, airport kiosks, even wireless devices—anywhere employees can use a simple browser.

The e-Gap Webmail Appliance for Microsoft Exchange provides a secure front end to Microsoft Exchange (5.5 and 2000) enabling Outlook® Web Access from any browser anywhere in the world. It is a cost-effective, rapidly deployable alternative to VPNs. e-Gap Webmail protects against IIS vulnerabilities like Code Red and even unknown future exploits. There's no need to open dangerous holes in your firewall. The e-Gap Webmail Appliance also overlays strong authentication like RSA SecurID® Authentication and provides additional security features such as a patent-pending "secure log-off." Installation is quick and nonintrusive, requiring no intervention with production Exchange servers or firewalls.

The e-Gap Webmail Appliance for Lotus Domino enables secure web access to corporate Lotus Domino servers from any Internet browser, without the need for a VPN. It acts as a secure front end to the back end Domino servers, in a scalable, one-to-many network architecture. It thus eliminates the cost—i.e. security price, administrative overhead, and dollar expense—of replicating the Domino servers to the DMZ. Dangerous holes do not need to be opened in the firewall due to the network isolation and application-level security the appliance provides. It overlays strong authentication like RSA SecureID® and provides security features such as strict application level filtering.

The e-Gap Application Firewall Appliance enables organizations to rapidly deploy secure web-based access to sensitive core applications. The System may be used to protect e-business applications for customers or partners (such as eCRM, supply chain integration or e-billing). It protects against known and unknown threats by isolating application servers—via Air Gap technology—and tightly controlling application layer access to them. It also significantly reduces the urgency to patch production web servers. It unites all of the application-protection components into a single application-centric appliance, and features automatic learning of the application to generate and enforce application-level rule sets. Encryption, authorization, authentication, PKI, HTTP payload screening, automatic rule-set generation and a physical air gap all reside within an integrated software/hardware platform.

The e-Gap Network Separator Appliance enables organizations to securely transfer data in real-time between disconnected networks. Organizations may utilize this to transfer files between DMZs and the back office, upload files to web servers situated in DMZs, or provide e-mail/file connectivity between networks of different security classifications—all without opening up communication ports between the networks. It can also be used to secure other standard and proprietary client/server applications. It includes stringent application-level inspection capabilities for file and mail applications and an API for custom filtering.

General protection

Company Name:	CyPost Corporation
Address:	900–1281 West Georgia Vancouver, BC V6E 3J7
Phone Number:	(604) 904-4422
E-mail Address:	info@cypost.com
URLs:	http://www.cypost.com
Category:	General Protection
Product Name:	Navaho ZipSafe

Product Description: Navaho ZipSafe is the easiest and fastest way to ensure no one reads confidential data on hard disks, network drives, or floppies.

Navaho ZipSafe compresses (by up to 70%) and protects data in one step, enabling you to instantly organize documents files and folders for secure storage or transport.

- Built-in Compression: Reduces file size on hard drives and floppy disks by as much as 70%.

- Drag-and-Drop Feature: Application works behind the scenes allowing users to encrypt and compress files by simply dragging and dropping them into the Drop area.

- Shredder: This feature makes files unrecoverable to programs that rebuild files after deletion.

- Choice of Encryption: Navaho ZipSafe supports a variety of algorithms including 40-, 56-, 112-, 128-, and 168-bit.

Works with all file formats: Navaho ZipSafe quickly and easily encrypts and compresses digital images, spreadsheets, Word documents, files, folders, and even entire directories.

Company Name:	Delta Design UK.com
Address:	10 Wratting Road Haverhill, Suffolk, CB9 0DD, United Kingdom
Phone Number:	n/a
E-mail Address:	marketing@deltadesignuk.com/ for publication: mail@deltadesignuk.com
URLs:	http://www.deltadesignuk.com/
Category:	General Protection
Product Name:	Net-Commando 2000

Product Description: Hacker Protection/Prevention/Detection, Trojan Horse virus Protection/Prevention/Detection/Removal, System Analysis, and Internet Tracing. This package uses various methods of detection, prevention, and monitoring to deny remote access to your computer. It does this by monitoring areas of your computer where Internet viruses aim their auto-start procedures. It warns of hackers attempting to access your computer, and provides an address for you to back track them, as well as tools to assist you in reporting the hacker to the ISP. The program also includes many system analysis tools, including NetStat (protocol statistics), which lists all open ports and allows one to terminate an established TCP port.

Company Name:	Finjan Software
Address:	2860 Zanker Road, Suite 201 San Jose, CA 95134
Phone Number:	(408) 324-0228
E-mail Address:	info@finjan.com
URLs:	www.finjan.com
Category:	General Protection
Product Name:	SurfinShield Corporate

Product Description: SurfinShield Corporate is a centrally managed PC security solution that proactively monitors the actual behavior of downloaded active content, including executables, scripts, ActiveX, and Java. By monitoring code behavior in its protected "SafeZone," SurfinShield enforces its security policy and automatically blocks malicious activity before damage can be inflicted. Unlike traditional antivirus technology, SurfinShield represents a new way to combat Trojans, Internet worms, and hostile web pages based on code behavior, not by static signature recognition. Because SurfinShield does not rely on database updates, it defends against new variants, unknown and "yet-to-be-created" attacks on the "first strike."

Features and benefits

- Behavior Monitoring of active content in real-time in SurfinShield's sandbox including executables, ActiveX controls, Java applets, Scrap files (.shs), and all Windows scripting host files (e.g., .VBS, .JS, .WSH). Companies can have protection from all "ILOVEYOU" type worm attacks as they surface without having to wait for antivirus updates.

- Palm-to-PC Sync Protection: Palm Pilots can be used to deliver malicious programs or Trojans to PCs using the synchronization process. SurfinShield monitors all Palm OS-based PDA sync processes for executable programs and protects PCs from sync attacks.

- Multimedia Surveillance Protection: SurfinShield now protects against Audio/Video recording from Trojans by preventing a PC's microphone or camera from automatically being turned on, and by monitoring network connections.

- White Listing of applications from trusted partners enables secure e-business. Companies can allow trusted applications to enter the network with full permissions while unknown code is still subject to monitoring.

- Application Auto-Launch Blocking: prevents Microsoft Office Suite applications from being automatically launched by web browsers, Microsoft Outlook, and Qualcomm's Eudora e-mail client.

- SurfinConsole™: centralized management console enabling security managers to easily implement and enforce group and individual security policies for all computer users throughout an organization.

- Smart Kill: SurfinShield can identify and surgically kill specific malicious code. Applications and web browsers are left undisturbed and user productivity is not hindered.

- Mobile PC Protection: SurfinShield Corporate's monitoring "engine" resides on the PC and will continue to operate when taken on the road. This results in ongoing protection for PC users who are connecting to the Internet from outside the corporate network.

SurfinShield Corporate consists of a console, server, and client module.

The central console is designed for ease of use, allowing administrators to set both granular and corporatewide security policies.

The central server holds security policies and logs the security events of each desktop. Should one client face an attack, it will update all other SurfinShield Corporate clients, automatically blocking the hostile element upon contact.

The client module of SurfinShield Corporate houses the behavior monitoring "engine." The client is not dependent on the server for protection and will continue to defend against attacks when removed from the corporate network.

First-strike security

A "first strike" is the first time a new malicious code attack is launched. First-strike security uses content inspection and behavior-monitoring technology to detect and prevent malicious attacks before damage is caused. Because Finjan products do not rely on database updates, they defend against new variants, unknown and even "yet-to-be-created" attacks on the "first strike."

System requirements

SurfinShield client

- Pentium 133 processor and above
- Windows 9x/ME/NT 4.0/2000
- 16 MB RAM (32 MB RAM recommended)
- 15 MB of free disk space

SurfinShield server

- Pentium 266 processor and above
- Windows NT 4.0/2000/Solaris 2.6
- 64 MB RAM (128 MB recommended)
- 24 MB of free disk space

SurfinConsole

- Pentium 200 processor and above
- Windows 9x /NT 4.0/2000
- 64 MB RAM (128 MB recommended)
- 15 MB of free disk space

Company Name:	Intego, Inc.
Address:	6301 Collins Ave., Suite #1806 Miami, FL 33141
Phone Number:	(305) 868-7920
Contact Name:	Olivier Depoorter
E-mail Address:	odepoorter@intego.com
URLs:	www.intego.com
Category:	General Protection
Product Name:	ContentBarrier
Product Description:	Blocks all offensive material from the Internet.

San Francisco, CA, January 9, 2001—Intego, a leading provider of Macintosh Internet security utilities, today announced ContentBarrier, thorough and efficient Internet filtering software for Macintosh. Content-Barrier 1.0 helps parents protect their children by monitoring Internet usage to avoid contact with dangerous web sites, chat rooms, e-mail, news-groups, and downloads.

ContentBarrier allows parents to select or customize specific categories of potential danger; log Internet usage; control access days and times; and receive e-mail alerts when certain activity occurs. ContentBarrier works with multiple users, so if there are several children in a household, different criteria can be set according to their age.

ContentBarrier has a high-performance content filter engine for sophis-ticated filtering. Its predefined categories let you choose what you don't want your children to see. Inappropriate web sites are blocked, shielding your children from things they are too young for.

ContentBarrier also supports the new version of Intego's NetUpdate, the automatic software update engine. Users can program updates for specific days and times, and NetUpdate will check the Intego server to find out if updates are available for all of Intego's Barrier products installed on your computer.

Intego's programs have received many awards in the U.S., Europe, and Asia, such as awards from *Macworld, MacRame, MacNN, MacAddict*. In France, *UniversMacWorld* recently gave NetBarrier its 2000 trophy for the best Internet program.

"When children surf the Internet, they can see whatever they want, unless a parent is there to watch over their shoulders," said Laurent Mar-teau, CEO, Intego. "ContentBarrier sets up a protective wall around your computer making the Internet a safer place for children."

ContentBarrier features

- Blocks and filters all offensive material from the Internet

- Multiple users—if you have several children, you can adjust the settings for their age and maturity

- Multiple levels of protection

- Predetermined categories for safe and easy content filtering (sexually explicit sites, violence, hate/racism, on-line chat, etc.)

- Limits Internet access by day and time

- Allows you to inspect your child's computer and make a full inventory of all pictures, movies, music files, or web pages

- Antipredator function to block predatory language in chat sessions

- Trusted site selection—you can set the program to block all sites except those you select

- Keeps a detailed log of each user's Internet sessions, and records traffic data for an overview of Internet use

- Automatic updates with Intego's NetUpdate function

- Password protection to prevent unauthorized users from changing program settings

- Automatic e-mail notification of certain events

ContentBarrier is also used by companies to restrict inappropriate employee web site usage. Many employees do their shopping on the Internet, play network games, send and receive personal e-mail, or download MP3 files while at work, reducing productivity and using valuable network bandwidth. ContentBarrier can solve this problem by blocking access to many different types of sites, and contains specific categories of web sites designed for business use.

If your employees spend their working time surfing sexually explicit sites, this not only reduces productivity, but it may even expose you to liability for sexual harassment. Sending private e-mail over your mail server can also expose you to liability, and even prosecution, since your business is responsible for what circulates on its network.

ContentBarrier business features

- Helps increase productivity, optimizes bandwidth

- Protects your company from liability

System requirements are a MacOS compatible computer with a Power PC processor, OpenTransport, Mac OS 8.1 or higher, and 32 MB RAM. It is also compatible with Mac OS 9.1. Also available in French and Japanese versions.

ContentBarrier is available immediately from retailers including buy.com, CompUSA, MacZone, Outpost.com, Computertown, Club Mac, MacWarehouse, MacMall, ComputerWare, Computer Store Northwest, J&R, Microcenter, CDW, Developer Depot, and from 200 Apple Specialists (see list on the Intego web site) and on-line at http://www.intego.com.

For more information, contact Intego, 6301 Collins Ave., Ste. 1806, Miami, FL 33141 tel: (305) 868-7920 fax: (305) 868-7938 web site: http://www.intego.com, info@intego.com.

Company Name:	Intego, Inc.
Address:	6301 Collins Ave., Suite #1806 Miami, FL 33141
Phone Number:	(305) 868-7920
Contact Name:	Olivier Depoorter
E-mail Address:	odepoorter@intego.com
URLs:	www.intego.com
Category:	General Protection
Product Name:	Internet Security Barrier
Product Description:	The Internet Security Suite for the Mac

San Francisco, CA, January 9, 2001—Intego, a leading provider of Macintosh Internet security utilities, today announced Internet Security Barrier, a total Internet security suite for the Macintosh. Internet Security Barrier includes NetBarrier and its three powerful modules: Firewall, Anti-vandal, and Internet Filter; VirusBarrier, the acclaimed antivirus program for Macintosh; and ContentBarrier, the thorough and efficient Internet filtering program for a full security suite to protect Macs from all Internet dangers. This suite is the perfect solution to Internet security problems.

Intego's programs have received many awards in the U.S., Europe, and Asia, such as awards from *Macworld, MacHome, MacNN, MacAddict*. In France, *UniversMacWorld* recently gave NetBarrier its 2000 trophy for the best Internet program.

Internet Security Barrier 1.0 also supports the new version of Intego's NetUpdate, the automatic software update engine. Users can program updates for specific days and times, and NetUpdate will check the Intego server to find out if updates are available for all of Intego's Barrier products installed on your computer.

"Security issues are the biggest computer problem in recent years," said Laurent Marteau, CEO, Intego. "Hackers, viruses and inappropriate content are a plague. Our goal was to develop a full suite of security software for the Macintosh, so Mac users can be protected from every security risk. We're proud to be able to offer such a comprehensive package."

Internet Security Barrier Features include:

- NetBarrier's fully customizable Firewall

    —Antivandal to protect your computer from hacker attacks

    —Internet Filter

    —Spam Filtering

    —Ad banner blocking

- VirusBarrier's protection against all known viruses

    —Protection against Word and Excel macro viruses

    —Scans compressed files—checks all types of archives recognized by Stuffit Expander (Zip, CompactPro, DiskDoubler, tar, BZip, arc, etc.)

    — Turbo Mode makes scanning from 5 to 40 times faster

    — Contextual Menu module for quick virus scanning

- ContentBarrier's predetermined categories for safe and easy content filtering (sexually explicit sites, violence, hate/racism, on-line chat, etc.)

    —Blocks and filters all offensive material from the Internet

    —Multiple users—if you have several children, you can adjust the settings for their age and maturity

    —Multiple levels of protection

System requirements are a MacOS compatible computer with a Power PC processor, OpenTransport, Mac OS 8.1 or higher, and 32 MB RAM. It is also compatible with Mac OS 9.1. A Mac OS X version will be available Q1 2001. Also available in French and Japanese versions.

Internet Security Barrier is available immediately from retailers including buy.com, CompUSA, MacZone, Outpost.com, Computertown, Club Mac, MacWarehouse, MacMall, ComputerWare, Computer Store Northwest, J&R, Microcenter, CDW, Developer Depot, and from 200 Apple Specialists (see list on the Intego web site) and on-line at htm://www.intego.com.

For more information, contact Intego, 6301 Collins Ave., Ste. 1806, Miami, FL 33141 tel: (305) 868-7920 fax: (305) 868-7938 web site: htm://www.intego.com, info@intego.com.

About Intego

Intego, the i-security software company, publishes security software for the Macintosh, and its products are currently sold in 65 countries. With three essential products, Intego focuses on all aspects of the computer security market: antivirus protection, intrusion prevention, and content control.

In less than two years, NetBarrier has become the world leader in personal firewalls for the Macintosh. VirusBarrier, Intego's acclaimed antivirus solution, has been a resounding success since its launch in July 2000. ContentBarrier, Intego's new parental control program, has been available to reinforce its product line since January 2001.

Intego was founded in May 1999 by a collection of highly motivated engineers and high-profile marketing, finance, and sales managers to leverage their extensive knowledge of network security and the Mac environment to corporate, individual, and educational users worldwide. The privately held company has its headquarters in Miami, Florida and in Paris, France.

Company Name:	MFX Research
Address:	19 – 23 Bridge Street Pymble NSW 2073 Australia
Phone Number:	+61 2 9440 0200
E-mail Address:	info@mfxr.com
URLs:	www.mfxr.com
Category:	General Protection
Product Name:	MFX Verify

Product Description: MFX Verify is a toolset designed to monitor and protect the condition of your applications and operating systems files from *any* form of corruption, decay, or degradation.

MFX Verify continuously checks critical system and application files, and as soon as any corruption is detected, irrespective of the cause, the files are immediately restored to their original state.

Examples of some of the day-to-day problems MFX Verify solves :

- Your PC "hangs."

- Your system has not closed properly.

- Your .exe or .d II files have become corrupted.

- You inadvertently delete a monitored file.

- A virus attaches to an .exe file.

In all of the preceding examples, MFX Verify immediately detects what has happened, and undoes any damage done to the file.

MFX Verify is unique, and being complementary to other utility software, finally "plugs the holes" in the control of systems and applications.

Unlike other so-called restoration systems, MFX Verify operates by making a byte-by-byte comparison, not simply a checksum, file size, or date stamp comparison. It offers users the ability to define which files they wish to protect.

The major cause of errors in PCs is the corruption of application and system executable and library files. By keeping these files in their original condition, "up time" is dramatically improved.

Rather than permitting a problem to occur, and then trying to fix it, MFX Verify prevents the problem from happening in the first place.

MFX Verify also permits the frequency of scan to be run continuously or set at intervals.

MFX Verify operates in a fully automated or user selected format, on compiled file types eg .exe, .com, .dll, and .sys.

MFX Verify is very fast—the throughput is up to 20Mb per second.

With full log and reporting facilities, MFX Verify maintains the integrity of the files from the time of installation.

MFX Verify SDK provides the same protection on Windows NT and 2000 systems.

Company Name:	MFX Research
Address:	19–23 Bridge Street : Pymble NSW 2073 Australia
Phone Number:	+61 2 9440 0200
E-mail Address:	info@mfxr.com
URLs:	www.mfxr.com

| Category: | General Protection |
| Product Name: | MFX ValidSite |

Product Description: "How do I ensure that my web site is fully protected? My site is hosted on an Internet Service Provider! This was the challenge posed to us by a recent client.

The solution is . . . ValidSite. ValidSite from MFX Research ensures that *only* the information *you* want to display is published on your web site.

ValidSite's unique "file trap procedure" provides for:

- Total and automatic revalidation of a web site's contents.

- Regular updates to the site's contents, ensuring that only the correct information is being seen by visitors to the site.

- Approved updates of information on the site.

- Elimination of any site rebuild costs should an attack take place.

Should a hacker enter the site, ValidSite will automatically remove all traces of the attack. ValidSite dramatically reduces web site maintenance and update costs.

Other benefits

- ValidSite is simple to use; does not require any extra hardware; requires little or no systems knowledge; and can be installed in seconds.

- ValidSite ensures that only the "authorized version" of your site can be viewed by your customers, staff, investors, or any visitor to the site.

As more companies are relying upon their web sites to act as both a shop front for their products and services, and as a window to their company, the need to protect the contents of their web site is critical. The protection of this investment is paramount to companies and organizations.

Company Name:	MFX Research
Address:	19–23 Bridge Street Pymble NSW 2073 Australia
Phone Number:	+61 2 9440 0200

E-mail Address:	info@mfxr.com
URLs:	www.mfxr.com
Category:	General Protection
Product Name:	MFX WebSiteLock
Product Description:	Protect your web site from attack and alteration.

WebSiteLock is the world's first software toolset to "lock" and protect the contents of an organization's web site.

- Automatically monitors and secures your web site.

- Can constantly monitor all files on a web site.

- Monitors each byte, and at the first change, reverts to the original and correct byte.

- Permits an immediate and automatic rebuild of any "tampered" files with the original files.

- Immediate reporting of any attack to the System Administrator.

- Not just an intrusion detection system—WebSiteLock actually maintains the integrity of your web site.

- Prevents the web site files from being corrupted, which is essential for the protection of full e-commerce sites.

- Can protect both dynamic and static files.

- Allows authorized users to make changes to the web site, but blocks anyone else.

- Protects your critical firewall files.

- Prevents corruption of vital web site files.

As more companies are relying upon their web sites to act as both a shop front for their products and services, and as a window to their company, the need to protect the contents of their web site has become of critical importance. The protection of this investment is paramount to companies and organizations.

Significant amounts of interest, time, and money are spent on firewalls and other software and hardware solutions to prevent intrusion. In spite of this, we all know that even the most secretive and security-conscious organizations have been "hacked"—from our own prime minister's site to the CIA site in Washington.

Commercial sites such as Nike and MGM have been entered and details altered, deleted, or added. The British PM's site and the GST site have been altered.

Many smaller companies and organizations have been targeted and the costs suffered by the disruption have been experienced by all sectors of business, the utilities, and the government. Hackers often attack a site out of curiosity, mischief, and for "fun," to prove how clever they are—not necessarily to prove how negligent you are.

Regardless of the motive, the impact is the same: You pay for the consequences! Because your firewall alone is never enough....

Further, the damage being caused by someone from within, or someone with inside knowledge who has recently left the company, can be of greater impact. This person can be far more "focused" and specific in the damage he or she causes.

WebSiteLock is aimed at organizations that have their own server(s) to manage their site.

Truly, your web sites' last line of defense...

To meet the needs of companies who use Internet Service Providers (ISPs) to host their web sites, MFX Research has developed ValidSite. Full details of the features and functions of ValidSite can be obtained from the MFXR web site.

A version, aimed at meeting the specific requirements of ISPs and Application Service Providers (ASPs) themselves, is also available.

Company Name:	Neoteris, Inc.
Address:	161 East Evelyn Avenue Mountain View, CA 94041
Phone Number:	(605) 605-4800
E-mail Address:	info@neoteris.com
URLS:	www.neoteris.com
Category:	General Internet Protection

Neoteris, Inc. is the industry leader in the Instant Virtual Extranet (IVE) category of Internet security appliances. Neoteris' IVE provides secure access to private network resources over the Internet using a standard web browser. The IVE requires neither client software/hardware nor LAN configuration changes, thus dramatically reducing secure access implementation and maintenance costs over conventional methods such as dial-up networks, VPNs, or custom extranet deployments. Additionally, Neoteris increases security by limiting users to authorized application resources versus conventional methods that provide broad network layer access.

Customers typically deploy Neoteris' IVE as an employee remote access solution or as a secure partner extranet solution. Private dial network connections are for today's applications and prohibitively expensive for large deployments. Virtual private networks (VPNs) using the Internet require client software or special hardware that are plagued with network incompatibilities and support costs. Also, VPNs provide broad network layer access, which may introduce security risks. Neoteris' IVE limits users to authorized application resources, thus increasing security.

Custom extranet deployments are expensive to implement and maintain and limit the network resources available to users. Furthermore, unlike custom extranet deployments that may be exposed to security vulnerabilities through set-up or maintenance errors, Neoteris' IVE is a secure, hardened, dedicated appliance.

Neoteris' IVE appliances provide clientless, secure access to enterprise resources such as web-based applications, client-server applications, proprietary messaging servers (Lotus Notes, MS Exchange), file servers (MS CIFS and NFS), Telnet and SSH hosts, and standards-based e-mail servers (IMAP, POP, SMTP)

Company Name:	Palisade Systems Inc.
Address:	2625 North Loop Drive, Suite 2120 Ames, IA 50010
Phone Number:	(515) 296-6500 or (888) 824-0720
E-mail Address:	info@palisadesys.com
URLs:	http://www.palisadesys.com
Category:	General Protection
Product Name:	PacketPup

Product Description: PacketPup is free-to-download software (available from www.packetpup.com) that quickly and easily shows you whether you should be concerned about bandwidth allocation on your network. PacketPup tracks the use of file-sharing and streaming applications like Napster, Gnutella, iMesh, RealAudio/RealVideo, Scour Exchange,

Shoutcast, and Windows Media, displaying its data in graphical form. It then provides a Return on Investment (ROI) interface that helps you determine both usage and how much that usage costs your organization. If PacketPup shows you that you have a bandwidth problem, PacketHound—a hardware-based blocking appliance—is a great solution.

PacketPup protects PC networks by alerting administrators to possible bandwidth and security issues associated with the use of file-sharing and streaming applications. Used unchecked, these applications (including Napster, Gnutella, RealAudio/RealVideo) can make PCs vulnerable to problems, clogging network bandwidth and exposing the network to security holes by opening back doors and creating virus vulnerabilities.

Company Name:	Palisade Systems Inc.
Address:	2625 North Loop Drive, Suite 2120 Ames, IA 50010
Phone Number:	(515) 296-6500 or (888) 824-0720
E-mail Address:	info@palisadesys.com
URLs:	http://www.palisadesys.com
Category:	General Protection
Product Name:	PacketHound

Product Description: PacketHound is a network appliance that allows system administrators to manage or block access to bandwidth- and productivity-eating Internet technologies like Napster, Gnutella, iMesh, RealAudio!RealVideo, Scour Exchange, and Windows Media. PacketHound protects your organization by allowing you to impose a flexible, organization-specific rule set. You can, for example, block an entire network, or block all access except in one computer lab, or block on a machine-by-machine basis. You can also use time-based rules to shut down access during critical hours but allow it at other times.

PacketHound protects PCs from the bandwidth and security issues associated with the use of file-sharing and streaming applications. Networked PCs are vulnerable to the actions of others on the network; if others are running Napster or Gnutella, all computers have less bandwidth and are potentially vulnerable to security issues: network use of peer-to-peer clients can open security holes and expose an organization to viruses and Trojan horses.

Company Name:	Pedestal Software
Address:	11 Medway Branch Road Norfolk, MA 02056
Phone Number:	(888) 664-7174
E-mail Address:	info@pedestalsoftware.com
URLs:	http://www.pedestalsoftware.com
Category:	General Protection
Product Name:	SecurityExpressions

Product Description: Enterprise security management, administration, reporting, and lockdown. SecurityExpressions automates the process of deploying, assessing, and maintaining consistent security policies on networks of Windows NT and 2000 systems. It helps organizations with security management and large-scale systems lockdown.

SecurityExpressions helps protect Internet PCs by locking them down according to industry-standard guidelines. Security "expressions," similar to mathematical ones, are at the core of this host and application policy management system. SecurityExpressions first assesses the vulnerability state by seeing how well the PC complies with the lockdown policy. Changes are recommended for noncompliant settings and SecurityExpressions automatically fixes them either interactively or in unattended mode. History logging provides an audit trial of changes, and modifications may be rolled back to their previous state if problems arise.

Company Name:	Redline Networks®
Address:	675 Campbell Technology Parkway Suite 150 Campbell, CA 95008
Phone Number:	(408) 369-3800
E-mail Address:	info@RedlineNetworks.com
URLs:	http://www.redlinenetworks.com
Category:	General Protection

Total security and acceleration

With Redline Networks' Web I/O Accelerator sites and enterprises achieve advanced HTTP security. Performing all functions in a completely secure environment, Web I/O Accelerators offer speed, capacity, cost savings, and HTTP security for public facing web sites and enterprise applications.

Secure connection management

Once a user is connected to a web server, the user can do any number of things to harm the network connected to the web server. But with a Web I/O Accelerator, two distinct sets of connections are maintained—one set to users and a separate set to internal servers. The barrier created by this secure connection management ensures that users never directly access content holding or content generating devices.

Complete server offload

Servers simply maintain a few connections to the Web I/O Accelerator and no connections to users. This offloads all end-user SSL key exchange work from the servers. By performing key exchanges a few times per day versus 200 times per minute, more resources are available for the server to quickly generate content. Additionally, by offloading the server, Web I/O Accelerators enable end-to-end SSL without requiring an SSL card in the server.

HTTP(S) request balancing

To enable true end-to-end SSL security, an SSL accelerator must be able to load balance directly rather than rely on an external load balancer for this functionality. Web I/O Accelerators provide fine-grained Request Balancing, rather than coarse-grained connection balancing.

Multiprotocol transaction integrity

An SSL device not only needs to balance requests, it must also support multiprotocol sticky cookies. This ensures that a user returns to the same content server not only on successive requests, but also when switching between HTTP and HTTPS requests. Web I/O Accelerators support multiprotocol sticky cookies.

Full payload parsing

Unlike other products that simply parse HTTP headers, Web I/O Accelerators can perform full HTTP payload parsing and content rewriting at wirespeed. Web I/O Accelerator can utilize any defined set of rules to make security decisions based on the entire payload rather than simple header information.

No cache

Caching secure data gives hackers an opportunity to steal secure files and decrypt them off-line, increasing the risk of a security breach. Additionally, caching is irrelevant for SSL transactions where each user gets a unique, encrypted file. Instead, Web I/O Accelerators increase application performance and decrease latency without caching and without risk of content corruption.

Data optimization and compression

Increasingly, sites are deploying data optimization and compression devices. To maintain end-to-end SSL and benefit from bandwidth savings, an SSL device must perform data optimization and compression internally. Throughput must be at full wire-speed and the implementation must support chunked transfer encoding and request pipelining to accelerate modem and broadband users. Web I/O Accelerators provide all of these data optimization and compression benefits for static, dynamic, and secure content.

Web DMZ

Web I/O Accelerators have the unique ability to protect servers from hackers by maintaining two completely separate sets of TCP connections:

- Users are never allowed to connect directly to the servers; client connections terminate at the Web I/O Accelerator

- Servers are never allowed to connect to the users; server connections terminate at the Web I/O Accelerator

Thus, the outside world never comes into direct contact with any content holding or content creating device. This effectively creates a Web DMZ inside the network where only valid, well-formed requests and responses can pass.

AutoSSL

Revolutionary security functionality enabled by the Web I/O Accelerator is automatic transformation of HTTP requests and clear text into HTTPS requests and secure content. With the Web I/O Accelerator AutoSSL functionality, enterprise applications, all site content, or even a particular VIP can be instantly secured with no rewriting of content, no modification to applications, and no change in user behavior. Users continue to make HTTP requests over port 80, and the Web I/O Accelerator automatically changes the request to HTTPS over port 443. The returning page is secured, with both redirects and the in-line objects rewritten to HTTPS.

Summary

Redline Networks' Web I/O Accelerator enables advanced HTTP security and true acceleration of SSL transactions. The Web I/O Accelerator performs all essential activities in a secure environment (connection management, sticky request balancing, parsing, compression, etc.), which enables high-performance end-to-end SSL. The Web I/O Accelerator offloads connections and key generation from servers so they focus on generating pages quickly. Web I/O Accelerators securely balance request load to servers and support multiprotocol sticky cookies so session integrity is always maintained. Once the server generates a response, the Web I/O Accelerator optimizes and compresses the response data before encrypting it for delivery to the user. In this way the Web I/O Accelerator sends fewer encrypted bits to the end user, reducing bandwidth while further speeding download and decryption times for modem and broadband users alike. Web I/O Accelerators can do this for clear text as well, enabling faster downloads of both HTTP and HTTPS data. With Redline Networks technology, a site can enjoy all of the benefits of advanced HTTP security with the speed and performance of clear text.

Company Name:	Secure Computing Corporation
Address:	One Almaden Blvd., Suite 400 San Jose, CA 95113
Phone Number:	(800) 379-4944
URLs:	www.securecomputing.com
Category:	General Protection
Product Name:	SafeWord Plus

Product Description: Supports smart cards, Secure Computing's Server for Virtual Smart Card, and general smart cards.

Company Name:	Secure Computing Corporation
Address:	One Almaden Blvd., Suite 400 San Jose, CA 95113
Phone Number:	(800) 379-4944
URLs:	www.securecomputing.com
Category:	General Protection

Product Name: Sidewinder 5

Product Description: Provides internal and perimeter security.

Company Name: Texar Software Corp.

Address: 1101 Prince Of Wales Dr.
                                 Ottawa K2H 9N6 Canada

Phone Number: (613) 274-2200

E-mail Address: info@texar.com

URLs: www.texar.com

Category: General Protection

Product Name: Secure Realms

Product Description: An access control solution that controls access to both legacy-based applications and the Web.

Company Name: WatchGuard Technologies

Address: 316 Occidental Ave. S., Ste. 2000
                                 Seattle, WA 98104

Phone Number: (206) 521-8340

E-mail Address: information@watchguard.com

URLs: www.watchguard.com

Category: General Protection

Product Name: WatchGuard LiveSecurity System
                                 w/FBII Plus and w/FBIFast VPN

Product Description: Provides VPN and security for the Internet.

Company Name: Webroot Software, Inc.

Address: PO Box 3531
                                 Boulder, CO 80307

Phone Number: (800) 772-9383

E-mail Address: info@webroot.com

URLs: www.webroot.com

Category: General Protection

Product Name: Window Washer

Product Description: Window Washer^{TM} is a utility, not unlike Scan-Disk, Disk Defragmenter, etc., that every computer should have, whether it is used in the home or office. Window Washer^{TM} automates the cleaning of all unnecessary system and Internet files.

In the case of system files, Window Washer^{TM} cleans the following:

Recycle Bin   This area continues to hold deleted information long after it is useful. Deleting its contents is important for home users as many do not know the Recycle Bin does not empty itself. In the case of businesses, this serves the important function of completely removing sensitive material.

Registry Streams   This area tracks programs that are used most often. Clearing the registry streams is important for home users since it contains useless data that takes up space. In the case of businesses, eliminating this information prevents others from finding information regarding the computer's recent activity .

Windows Run and Find History   These memory blocks were created for convenience, but only take up space in the average consumer's computer. On business computers, they can also act as an open window into the user's activity.

CHK Scan Disk Files   These files can be used to reconstruct old, deleted files. Eliminating these files removes useless fragments and, in the case of businesses, prevents other users from reconstructing old files.

Recently Viewed Pictures   Deleting these items can protect children from inappropriate material parents do not wish them to view. For businesses, this can prevent the theft of on-line schematics and PowerPoint presentations.

Recently Opened Documents   Removing the information stored in this area keeps others from discovering which documents recently have been opened.

MS Office 97 and 2000 Tracks   These files are similar to Recently Opened Documents. By deleting the MS Office tracks, a user keeps secret the documents that have been recently modified, whether it is changes to a home checking account or changes to the company's new formula for household cleaners.

Windows Temporary Files Folder   By eliminating these files, users prevent anyone from determining which programs have been recently installed and what items have been downloaded.

This list is considerably expandable through the use of Window Washer's™ free plug-in and the custom cleaning feature. The plug-ins enable the user to clean programs such as Adobe Acrobat Reader, MSNInstant Messenger, and Real Player.

For browsers such as Internet Explorer, Netscape, Opera, Neoplanet, etc. Window Washer cleans:

Cache   This area stores accessed Internet pages. By deleting this, users do not have to worry about anyone seeing which sites recently have been viewed.

Cookies   By deleting the cookies from a user's browser, it prevents third-party services from tracking the sites to which the user has gone.

History   By deleting this, the user prevents others with access to the computer from being able to find out which sites have been visited. This can help keep research and financial information secret.

Mail Trash   This function of Window Washer completely eliminates e-mails once they have been removed from the deleted folder in mail managers. Many users believe that when the deleted items folder is emptied, the e-mails are gone forever. Window Washer completely secures old correspondence by deleting them from the system entirely.

Drop Down Address Bar   As this area tracks all URLs that have been input into the browser, deleting this information helps secure a user's browsing history.

Auto Complete Data Forms   By removing this information, home users can protect their credit card information and business users can keep log-in and password information secure.

Downloaded Program Files   Deleting this information gives both home and business users the comfort of knowing that no one can discover which Internet programs have been downloaded onto the computer.

The functionality of Window Washer offers the user two major benefits: privacy and performance. Whether it is the home user who doesn't want friends, spouses, or children to view his or her latest letter to the IRS, or whether it is a business person writing a letter to the human resources department, Window Washer protects their privacy to DOD standards.

In the process of protecting the user's privacy, Window Washer ™ also recovers valuable hard drive space, restoring overall performance to the machine's original speed. Unless these areas are routinely cleaned, they accumulate rapidly, using more and more hard drive space. Most computer users are not aware of how to clean these areas and those that do know tend to avoid doing so because of the tedious and boring nature of the task.

The Windows™ operating system was designed for convenience and ease of use, not security. Hackers can enter computer systems through a variety of surreptitious means. This enables them to access private information, thereby compromising an individual's safety and right to privacy. Window Washer, when used routinely, plugs many of the security holes left open by the operating system's original design.

Window Washer™ is currently available on the Webroot web site, http://www.webroot.com and through a variety of Internet resellers. In the retail channel, Window Washer™ is carried by AOL, CompUSA, Fry's Electronics, Hastings, etc.

Company Name:	Webroot Software, Inc.
Address:	PO Box 3531 Boulder, CO 80307
Phone Number:	(800) 772-9383
E-mail Address:	info@webroot.com
URLs:	www.webroot.com
Category:	General Protection
Product Name:	WinGuardian

Product Description: As children begin to use computers at younger and younger ages, they often become sophisticated enough to disable filtering and blocking software. WinGuardian is a Windows™ monitoring utility that is an alternative to filtering and blocking for parents, schools, and other organizations. This helpful tool runs completely hidden and is able to monitor everything a user does on a system. WinGuardian can keep track of which programs a user runs, log any text that is typed into a program, log all web sites that are visited, and even capture screenshots at specified intervals. The logs can be reviewed to determine if a user is running inappropriate programs such as games or visiting web sites that the system owner considers offensive. Alternatively, WinGuardian can display an acceptable use policy (AUP) on the computer screen. A user must read the AUP and then click on the AGREE button before he or she is allowed to access the system. Knowing that the system is being monitored is a strong deterrent from using inappropriate programs or viewing inappropriate web pages. WinGuardian also gives you the option to "lock down" the Windows *95/ 98/Me* environment so that users can only run authorized programs.

Company Name:	World Wide Digital Security, Inc. (WVVDSI)
Address:	4720 Montgomery Lane, Suite 800 Bethesda, MD 20814
Phone Number:	(301) 656-0521, extension 0085
E-mail Address:	isolav@wwdsi.com
URLs:	http://www.wwdsi.com
Category:	General Protection
Product Name:	SAINT^{TM} (System Administrator's Integrated Network Tool)

Product Description: The most current version is bundled with SAINT-writer^{TM} and/or SAINTexpresss^{TM}. Older versions can be downloaded separately. SAINT^{TM} is a vulnerability assessment tool used to scan networks for vulnerabilities that hackers might exploit to gain access. SAINT^{TM} also supports extensive documentation on how to use the product, about the vulnerability, and how to fix the vulnerability. SAINT^{TM} provides links to more information on the vulnerabilities found, and when possible, links to sites where patches can be downloaded to fix vulnerabilities. SAINT^{TM} provides a variety of scanning intensity options ranging from *light* to *heavy plus*. Additional options include the SANS Top 10 and user-customized scans.

Company Name:	World Wide Digital Security, Inc. (WVVDSI)
Address:	4720 Montgomery Lane, Suite 800 Bethesda, MD 20814
Phone Number:	(301) 656-0521, extension 0085
E-mail Address:	isolav@wwdsi.com
URLs:	http://www.wwdsi.com

Category: General Protection

Product Name: SAINTwriter^{TM}

Product Description: SAINTwriter^{TM} is a report writing module that attaches seamlessly to SAINT^{TM}. SAINTwriter^{TM} allows the user to generate easily various types of reports, ranging from executive summaries to technical detail reports. Users can quickly and easily create customized reports and save the report formats for future use.

Company Name: World Wide Digital Security,
                             Inc. (WVVDSI)

Address: 4720 Montgomery Lane, Suite 800
                             Bethesda, MD 20814

Phone Number: (301) 656-0521, extension 0085

E-mail Address: isolav@wwdsi.com

URLs: http://www.wwdsi.com

Category: General Protection

Product Name: SAINTexpresss^{TM}

Product Description: SAINTexpresss^{TM} is an automatic service that updates SAINT^{TM} every time it is used. When a SAINT^{TM} scan is initiated, SAINTexpress^{TM} checks the WWDSI web site to see if a newer version of SAINT^{TM} is available. If available, SAINTexpresss^{TM} downloads the newer version of SAINT^{TM} and runs the scan using this newer version. This guarantees that the scan is testing for the most recently discovered vulnerabilities and using the most advanced version of SAINT^{TM}. This service is important because SAINT^{TM} is updated at least once every two weeks or whenever a new critical vulnerability is discovered.

Company Name: World Wide Digital Security,
                             Inc. (WVVDSI)

Address: 4720 Montgomery Lane, Suite 800
                             Bethesda, MD 20814

Phone Number: (301) 656-0521, extension 0085

E-mail Address: isolav@wwdsi.com

URLs: http://www.wwdsi.com

Category: General Protection

Product Name: WebSAINTTM

Product Description: WebSAINT^{TM} is WWDSI's web-based vulnerability assessment scanner. The network scan is run from the WWDSI web site and the report of the findings is sent to the user via secure HTTP. WebSAINT^{TM} is designed for people who are responsible for the security of their networks but do not have the time or expertise to download and configure the software, perform the scan, and create the reports.

Personal firewall

Company Name: Computer Peripheral Systems, Inc. (CPS)

Address: 5096 Bristol Industrial Way, Suite B
                                   Buford, GA 30518

Phone Number: (770) 945-0643

E-mail Address: sales@cpscom.com

URLs: http://www.cpscom.com

Category: Personal Firewall

Product Name: Mini Firewall

Product Description: Hardware security product for LANs with modem connections. Used to prevent modem connections to the Internet from gaining backdoor access to the corporate LAN. It connects between the modem and the LAN and physically breaks the LAN connection when the modem is in use. The LAN connection is reestablished when the modem goes back on-hook or after user-specified software is executed.

Company Name: DSEnet

Address: 5201 South Westshore Blvd.
                                   Tampa, FL 33611

Phone Number: (813) 902-9597

E-mail Address: questions@dsenet.com

URLs: www.dsenet.com

Category: Personal Firewall

Product Name: DSEnet Firewall

Product Description: DSEnet Firewall is a personal firewall that protects networked PCs from remote attacks. Install DSEnet Firewall on a PC using the friendly interface, and apply the necessary access rights for the Internet.

DSEnet Firewall is an ideal low-cost solution for small to medium sized businesses, home offices, and home users. Now, connecting to the Internet does not require the resources or support of a large corporate security infrastructure. Put DSEnet Firewall on a PC and browse the Internet safely and securely.

Use DSEnet Firewall to restrict access to specific services (e.g., web browsing or e-mail). Even advanced rules can be created on a per-user basis. Allow and block various users from web addresses, ports, and protocols.

Parents can blacklist web sites that are off limits to children, or "whitelist" only the acceptable web sites children are allowed to browse.

Businesses can limit employees to work related web sites, prevent downloads, and restrict Internet e-mail.

Using DSEnet firewall

Access DSEnet Firewall with the icon located in the lower right corner of the taskbar. Logging in provides users with their profiles.

The Configuration Panel is accessible only with an administrator password. All user profiles, settings, and rights can be configured in this panel.

DSEnet firewall

- prevents unauthorized access from the Internet
- stealth mode hides your PC from the Internet world
- runs seamlessly while surfing the Internet
- has great help files and instructions
- basic users can use the firewall with minimal effort
- computer wizards can, in detail, control every TCP and UDP port
- runs on windows 95, 98, NT 4.0
- control access to unacceptable web sites
- low cost solution with no additional hardware required
- supports multiple-user profiles
- simultaneously notifies the user and blocks intrusion attempts

- flexible control of web browsing
- restricts access by IP address, URL, port, and protocol
- easy to install and easy to use explorer style interface

System Requirements: Win 95, 98, NT, Me, 2000; 32MB RAM & TCP/IP

Company Name:	Intego, Inc.
Address:	6301 Collins Avenue Suite # 1806 Miami, FL 33141
Phone Number:	(305) 868-7920
Contact Name:	Olivier Depoorter
E-mail Address:	odepoorter@intego.com
URLs:	www.intego.com
Category:	Personal Firewall
Product Name:	NetBarrier
Product Description:	First personal firewall for the Mac

NetBarrier wins Univers Macworld Award

Miami FL, December 26, 2000—Intego, a leading provider of Macintosh Internet security utilities, today announced that it has won the prestigious International award, the Univers Macworld Award for the Best Internet Software of 2000 for NetBarrier. NetBarrier is the first personal Firewall for Macintosh with Firewall, Antivandal, and Internet Filter components that make NetBarrier the all-in-one solution for complete personal Internet security.

Intego has won over 20 awards in the U.S., Europe, and Asia, such as the *Macworld, MacHome, MacNN,* and *MacAddict* Awards. In just two years, NetBarrier has become the worldwide leader in personal firewall software for the Mac.

"We are extremely excited about winning this international award for our Internet security software," said Laurent Marteau, CEO, Intego. "To be chosen the Best Internet Software among this fast-paced Internet community is truly an honor."

Macworld

San Francisco, CA, January 9, 2001—Intego, a leading provider of Macintosh Internet security utilities, today announced NetBarrier 2.0, the new version of the first personal firewall for Macintosh. NetBarrier provides three powerful modules: Firewall, Antivandal, and Internet Filter to make NetBarrier the all-in-one solution for complete personal Internet security. Designed with maximum ease of set-up and use, NetBarrier is the "must have" in Internet security software.

New security features in NetBarrier 2.0 include control of unwanted Internet cookies, banner ads, and spam; the ability to filter personal information sent when connected to a web site; updates to the program's Firewall settings; gauges to monitor data traffic by protocol or application; and log exporting.

NetBarrier 2.0 also supports the new version of Intego's NetUpdate, the automatic software update engine. Users can program updates for specific days and times, and NetUpdate will check the Intego server to find out if updates are available for all of Intego's Barrier products installed on your computer.

Intego's programs have received many awards in the U.S., Europe, and Asia, such as awards from *Macworld, MacRame, MacNN, MacAddict*. In France, *UniversMacWorld* recently gave NetBarrier their 2000 trophy for the best Internet program.

"All Macs connected to the Internet are susceptible to security problems without exception," said Laurent Marteau, CEO, Intego. "Some Internet users falsely believe that using a modem or ISDN dial-up connection does not expose them to hackers. Hackers can get in through flaws in the OS. For example, a flaw discovered in port 49152 of Mac OS 9 allows hackers to send data that instantly freezes up a Mac, a problem that NetBarrier solves easily."

New NetBarrier Features include:

- Quick access to many settings via a new Control Strip module
- New Aqua interface
- Spam Filtering
- Filtered spam is deleted directly on POP3 servers
- Filtering of message subject, author, and sender
- Filtering of URLs

- Updates to the program's Firewall settings

- Definition of port intervals

- Predefined rule sets

- Monitor data traffic by protocol or application

- Blocks cookies and counts the number of cookies received

- Allows the user to erase cookies received by Internet Explorer, Netscape Communicator, and iCab

- Blocks banner ads

- Allows the user to filter information sent when connected to a web site

- Choose to not send your type of computer and browser

- Choose to not identify the last web page visited

- Support for the new version of NetUpdate

- Information on Macintosh network configuration

System requirements are a MacOS compatible computer with a Power PC processor, OpenTransport, Mac OS 8.1 or higher, and 32 MB RAM. It is also compatible with Mac OS 9.1. A Mac OS X version will be available Q1 2001. Also available in French and Japanese versions.

NetBarrier is available immediately. It can be purchased from www.intego. com, from retailers including buy.com, CompUSA, MacZone, Outpost.com, Computertown, Club Mac, MacWarehouse, MacMall, ComputerWare, Computer Store Northwest, J&R, Microcenter, CDW, Developer Depot, and from 200 Apple Specialists (see list on the Intego web site) and on-line at htm://www.intego.com.

For more information, contact Intego, 6301 Collins Ave, Miami, FL 33141 tel: (305) 868-7920 fax: (305) 868-7938 Web site: htm://www. intego.com info@intego.com.

About Intego

Intego, the i-security software company, publishes security software for the Macintosh, and its products are currently sold in 65 countries. With three essential products, Intego focuses on all aspects of the computer security market: antivirus protection, intrusion prevention, and content control.

In less than two years, NetBarrier has become the world leader in personal firewalls for the Macintosh. VirusBarrier, Intego's acclaimed antivirus solution, has been a resounding success since its launch in July 2000. And ContentBarrier, Intego's new parental control program, has been available to reinforce its product line since January 2001.

Intego was founded in May 1999 by a collection of highly motivated engineers and high-profile marketing, finance, and sales managers to leverage their extensive knowledge of network security and the Mac environment to corporate, individual, and educational users worldwide. The privately held company has its headquarters in Miami, Florida and in Paris, France.

Company Name:	Network ICE
Address:	2121 S. El Camino Real, Suite 1100 San Mateo, CA 94403
Phone Number:	(650) 532-4100
E-mail Address:	info@networkice.com
URLs:	www.networkice.com
Category:	Personal Firewall
Product Name:	BlackICE Defender
Product Description:	Personal Firewall and Intrusion Detection System

Everyone on the Internet is at risk of attack by hackers. "Always-on" DSL or cable modem, and dial-up Internet connections provide hackers the ability to violate the security of your computer.

BlackICE Defender is an industrial-strength antihacker system that automatically blocks unauthorized intrusions into your computer. It scans your DSL, cable modem, or dial-up Internet connection looking for hacker activity. When it detects an attempted intrusion, it automatically blocks traffic from that source, keeping intruders from accessing your computer. BlackICE Defender works silently in the background, keeping hackers at bay so you can safely stay connected to the Internet.

BlackICE Defender installs automatically and is up and running in a matter of seconds. It has a simple easy-to-use interface, provides audible or visual alerts, and a display that identifies who's trying to break into your computer.

BlackICE technology has been recognized with over 12 industry awards for superior technology and usability by leading organizations such as

Business Week, PC World, Network World, PC Computing, PC Magazine, Info World, and Internet Week.

Company Name:	Open Door Networks, Inc.
Address:	110 S. Laurel St. Ashland, OR 97520
Phone Number:	(541) 488-4127
E-mail Address:	sales@opendoor.com
URLs:	http://www.opendoor.com/doorstop/
Category:	Personal Firewall
Product Name:	DoorStop Server Edition

Product Description: A software-based "firewall" product for Macintosh servers. Unlike conventional firewalls, which are usually expensive, dedicated hardware devices, DoorStop is software you install directly on the servers you wish to protect. DoorStop is significantly easier to set up and use than a hardware firewall and provides the same capabilities at lower cost. With DoorStop, you can specify precisely which machines should have access to which services, and you can keep track of both allowed and denied access attempts to those services. DoorStop works well with a wide range of Macintosh-based Internet servers, including AppleShare IP, Web-STAR, and Open Door's ShareWay IP product line. Also acts as a machine-specific firewall to deny TCP access attempts as desired. Also logs access attempts.

Company Name:	Open Door Networks, Inc.
Address:	110 S. Laurel St. Ashland, OR 97520
Phone Number:	(541) 488-4127
E-mail Address:	sales@opendoor.com
URLs:	http://www.opendoor.com/whosthere/
Category:	Personal Firewall
Product Name:	Who's There? Firewall Advisor

Product Description: Who's There? Firewall Advisor helps users analyze and react to access attempts detected by their firewall. Who's There? is essential for understanding the ever-increasing access attempts from the Net. It provides advice and helps users take action to combat access attempts. It works with Open Door's DoorStop and Symantec's Norton Personal Firewall for Macintosh. Lets users understand and react to access attempts detected by their machine-specific firewall.

Company Name:	Presinet Sytems
Address:	Suite L109 - 645 Fort Street Victoria, British Columbia Canada V8W 1G2
Phone Number:	(250) 405-5380
E-mail Address:	solutions@PresiNET.com
URLs:	http://www.PresiNET.com
Category:	Personal Firewall
Product Name:	Deadbolt Managed Internet Firewall and Virtual Private Networking Services

Product Description: PresiNET provides a range of managed Internet Firewall security services, Network Activity Reporting, and Virtual Private Networking services for small to enterprise-sized organizations for their computer networks of 1 to 250 units. As part of the service, PresiNET provides its robust firewall server, firewall management and reporting services, event and activity monitoring services, expert consulting and support—wherever your business is located.

Company Name:	SOLSOFT
Address:	130 rue Victor Hugo 92300 Levallois Perret, France
Phone Number:	00 33 1 47 15 55 00
E-mail Address:	info@solsoft.com
URLs:	www.solsoft.com/np-lite/
Category:	Personal Firewall
Product Name:	Solsoft NP^{TM}-Lite 4.1

Product Description: Solsoft NP^{TM}-Lite 4.1 is a free version of Solsoft NP^{TM} specially created for Linux users. Combining a powerful visual interface and compiler engine, Solsoft NP™-Lite automatically translates visual representations of a security policy into consistent, error-free IP Filters.

Solsoft NP™-Lite configures up to 3 interfaces on Linux IP Firewall 2.0.x, Linux IP Chains 2.2.x and Linux NetFilter version 1.2.

Solsoft NP™-Lite 4.1 is a free security solution and can be downloaded from Solsoft's web site (www.solsoft.com/np-lite/).

Solsoft NP™-Lite is the ideal solution for any user or small companies directly connected to the Internet (ADSL, cable, high speed connection) that want to protect themselves without wasting time.

The firewall will not give you the security needed all by itself; it depends on the way you manage it.

Company Name:	SonicWALL, Inc.
Address	1160 Bordeaux Drive Sunnyvale, CA 94089
Phone Number:	(408) 745-9600
E-mail Address:	info@sonicwall.com
URLs:	www.sonicwall.com
Category:	Personal Firewall
Product Name:	SonicWALL SOHO2 Internet Security Appliance

Product Description: Integrated Internet Security. The SonicWALL SOHO2 Internet Security Appliance is a high-performance, integrated security platform. It includes a stateful packet inspection firewall, IP address management, and support for an expanding array of SonicWALL security services, including VPN (virtual private networking), network antivirus, and content filtering. The SonicWALL SOHO2 is an ideal solution for broadband-connected small offices to provide Internet security for all the computers on a LAN. By offloading security from each PC on the LAN to a high-performance appliance, security is dramatically enhanced.

Physical security

Company Name:	Codex Data Systems, Inc.
Address:	143 Main Street Nanuet, NY 10954

Phone Number:	(845) 627-0011
E-mail Address:	sales@codexdatasystems.com
URLs:	www.codexdatasystems.com
Category:	Physical Security
Product Name:	PC PhoneHome
Product Description:	Tracks and locates a stolen computer throughout the world.

Company Name:	Digital Asset Protection
Address:	617 Myrtle St. Arroyo Grande, CA 93420
Phone Number:	(877) 752-7364
E-mail Address:	info@DAProtect.com
URLs:	www.DAProtect.com
Category:	Physical Security
Product Name:	Lock & Go^{TM}

Product Description: Lock & Go^{TM} offers premier mechanical protection for notebook computers. Nearly 700 pounds of resistance offers a level of asset protection unmatched by traditional cables. For quick and effective notebook protection, the Lock & Go^{TM} simply snaps into place; no awkward cabling is required. Upon your return, one twist of the key allows you to access your computer.

Company Name:	Digital Asset Protection
Address:	617 Myrtle St. Arroyo Grande, CA 93420
Phone Number:	(877) 752-7364
E-mail Address:	info@DAProtect.com
URLs:	www.DAProtect.com
Category:	Physical Security
Product Name:	DAP Watchman^{TM}

Product Description: The DAP Watchman^{TM} is a stand-alone electronic alarm that may be used to protect a single piece of computer hardware or other electronic equipment. Ideally suited for the SOHO, or for isolated equipment distributed throughout a large facility. If the sensor is removed, or the wire severed, an 85 dB tone notifies personnel in the vicinity of an attempted theft.

Company Name:	Digital Asset Protection
Address:	617 Myrtle St.
	Arroyo Grande, CA 93420
Phone Number:	(877) 752-7364
E-mail Address:	info@DAProtect.com
URLs:	www.DAProtect.com
Category:	Physical Security
Product Name:	DAP Marshall^{TM}

Product Description: Ideally suited for environments that contain note-books that are frequently taken on the road, the DAP Marshall^{TM} is a stand-alone electronic alarm system for computer hardware that combines state-of-the-art asset protection with hassle-free mobility. The DAP Marshall's infrared remote access allows the end-user to engage the system from a distance of up to 20 feet and protects your computer hardware without compromising the mobility of portable equipment.

Company Name:	Digital Asset Protection
Address:	617 Myrtle St.
	Arroyo Grande, CA 93420
Phone Number:	(877) 752-7364
E-mail Address:	info@DAProtect.com
URLs:	www.DAProtect.com
Category:	Physical Security
Product Name:	DAP Sentry^{TM}

Product Description: Ideally suited for environments with distributed computer hardware, The DAP Sentry^{TM} is a stand-alone electronic alarm system that allows for complicated configurations with minimal impact. Touch-pad or optional remote infrared access allows authorized users to quickly and effectively engage the system.

Company Name:	Digital Asset Protection
Address:	617 Myrtle St. Arroyo Grande, CA 93420
Phone Number:	(877) 752-7364
E-mail Address:	info@DAProtect.com
URLs:	www.DAProtect.com
Category:	Physical Security
Product Name:	DAP Guardian^{TM}

Product Description: The DAP Guardian^{TM} is a stand-alone electronic alarm system for computer hardware that pinpoints the exact location of a security breach. In the event of an attempted theft of your high-tech equipment, the information provided by the alarm panel allows your personnel to execute an effective stealth response.

Company Name:	Digital Asset Protection
Address:	617 Myrtle St. Arroyo Grande, CA 93420
Phone Number:	(877) 752-7364
E-mail Address:	info@DAProtect.com
URLs:	www.DAProtect.com
Category:	Physical Security
Product Name:	DAP Monitor^{TM}

Product Description: The DAP Monitor^{TM} is an integrated system ideally suited for unsupervised environments where round-the-clock protection of computer hardware is critical. The DAP Monitor^{TM} provides an interface with a central alarm system point panel. The DAP Monitor^{TM} uses a zone within a normally open or normally closed alarm loop circuit to protect computer equipment and allows organizations to take advantage of their existing access control infrastructure.

Company Name: Fastening Solutions, Inc.

Address: 15230 Burbank Blvd., Ste. 106
                          Van Nuys, CA 91411

Phone Number: (818) 994-3698; (800) 232-7836

Category: Physical Security

Product Name: LockGuard

Product Description: Provides fastening protection in combination with a key and lock security system. Can be used with PCs and peripherals.

Company Name: Kensington Technology Group
                          ACCO Brands

Address: 2855 Campus Dr.
                          San Mateo, CA 94403

Phone Number: (650) 572-2700

Category: Physical Security

Product Name: Notebook MicroSaver Security Cable

Product Description: A lock and cable device that can be attached to the security slot of a desktop sytem or notebook.

Company Name: PC Guardian

Address: 1133 E. Francisco Blvd.
                          San Rafael, CA 94901-5427

Phone Number: (415) 459-0190; (800) 288-8126

E-mail Address: pcg@pcguardian.com

URLs: www.pcguardian.com

Category: Physical Protection

Product Name: Perma Dome Cable Anchor

Product Description: Security cable anchor.

Company Name:	PC Guardian
Address:	1133 E. Francisco Blvd. San Rafael, CA 94901-5427
Phone Number:	(415) 459-0190; (800) 288-8126
E-mail Address:	pcg@pcguardian.com
URLs:	www.pcguardian.com
Category:	Physical Protection
Product Name:	Partition Furniture Cable Anchor
Product Description:	Security cable anchor that can be inserted into cubic walls.

Company Name:	Philadelphia Security Products, Inc.
Address:	405-R Baily Road Yeadonm, PA 19050
Phone Number:	(800) 456-1789
E-mail Address:	info@flexguard.com
URLs:	www.flexguard.com
Category:	Physical Security
Product Name:	FLEXGUARD security system
Product Description:	Anti-theft security hardware for laptop computers, desktop computers, and other electronic equipment.

Company Name:	Se-Kure Controls, Inc.
Company Address:	3714 Runge St. Franklin Park, Il. 60131-1112
Phone Number:	(847) 288-1111; (800) 322-2435
E-mail Address:	info@se-kure.com
URLs:	www.se-kure.com
Category:	Physical Security

Product Name: Laptop Holder #PTR-200

Product Description: Provides protection for the glass screen
                           with a metal enclosure.

User authentication

Company Name: American Biometric Company

Address: DFW Engineering & Development Ltd.
                           3429 Hawthorne Rd.
                           Ottawa KIG 4G2 Canada

Phone Number: (613) 736-5100; (888) 246-6687

Category: User Authentication

Product Name: BioMouse Fingerprint Scanner

Product Description: Plug and play peripheral that uses a desktop fingerprint scanner to replace password protection.

Company Name: Ankari

Address: 3429 Hawthorne Road
                           Ottawa, Ontario K1 G 4G2

Phone Number: (613) 736-5100; (888) 246-6687

E-mail Address: info@ankari.com

URLs: www.ankari.com

Category: User Authentication

Product Name: BioMouse

Product Description: Combined fingerprint scanner and smart card
reader. The BioMouse Plus integrated fingerprint scanner and smart card
reader lets you store credentials on a secure portable token whose use
depends on a method of positive identification that cannot be lost, stolen,
shared or forgotten—your fingerprint. When applied to Internet security, a
user can store a Verisign digital certificate on a smart card and use a fingerprint instead of a password to enter secure web sites.

Company Name: Ankari

Address: 3429 Hawthorne Road
                           Ottawa, Ontario K1 G 4G2

Phone Number:	(613) 736-5100; (888) 246-6687
E-mail Address:	info@ankari.com
URLs:	www.ankari.com
Category:	User Authentication
Product Name:	Trinity

Product Description: Trinity is a software authentication infrastructure that enables secure and convenient verification of user identities to protect access to a wide range of platforms and applications. Trinity allows a user to consolidate all their web-based passwords into a single digital identity and protect that identity through the use of a biometric or smart card.

Company Name:	Litronic Inc
Address:	17861 Cartwright Road Irvine, CA 92614
Phone Number:	(949) 851-1085
E-mail Address:	info@litronic.com
URLs:	www.litronic.com
Category:	User Authentication
Product Name:	NetSign
Product Description:	Secure the Internet for Business

NetSign provides users with the foundation to secure the web for electronic business and to protect user desktops from unauthorized access. By integrating smart cards with browsers, e-mail and desktop applications, NetSign delivers a high level of security for digital communications. In addition to security, NetSign offers its users the convenience of multiple application support on a single portable smart card. With NetSign, users can digitally sign and encrypt e-mail in both Netscape and Microsoft suites, lock desktop stations, automatic launching of applications, and securely connect to remote network services.

NetSign secures the Internet for communications by adding smart card functionality to Microsoft and Netscape e-mail/browser packages. A user's digital identity is stored on the smart card to increase security. Mission-critical security functions such as private key storage and digital signature are performed on the smart card for significantly greater security that is completely portable for use with a desktop or laptop at the office, from home, or while traveling.

NetSign includes: SecureDial, SecureStart, and CardStart features, which enhance network and desktop security and control desktop applications.

NetSign CardStart features

- Automatic registration of new certificates
- Windows log-off capabilities when the smart card is removed from the reader
- Automated launching of applications upon insertion of the smart card into the reader

NetSign SecureDial features

- Secure remote network access using the RAS, RADIUS, TACACS or PPTP protocols to enable smart card secured dial-up sessions and ISP access
- Storage of account information on the smart card to protect dial-up passwords

NetSign SecureStart features

- Log-on protection for Windows 95/98 & Windows NT PCs requiring the insertion of the user's smart card and PIN for PC access (Windows 2000 support provided through native Windows 2000 Log-on)
- Locking capabilities for Windows PC NT stations upon the removal of the user's smart card
- System lock override with the use of an administrator card

Browser and e-mail security features

- Authenticated web page access with SSL
- Digitally signed and encrypted email using S/MIME (VeriSign™ Digital ID included)
- Form and object signing using Microsoft Internet Explorer 4.0 or higher, Outlook 98/2000 or Outlook Express 4 or higher, or Netscape Communicator 4.05 or higher
- Support for custom smart card enabled Java applets

Company Name:	Litronic Inc
Address:	17861 Cartwright Road Irvine, CA 92614
Phone Number:	(949) 851-1085
E-mail Address:	info@litronic.com
URLs:	www.litronic.com
Category:	User Authentication
Product Name:	Profile Manager
Product Description:	

Profile Manager

Profile Manager provides organizations with a flexible solution by offering token interoperability. Because Profile Manager can initialize and maintain both smart cards and the exporting of PKCS#12 files, organizations can implement an adaptable PKI scheme that supports a multilevel security approach. Profile Manager is integrated with a variety of Certificate Authorities (CAs) offering trusted certificate issuance and integrated directory service. The CAs currently supported are Microsoft Certificate Server, VeriSign^{TM} OnSite, Netscape Certificate Management System, and Cyber-Trust. In addition, Profile Manager supports international standards such as SSL, S/MIME, PKCS #11, and PC/SC while enabling the generation of X.50gv3 certificates, RSA keypairs, and other custom data objects.

Deploy security tokens quickly and securely

Efficiency and security are critical to the success of a large-scale PKI deployment. Profile Manager enables organizations to quickly generate security tokens for any user in the system. To increase efficiency and decrease the risk of third party interception, token generation is removed from the user's desktop and performed by the security administrator for fail-safe installation of the certificate on the token. Security administrators can control security by generating and backing up keys and certificates in a restricted environment.

Profile Manager conveniently integrates with your existing employee or customer database so that the security administrator does not have to rekey user data for token personalization. User information can be imported from several sources including existing ASCII files, directories, and various databases. For large-scale deployments, Profile Manager integrates with Datacard^{TM} printers to provide bulk smart card initialization and custom printing.

Easily recover token information

The ability to recover user information, including keys and certificates, is necessary to replace lost or damaged tokens. Profile Manager provides optional secure database integration for the recovery of token information. User data and profile information is encrypted with the security administrator's Triple DES key/PIN-protected smart card and stored in the database. The security administrator can access this information from the database to issue a user a duplicate smart card when a card is lost or damaged.

Facilitate security token management

The routine maintenance of a PKI can be burdensome for security administrators without the proper tools for the management of security tokens. Profile Manager can be used to modify user privileges or alter user data by adding, deleting, or modifying items on an existing user token. If necessary, a user's keys and certificates can be revoked using Profile Manager. Data on a card or other token can be changed and updated after that token has been issued using Profile Manager. Changing user data after token issuance also creates a new backup entry in the database.

Profile manager supports

- Hardware key generation
- Integration with leading X.509v3 Certificate Authorities
- Security policy profiling
- Integration with various databases and directories
- Bulk token issuance
- Key recovery
- Certificate revocation

Profile Manager includes: Profile Manager software

Two NetSignia™ Smart Card Reader/Writers Argus 2000 PC Card Reader/Writer Chrysalis Luna™ 2 PCMCIA Token Thirteen smart cards

Company Name:	Mytec Technologies, Inc.
Address:	1220 Sheppard Ave. E., Ste. 200 Toronto, M2K 2S5 Canada
Phone Number:	(416) 467-6000
E-mail Address:	sales@mytec.com

URLs: www.mytec.com

Category: User Authentication

Product Name: Mytec® Gateway

Product Description: Compares the user's fingerprints with those contained in an encrypted template.

Company Name: Recognition Systems, Inc.

Address: 1520 Dell Ave.
                               Campbell, CA 95008

Phone Number: (408) 364-6960

E-mail Address: sales@regosys.com

URLs: www.handreader.com

Category: User Authentication

Product Name: Id3D-R Handkey

Product Description: A biometric access control system that responds to and recognizes people.

Company Name: Secure Computing Corporation

Address: One Almaden Blvd., Suite 400
                               San Jose, CA 95113

Phone Number: (800) 379-4944

URLs: www.securecomputing.com

Category: User Authentication

Product Name: SafeWord 5.1

Product Description: Authentication methods can be mixed and matched as needed.

Company Name: SHYM Technology Inc.

Address: 75 Second Ave.
                               Needham, MA 02494

Phone Number: (781) 455-1100

E-mail Address: info@shym.com

URLs: www.shym.com

Category: User Authentication

Product Name: snAPPsecure

Product Description:

Target audience

snAPPsecure^{TM} targets organizations moving off-line processes to the Web to achieve increased efficiencies. Most of these organizations do not have the vast resources required to implement a custom-built infrastructure for strong authentication and eSignatures. Initial target market segments include healthcare, manufacturing, financial services, pharmaceuticals, and government.

Every organization is working fast and furiously to determine which core processes should be e-enabled. However, without the necessary security precautions, mission-critical Web, e-mail, and enterprise applications, like SAP and PeopleSoft, are at serious risk. The latest version of Microsoft's server operating system, Windows 2000, has been developed with built-in security capabilities including a standards-based public key infrastructure (PKI) to deliver a complete Internet-enabled business operating system. SHYM's snAPPsecure^{TM} utilizes no-cost certificates from Microsoft's Windows 2000 as a low-cost and easy-to-deploy solution for small and medium enterprises to secure critical applications.

Description of product

SHYM's snAPPsecure is a turnkey application security solution powered by the Microsoft Windows 2000-based public key infrastructure (PKI) that dramatically accelerates the deployment of application security using digital certificates to protect today's e-business initiatives. snAPPsecure^{TM} allows organizations to look beyond individual security point-solutions to a complete product solution that is centrally managed, covering all organizational domains. snAPPsecure^{TM} lets organizations easily leverage the integrated PKI of Windows 2000 with their choice of Web, e-mail, and client/server applications without the time-consuming and costly custom integration traditionally needed for a complex and powerful PKI security. snAPPsecure^{TM} combines PKEnable, SHYM's flagship product, the Windows 2000 Certificate Server and professional services to enable organizations to rapidly secure critical e-business applications in just a few days, as opposed to the months of integration needed with today's digital certificate toolkits.

SHYM's application library includes support for popular Web, e-mail, and enterprise applications, providing snap-in application security, eliminating the pain of integrating and maintaining custom development. snAPPsecure^{TM} does not require a homogenous Windows 2000-based network. It provides clean integration with existing Windows NT, Novell, and UNIX environments.

Business problem

Today, enterprises engaging in business over public networks are doing it at a great risk. The idea of conducting high value transactions, such as contract negotiations and the exchange of product ideas with today's security technology gives most organizations reason for concern. PKI is poised to meet these security needs with its combination of strong authentication, message integrity, and eSignature capabilities, but PKI is still too difficult to integrate, manage, and deploy. Recent PKI projects that were expected to be in full-scale deployment are still mired in the pilot stages, while other projects have been completely cancelled. Those very few who have started to roll out a PKI now realize that just issuing certificates is not enough; there must be a way to validate that credentials are trusted to perform certain transactions. SHYM's snAPPsecure^{TM} is the solution to this problem. It makes PKI less expensive, faster to deploy, and easier to manage.

SHYM's snAPPsecure^{TM} enables organizations to leverage the underlying digital certificate capabilities of their Windows 2000 operating system, thereby leveraging digital certificates for greater efficiency and competitive advantage. snAPPsecure^{TM} enables e-processes that result in greater efficiencies and competitive advantage. SHYM's snAPPsecure^{TM} also removes application security integration barriers, making the product far easier to install and manage. With Microsoft's integrated PKI software, customers can deploy PKI-based security services quickly, easily, and most importantly, cost effectively. SHYM's solution lets organizations reap the promise of streamlined business processes, without breaking the bank or missing the market window. SHYM's solutions have the added advantage of being both snap-in simple, and customized to fit each organization's needs. A snAPPsecure^{TM} pilot implementation can usually be installed in one day as opposed to weeks or months.

SHYM's snAPPsecure^{TM} allows companies to build strong strategic online relationships with suppliers, distributors, customers, and other entities. They can share important business information knowing that interactions are private, that the identity of each party is authenticated, and that any agreements cannot be forged or repudiated. These assurances allow companies to replicate the best practices of the brick and mortar marketplace in the e-business realm.

Company Name:	SILANIS TECHNOLOGY INC.
Address:	398 Isabey, 2nd Floor, Saint Lauren, Quebec H4T 1V3
Phone Number:	(888) SILANIS (745-2647)
E-mail Address:	info@silanis.com
URLs:	www.silanis.com
Category:	User Authentication
Product Name:	ApproveIt

Product Description: Silanis ApproveIt is an award-winning, electronic signature software that enables organizations to securely capture multiple, legally binding signatures in electronic documents and Web forms without additional hardware, software, or programming. Supported software includes Microsoft Word, Excel, Outlook, Adobe Acrobat, JetForm FormFlow, PureEdge and X.509 v3 digital certificates.

Company Name:	Secure Computing Corporation
Address:	One Almaden Blvd., Suite 400 San Jose, CA 95113
Phone Number:	(800) 379-4944
URLs:	www.securecomputing.com
Category:	User Authentication
Product Name:	SmartFiler
Product Description:	Allows control of Web access throughout the entire organization.

Virus protection

Company Name:	Computer Associates International, Inc.
Address:	1 Computer Associates Plz. Islandia, NY 11749

Phone Number:	(516) 342-5224; (800) 225-5224
E-mail Address:	info@ca.com
URLs:	www.ca.com
Category:	Virus Protection
Product Name:	eTrust AntiVirus
Product Description:	Provides anti-virus protection. Has built-in identifiers of new virus.

Company Name:	F-Secure, Inc.
Address:	675 N. First St., 5th Fl. San Jose, CA 95112
Phone Number:	(408) 938-6700; (888) 432-8233
E-mail Address:	info@f-secure.com
URLs:	www.f-secure.com
Category:	Virus Protection
Product Name:	F-Secure Anti-Virus
Product Description:	Protection against virus and other attacking codes for both mobile and site-based workers.

Company Name:	InDefense
Address:	303 Potrero St. #42-204 Santa Cruz, CA 95060
Phone Number:	831-471-1413; 877-472-3372
E-mail Address:	info@indefense.com
URLs:	www.indefense.com
Category:	Virus Protection
Product Name:	Achilles' Shield
Product Description:	A patented protection from virus. It detects worm, viral, and Trojans.

Company Name:	Intego, Inc.
Address:	6301 Collins Avenue, Suite #1806 Miami, FL 33141
Phone Number:	305 868 7920
Contact Name:	Olivier Depoorter
E-mail Address:	odepoorter@intego.com
URLs:	www.intego.com
Category:	Virus Protection
Product Name:	VirusBarrier

Product Description: San Francisco, CA, January 9, 2001—Intego, a leading provider of Macintosh Internet security utilities, today announced VirusBarrier 1.5, a new version of its acclaimed antivirus program for Macintosh. VirusBarrier provides protection against all known viruses on the Macintosh, and also protects against Word and Excel macro viruses. It offers thorough protection against viruses of all types, coming from infected files or applications, whether on floppy disks, CD-ROMs, removable media, or on files downloaded over the Internet or other types of networks.

VirusBarrier was designed so that, once it is installed and configured, the user does not have to do anything unless a virus is detected, no false positive alerts, and no need to disable VirusBarrier when installing other software. The VirusBarrier philosophy can be summed up in three words: simple, fast and nonintrusive. VirusBarrier works in the background and alerts the user if any viruses are detected.

VirusBarrier 1.5 also supports the new version of Intego's NetUpdate, the automatic software update engine. Users can program updates for specific days and times, and NetUpdate will check the Intego server to find out if updates are available for all of Intego's Barrier products installed on your computer.

Intego's programs have received many awards in the U.S., Europe, and Asia, such as awards from *Macworld, MacHome, MacNN, MacAddict*. In France, *UniversMacWorld* recently gave NetBarrier their 2000 trophy for the best Internet program.

"The virus threat is real. More and more viruses are being discovered every day," said Laurent Marteau, CEO, Intego. "This is even more of a problem today, in our wired world, where people exchange files daily via e-mail. VirusBarrier is your insurance against all kinds of viruses—it watches over your computer so you don't have to worry about them."

New VirusBarrier features include:

- Simple, fast, and nonintrusive
- Scans compressed file, checks all types of archives recognized by Stuffit Expander (Zip, CompactPro, DiskDoubler, tar, BZip, arc, etc.)
- Turbo Mode makes scanning from 5 to 40 times faster
- Contextual Menu module for quick scanning
- Self-protection ensures that VirusBarrier doesn't get infected
- Scans RAM after detection of system viruses
- Faster manual scans
- Compatible with Mac OS 9.1

The upgrade from VirusBarrier version 1.x is free for registered users. Available from the Intego web site, www.intego.com.

System requirements are a Mac OS compatible computer with a Power PC processor, OpenTransport, Mac OS 8.1 or higher, and 32 MB RAM. It is also compatible with Mac OS 9.1 A Mac OS X version will be available Q1 2001. Also available in French and Japanese versions.

VirusBarrier is available immediately from retailers including buy.com, CompUSA, MacZone, Outpost.com, Computertown, Club Mac, MacWarehouse, MacMall, ComputerWare, Computer Store Northwest, J&R, Microcenter, CDW, Developer Depot, and from 200 Apple Specialists (see list on the Intego web site) and on-line at httq://www.intego.com.

For more information, contact Intego, 6301 Collins Ave, Miami, FL 33141 tel: (305) 868-7920 fax: (305) 868-7938 web site: htm://www.intego. com info@intego.com.

About Intego

In less than two years, NetBarrier has become the world leader in personal firewalls for the Macintosh. VirusBarrier, Intego's acclaimed antivirus solution, has been a resounding success since its launch in July 2000. And ContentBarrier, Intego's new parental control program, has been available to reinforce its product line since January 2001.

Intego was founded in May 1999 by a collection of highly motivated engineers and high-profile marketing, finance, and sales managers to leverage their extensive knowledge of network security and the Mac environment to corporate, individual and educational users worldwide. The privately held company has its headquarters in Miami, Florida and in Paris, France.

Company Name:	McAfee
Address:	3965 Freedom Circle Santa Clara, CA 95054
Phone Number:	(888) VIRUS-NO
URLs:	www.mcafeeb2b.com
Category:	Virus Protection
Product Name:	VirusScan TC

Product Description: As the Internet becomes the hub of an increasing number of business transactions, and users—especially mobile users—depend on network availability to perform mission-critical functions, bandwidth becomes essential resource for IT to manage. And in a circular scenario, this trend leads to a lack of available bandwidth. VirusScan TC (Thin Client) not only requires less bandwidth to deploy and manage than any other antivirus solution on the market today, but it intelligently uses the little bandwidth it does require. Working in concert with McAfee's ePolicy Orchestrator, which sets the standard for enterprise antivirus management, VirusScan TC allows you to centrally update, configure, manage, and gather information about your entire network, while minimizing the bandwidth impact to your network.

Because ePolicy Orchestrator uses standard protocols to communicate between the desktop and the server (secured HTTP), managing remote sites across the Internet is a breeze. Got an office in Australia, but no VPN connectivity between here and there? Using ePolicy Orchestrator and VirusScan TC you're still secure. Remote users who dial in for e-mail and become frustrated with their antivirus protection because it took a long time to download updates will forget they ever had a problem once VirusScan TC is installed. Not only will they have the quicker download speed of VirusScan TC's incremental update technology, but they will have the peace of mind that secured agent-server communication provides.

Company Name:	Midwest Systems, Inc.
Address:	1303 Corporate Center Dr. Eagan, MN 55121

Phone Number:	(651) 406-4100; (888) 800-8339
E-mail Address:	moreinfo@midwest-sys.com
URLs:	www.midwest-sys.com
Category:	Virus Protection
Product Name:	Midwest Systems
Product Description:	A services company that specializes in storage, network, and messaging solutions that are secure.

Company Name:	SaferSite
Address:	2130 Walnut Bottom Road Carlisle, PA 17013
Phone Number:	(717) 243-6588
E-mail Address:	brose@safersite.com
URLs:	www.safersite.com
Category:	Virus Protection
Product Name:	PestPatrol

Product Description: PestPatrol detects and can delete any malicious nonvirus software found on PCs. Everyone knows what a virus scanner is and what it does. What people don't realize is that there is a wide variety of malicious software that can be more harmful than viruses, and are not being detected by your antivirus software.

"Pests" represent a whole new category of things that threaten the stability and integrity of your computer or network. You may not have been aware that these threats exist. Wouldn't you be surprised to find files containing information about hacking your PBX, password cracking, mail bombing, or a variety of hacker tools on your network or even on your own computer?

Where do these pests come from?

In some instances, these pests can be planted on your machine by hackers. Such things as Trojans, worms, or hostile applets are among the most common items that arrive from the "outside." Other items can be brought into your network, knowingly or unknowingly, by your own employees.

In any event, as a webmaster or system administrator, you should be aware that they exist and that they can be a source of disruption.

The vulnerability

Some pests can cause a great deal of damage, and some can live on your machine without you even knowing about them. There are thousands of pests and new ones are found each day and added to SaferSite's PestPatrol database. You should be as rigorous about scanning for pests as you are about scanning for viruses.

Categories of pests

There are dozens of categories of pests, including: worms, Trojans, spyware, hacker toolkits, and password crackers.

Continuous protection

With such a large variety of pests out there, doesn't it make sense to protect your network? PestPatrol only needs a few minutes to identify unwanted pests on your entire network. PestPatrol can also be updated in seconds to detect new pests as soon as they are discovered.

Company Name:	Trend Micro, Inc.
Address:	10101 N. De Anza Blvd., 2nd Fl. Cupertino, CA 95014
Phone Number:	(408) 257-1500; (800) 228-5651
E-mail Address:	sales@trendmicro.com
URLs:	www.antivirus.com
Category:	Virus Protection
Product Name:	InterScan Virus Wall
Product Description:	A three-in-one product that scans SMTP mail, HTTP, and FTP traffic, in real time.

Company Name:	Trend Micro, Inc.
Address:	10101 N. De Anza Blvd., 2nd Fl. Cupertino, CA 95014
Phone Number:	(408) 257-1500; (800) 228-5651

E-mail Address:	sales@trendmicro.com
URLs:	www.antivirus.com
Category:	Virus Protection
Product Name:	ScanMail for OpenMail
Product Description:	Virus protection system for Hewlett-Packard's e-mail.

Companies' Copyright Notices and Statements

Although the authors and editors have attempted to provide accurate information in this book, we assume no responsibility for the accuracy of the information.

Microsoft

Copyright notice. Copyright © 2000 Microsoft Corporation, One Microsoft Way, Redmond, Washington 98052-6399 U.S.A. All rights reserved. See www.microsoft.com for more information.

Trademarks

Microsoft, Windows, Windows NT, MSN, Outlook, The Microsoft Network, Windows98, Windows95, and/or other Microsoft products referenced herein are either trademarks or registered trademarks of Microsoft. See www.microsoft.com for more information.

Verisign

Copyright ® 2000 VeriSign, Inc. All rights reserved.

VeriSign, the VeriSign logo, Digital ID, OnSite, and Go Secure! are trademarks and service marks or registered trademarks and service marks of VeriSign, Inc. All other trademarks and service marks are property of their respective owners. See www.verisign.com for more information.

INTEL

http://www.intel.com/sites/corporate/tradmarx.htm?iid=intelhome+legal&

XEROX

http://www.xerox.com/go/xrx/template/
004.jsp?view=Legal&Xcntry=USA&Xlang=en_US&Xseg=corp

Whale Communications

e-Gap® Remote Access Appliance. www.whalecommunications.com

DEC/Compaq/HP

http://welcome.hp.com/country/us/eng/privacy.htm

HP

http://welcome.hp.com/country/us/eng/termsofuse.htm

Neoteris, Inc.

http://www.neoteris.com

Redline Networks

http://www.redlinenetworks.com

3COM

http://www.3com.com/legal/index.html

Spam (this is trademarked)

http://www.spam.com/ci/ci_in.htm

spam is not trademarked

http://www.spam.com/ci/ci_in.htm

GE

http://www.ge.com/

Zone Labs

http://www.zonealarm.com/aboutus/legal.html

LinkSys

http://www.linksys.com/contact/coinfo.asp

Network ICE

Network ICE, the Network ICE logo, the Defender logo, BlackICE, Black-ICE Sentry, BlackICE Defender, BlackICE Auditor, ICEpac, Enterprise ICEPAC, ICEPAC, ICEPAC Auditor, advICE, "Collective Awareness,"

"The Future of Network Security ... Today," "We Stop Hackers Cold," Intrusion Countermeasure Enhancements (ICE), Intrusion Defense System, and "Intrusion Detection at the Speed of Light" are trademarks or registered trademarks of Network ICE or its licencees in the United States and other countries.

APPLE

http://www.apple.com/legal/default.html

MICROWAREHOUSE

http://www2.warehouse.com/

IBM

IBM list is too large to list. See this URL; http://www.ibm.com/legal/copytrade.phtml.

RSA

The 'S/MIME-Enabled' logo is trademarked, for the purpose of promoting interoperability among products implementing S/MIME. (http://www.rsasecurity.com/) Vendors must demonstrate S/MIME compliance before using the logo on product packaging, promotional materials, advertising, signage, and/or web sites. See www.rsa.com for more information. S/MIME logo can be found at http://www.rsasecurity.com/standards/smime/logos.html.

Baltimore Technologies

Baltimore Technologies, Global E|Security, Global E-Security, E-Security, E|Security, TrustedWorld, PKI World, Zergo, ZSA and Baltimore product names including UniCERT, MailSecure, PKI-Plus, W/Secure, X/Secure and J/CRYPTO are all trademarks of Baltimore Technologies plc and its subsidiaries. See http://www.baltimore.ie/legalnotices.html.

Netscape

Netscape, Netscape Certificater Server, Netscape FastTrack Server, Netscape Navigator, Netscape ONE, SuiteSpot, and the Netscape N and Ship's Wheel logos are registered trademarks of Netscape Communications Corporation in the United States and other countries. The following list represents trademarks of Netscape Communications Corporation, which may be registered in other countries.

Netscape trademarks

Following are Netscape's trademarks. An ® following a name indicates that the trademark has been registered in the U.S. This list is not exhaustive. Netscape may own other trademarks that are not included here.

AutoConfig, AutoUpdate, BeanConnect, Client Registry, Client Version Registry, Collabra®, Collabra Share®, Contact, CoolTalk, Expert Alliance, ExpertDesk, Expert-to-Expert, In-Box Direct, ISP Select®, Live 3D, LiveCall, LiveConnect, Live Objects, LiveType, LiveWire, LiveWire Pro, MailCaster, Mozilla, Netcaster Netcenter, NetHelp, Netscape®, Netscape® Administration Kit, Netscape AffiliatePlus, Netscape® AgentXpert, Netscape Alliance, Netscape® AppFoundry, Netscape® Application Builder, Netscape® Application Server, Netscape® AutoAdmin, Netscape Business Community, Netscape Business Journal, Netscape® BuyerXpert, Netscape® Calendar, Netscape® Calendar Express, Netscape® Calendar Link, Netscape® Calender Server, Netscape CaseTracker, Netscape® Cash Register, Netscape Catalog Server®, Netscape Certificate Server®, Netscape® Channel Finder, Netscape Charters Program, Netscape® Chat, Netscape® Client Customization Kit, Netscape® Collabra®, Netscape® Collabra® Server, Netscape® Commerce Server, Netscape® CommerceXpert, Netscape® Commercial Applications, Netscape® Communications Server, Netscape® Communicator, Netscape® Communicator Deluxe Edition, Netscape® Communicator Internet Access Edition, Netscape® Communicator News, Netscape Community, Netscape® Community System, Netscape® Compass Server, Netscape® Component Builder, Netscape® Composer, Netscape® Conference, Netscape® Console, Netscape® Content Management Server, Netscape DevEdge®, Netscape DevEdge® Application Builder, Netscape DevEdge® Online, Netscape DevEdge® Open Studio, Netscape® DeveloperXpert, Netscape Direct, Netscape® Directory Server, Netscape® ECXpert, Netscape® Enterprise News, Netscape® Enterprise Server, Netscape® Enterprise Server with FORTEZZA, Netscape® Extension Builder, Netscape FastTrack Server®, Netscape Guide, Netscape Industry Watch, Netscape Insight, Netscape® Install Builder, Netscape® Internet Applications, Netscape® Internet Foundation Classes, Netscape Internet Learning Academy, Netscape® Internet Service Broker, Netscape® Istore, Netscape® JAR Installation Manager, Netscape® JAR Packager, Netscape® LiveMedia, Netscape® LivePayment, Netscape® Mail, Netscape® Mail Server, Netscape® Mailing List Manager, Netscape® Media Converter, Netscape® Media Player, Netscape® Media Server, Netscape® Merchant System, Netscape® MerchantXpert, Netscape® Messaging Server, Netscape® Messenger, Netscape® Messenger Express, Netscape® Migration

Toolkit, Netscape® Mission Control, Netscape® Mission Control Desktop, Netscape Navigator®, Netscape Navigator® with FORTEZZA, Netscape Navigator® Gold, Netscape Navigator® News, Netscape Navigator® Personal Edition, Netscape Netcenter, Netscape Netcenter Small Business Source, Netscape® News Server, Netscape ONE®, Netscape® Payment Kit, Netscape® Power Pack, Netscape® Process Manager, Netscape Professional Community, Netscape® Proxy Server, Netscape® Proxy Server with FORTEZZA, Netscape® Publishing Suite, Netscape® Publishing System, Netscape® PublishingXpert, Netscape® SellerXpert, Netscape Services Network, Netscape® Site Manager, Netscape Site Sampler, Netscape® SmartUpdate, Netscape Software Depot, Netscape Solution Expert, Netscape Subscribers Advantage, Netscape® SuiteTools, Netscape SupportEdge, Netscape® Update, Netscape Virtual Office, Netscape® WebTop, Netshare, ONE Stop Software, PowerStart®, ResponseDesk, ResponseLine, Secure Courier, ShopTalk Direct, SmartMarks, Suite Solutions, SuiteSpot®, SuiteSpot® Hosting Edition, TechVision.

Netscape trade names

Following are Netscape trade names:

> Netscape
>
> Netscape Communications
>
> Netscape Communications Corporation

Cisco

See http://www.cisco.com/public/copyright/trademark.html for a list.

Sun

JavaScript is a trademark of Sun Microsystems, Inc., used under license for technology invented and implemented by Netscape.

CERT

CERT® is a registered trademark and service mark of Carnegie Mellon University.

Computer Security Institute

http://www.gocsi.com/

Copyright © 2000, Computer Security Institute, 600 Harrison Street, San Francisco, CA 94107.

The above list is not exhaustive. All other companies not explicitly mentioned, and the names of actual companies and products mentioned herein may be the trademarks of their respective owners.

The example companies (example: The Company), organizations, products, people, and events depicted herein are fictitious. No association with any real company, organization, product, person, or event is intended or should be inferred.

Additions from Redline Network to chapter 5 printed with permission from Redline Networks

Additions from Whale Communications to chapter 5 printed with permission from Whale Communications

Additions from Neoteris to chapter 5 printed with permission from Neoteris.

Cert Permission for Reprint

Use of the foregoing CERT Reporting Guidelines constitutes acceptance of the terms and conditions of the release.

- The following acknowledgments and attributions to Carnegie Mellon University/Software Engineering Institute must be made as follows before the title page of the reproduced CMU/SEI document:

  Special permission to reproduce "CERT Reporting Guidelines," © 2002 by Carnegie Mellon University, is granted by the Software Engineering Institute.

  ®CERT and CERT Coordination Center are registered in the U.S. Patent and Trademark Office by Carnegie Mellon University.

  Original source link:
  (http://www.cert.org/tech_tips/incident_reporting.html)

- No warranty. This Carnegie Mellon University and Software Engineering Institute material is furnished on an "as is" basis. Carnegie Mellon University makes no warranties of any kind, either expressed or implied as to any matter including, but not limited to, warranty of fitness for purpose or merchantability, exclusivity or results obtained from use of the material. Carnegie Mellon University does not make any warranty of any kind with respect to freedom from patent, trademark, or copyright infringement.

- CMU Indemnification. Butterworth-Heinemann hereby agrees to defend, indemnify, and hold harmless CMU, its trustees, officers, employees, and agents from all claims or demands made against them (and any related losses, expenses, or attorney's fees) arising out of, or relating to Butterworth-Heinemann's and/or its sublicensees' negligent use or willful misuse of or negligent conduct or willful misconduct regarding CMU intellectual property, facilities, or other rights or assistance granted by CMU under this Agreement, including, but not limited to, any claims of product liability, personal injury, death, damage to property, or violation of any laws or regulations.

- Disputes. This Agreement shall be governed by the laws of the Commonwealth of Pennsylvania. Any dispute or claim arising out of or relating to this Agreement will be settled by arbitration in Pittsburgh, Pennsylvania in accordance with the rules of the American Arbitration Association and judgment upon award rendered by the arbitrator(s) may be entered in any court having jurisdiction.

- No Endorsement. The SEI and CMU do not directly or indirectly endorse Butterworth-Heinemann work.

- This permission is granted on a non-exclusive basis for commercial purposes.

Warning and Disclaimer

Every effort has been made to make this book as complete and accurate as possible, but no warranty or fitness is implied. The Security of any site is the responsibility of the owners, the authors and publishers are not liable for any person, company or sites security. The authors and the publisher shall have neither liability nor responsibility to any person or entity with respect to loss or damages arising from the information contained in this book. Purchase and read this book at your own risk. Every effort has been attempted to obtain permissions for extracts and quotes whenever possible. See listed URLs for quote sources. The products referenced or mentioned in this book are listed for informational purposes only. The publisher and authors may have received demo copies to review. The publishers and authors have not received any compensation from the software or hardware vendors mentioned in the book. Many different vendors are mentioned in this book and many vendor products are used for reference. The publisher and authors do not recommend any product, software, or hardware. You, the owner of your hardware, software, and data are responsible to make a determination of what is best for you. The authors DO advise that you take careful consideration in determining your security needs and review more than just one vendor. Remember, you own your security, not us!

From - RFC2026 -

ftp://ftp.isi.edu/in-notes/rfc2026.txt

© The following copyright notice and disclaimer shall be included in all ISOC standards-related documentation:

"Copyright © The Internet Society (date). All Rights Reserved.

From RFC2223

ftp://ftp.isi.edu/in-notes/rfc2223.txt

11. Copyright Section

Per BCP 9, RFC 2026 [2], "The following copyright notice and disclaimer shall be included in all ISOC standards-related documentation." The following statement should be placed on the last page of the RFC, as the "Full Copyright Statement."

assist in its implementation may be prepared, copied, published and distributed, in whole or in part, without restriction of any kind, provided that the above copyright notice and this paragraph are included on all such copies and derivative works. However, this document itself may not be modified in any way, such as by removing the copyright notice or references to the Internet Society or other Internet organizations, except as needed for the purpose of developing Internet standards in which case the procedures for copyrights defined in the Internet Standards process must be followed, or as required to translate it into Postel & Reynolds Informational [Page 11] RFC 2223 Instructions to RFC Authors, October 1997, languages other than English. The limited permissions granted above are perpetual and will not be revoked by the Internet Society or its successors or assigns.

This document and the information contained herein is provided on an "as is" basis and the Internet Society and the Internet Engineering Task Force disclaim all warranties, express or implied, including but not limited to any warranty that the use of the information herein will not infringe any rights or any implied warranties of merchantability or fitness for a particular purpose.

Index

Acceptable use policies, 59
Acquisitions, security and, 48–49
Addresses. *see also* Domains
    class A, 21–22, 23
    class B, 22, 23
    class C, 22, 23
    resolution protocol, 27–29
Air gap-based filtering proxies
    creation, 142
    description, 143
    external server, 143
    function, 143–144
    internal server
        authentication, 145
        benefits, 146–148
        inbound filtering, 145–146
        SSL management, 144–145
    switch, 144
Algorithms, 71–73
Andreesen, Marc, 10
Application gateway firewall, 112–114
Argus, 274
ARPANET
    creation, 3
    defense R&D, 7–8
    fruition, 4–5
    IMP, 4
    reliability, 6
Attacker 2.1, 276
Auditors, security responsibilities, 55
Authentication
    air gap-based proxies, 145
    basic, 84–85
    complexity, 150–151

    methods
        anonymous, 154–155
        biometric, 153–154
        certificates, 152–153
        password, 152
        smart cards, 154
        status codes, 155–157
        user name, 152
    service exchange, 163
Authorization
    complexity, 150–151
    description, 150, 158
    Kerberos
        description, 162–163
        development, 162
        protocols, 163–164
    passwords, 159–160
    single sign-on, 164–166
    smart cards, 166–168
    tokens, 160–162

Backup methods, 267
Bacon, Francis, 70
Baran, Paul, 3
Basic HTTP authentication, 84–85
Beranek, Bolt, 4
Berners-Lee, Tim, 9–10
Big Brother 1.3, 276
Biometric techniques, 153–154
BlackICE Defender, 274–275
Browsers, root certificates, 80–81
Buchanan, James, 2
Business
    continuity

Business *(cont'd)*
    backup methods, 267–270
    contingency plans, 270–271
    function, 264
    impact analysis, 265
    pilots, 271
    policy, 264–265
    roles/responsibilities, 265–266
    testing plans, 271
    impact analysis, 265
    partners, security and, 7

CCITT. *see* Consultative Committee on International
        Telephone and Telegraphy
Cerf, Vinton, 5, 6–7, 90
CERT. *see* Computer Emergency Response Team
Certificates
    authorities
        description, 80–81, 102–103
        information on, 103–104
        key recovery, 189–190
        owner, keys, 103
        private, creating, 106
        revocation, 104
        system types, 178–183
        trusted root, 104–106
    practice statements, 183–187
    revocation lists, 104, 187–189
Change control, 60
Ciphertext, definition, 69
Cipher Wheel, 69
Circuit-level gateways, 114
Clark, Dave, 7
Client/server exchange, 163–164
Clustering, 268–270
Cold sites, 270
CommView, 277
Competitive asset
    costs
        appraisal, 246
        external, 246–252
        internal, 246
        prevention, 245
    quality control, 243–244
Competitors, Internet security and,
        43–44
Compliance, 60
Computer Emergency Response Team
    description, 283–284

incident reporting guidelines
    definition of incident, 285–286
    reporting of incident
        contacts, 288–290
        data, 290–294
        procedures, 294–296
        reasons for, 286–288
        timing, 296–297
Consultative Committee on International Telephone
        and Telegraphy, 195
Control directory, 241–243
COPS, 276
Corp Comm, 218–220
Costs. *see under* Security analysis
Crack, 274
Crocker, Steve, 5
Cryptography, 68, 194–195. *see also* Encryption
Cryptology, definition, 69
Customer demographics, 43

DARPA. *see* Defense Advanced Research Projects
        Agency
Davies, Donald, 3
Defense Advanced Research Projects Agency,
        16–17, 18
Demilitarized zone
    acquisitions and, 48–49
    air gap architecture and, 147–148
    configuration, 47–48
    definition, 45
    function, 45–48
    mergers and, 48–49
Denial-of-service attacks
    description, 92
    examples, 93
    preventing, basic steps, 94–95
DES, 74
Developers, security responsibilities, 55
de Vere, Edward, 70
DHCP. *see* Dynamic Host Configuration Protocol
Disaster recovery
    backup methods, 267–270
    contingency plans, 270–271
    impact analysis, 265
    pilots, 271
    policy, 264–265
    roles/responsibilities, 265–266
    testing plans, 271
DMZ. *see* Demilitarized zone

Domains. *see also* Addresses
    description, 25–26
    function, 25
    name, fully qualified, 26–27
    name system, 8
    proper terminology, 26–27
DoS. *see* Denial-of-service attacks
Dynamic host configuration protocol, 32–37

Elron CommandView Message Inspector, 278
E-mail. *see* Messaging
E-mail bombing. *see* Spamming
Encryption. *see also* Cryptography
    applications
        scenario one, 76–78
        scenario two, 78–79
        scenario three, 79–83
        scenario four, 83–88
    export control, 99–100
    history, 69
    key types, 71–75
    SSL, 98–100
"Enigma" machine, 70
Environmental risk table, 241–243
ESMonitor, 277
Ethernet
    creation, 12–13
    definition, 12
    DHCP, 32–37
    domains, 25–27
    LAN, 15–16
    packet, in TCP/IP, 18–21, 24–25
    ports, 30–32
    routing, 27–29
ETRN, 226
Exchange Plus, 275
EXPN, 226
Extranets
    accessibility, 140
    description, 139–140
    instant virtual, 140–141
    secure access, 138–141
Eye scanners, 153

Feedback loops, 58–59
Filtering, inbound, 145–146
Fingerprints, 153
Firewalls
    application gateway, 112–114

architectural considerations, 109–110
building/buying, considerations,
        116–118
buyer's assessment form
    basic process, 125
    business section, 126
    considerations, 132
    information systems, 127–128
    Internet connectivity, 128–129
    product features, 130–131
    purpose, 124–125
circuit-level gateways, 114
evaluation guidelines, 115–118
function, 108
packet-filtering, 110–112
products, 119–124
proxy-server, 112–114
reasons for, 108
requirements, 115–116, 118
vendors, selecting, 132–134
Flaming. *see* Spamming
Friedman, William F., 70
FTP, 112–113

Gateway, description, 28
Generic routing encapsulation, description,
        95–96
Good times virus hoax, 207
GRE. *see* Generic routing encapsulation

Heart, Frank, 4
High Performance Computing and Communications
        Act, 9
Hoaxes, 206–207
HostScan, 275
Hot sites, 269

ICMP attack. *see* Ping of death
IMP, 4
Information technology
    business continuity
        backup methods, 267–270
        contingency plans, 270–271
        function, 264
        impact analysis, 265
        pilots, 271
        policy, 264–265
        roles/responsibilities, 265–266
        testing plans, 271

Information technology *(cont'd)*
  infrastructure damage
    CERT, incident reporting
      contacts, 288–290
      data, 290–294
      definition, 285–286
      procedures, 294–296
      timing, 296–297
    incident handling
      analysis system, 257
      components, 257
      procedures, 259–262
      processes, 257–258
      reporting system, 257
      requirements, 256
      steps, 254–256
      team implementation, 262–263
    recovery
      backup methods, 267–270
      contingency plans, 270–271
      description, 263–264
      pilots, 271
      roles/responsibilities, 265–266
      testing plans, 271
    Windows NT intruder
      listing 1, 299–306
      listing 2, 306–307
      listing 3, 307–311
      procedures, 297–299
  security, risks analysis, 237–241
  trusted network, 45–49
International Telecommunication Union,
      195
Internet
  activities board, 9
  addressing, 20–21
  anywhere toolkit, 277
  assigned numbers authority, 36–37
  birth of, 10
  definition, 11
  engineering task force, 195–196
  history
    1960's, 3–4
    1970's, 5–7
    1980's, 7–10
  infrastructure, analysis, 109–110
  security analysis (*see* Security analysis)
Intrusion detection systems, 142
IPSec. *see* IP security protocol

IP security protocol, description, 96–97
ITU. *see* International Telecommunication Union

Jefferson, Thomas, 69
Jobs, Steve, 7
Journaling, 267
Junk mail, 207–211

Kahn, Bob, 4, 6–7
Kerberos, 162–163
KEYFOB, 161
Keys
  basic, 71–73
  CA ownership, 103
  escrow, 189–190
  generation capacity, SSL, 135
  public, infrastructure
    certificate
      authority, 178–183
      practice statement, 183–187
      revocation lists, 187–189
    closed systems, 178–179
    components, 171–172
    cryptography standards, 194–195
    LDAP, 190–193
    open systems, 179–183
    recovery, 189–190
    service environments, applications, 170–171
    X.509
      attribute types and, 172
      certificate, 174–178
      concept of, 172
      infrastructure standards, 195–197
  RSA, 74–75
Kirstein, Peter, 7
Kleinrock, Leonard, 3, 5

Layer 2 forwarding, 96
Layer 2 tunneling protocol, 96
LDAP. *see* Lightweight Directory Access Protocol
Legal department, 54–55
L2F. *see* Layer 2 forwarding
Licklider, J.C.R., 3
Lightweight directory access protocol, 85–86, 190–193
Love Bug virus, 202–205
L2TP. *see* Layer 2 tunneling protocol

MailMarshal, 277
MailSweeper, 279

Marlowe, Christopher, 70
Mass-mail, 216–219
Mergers, security and, 48–49
Message Digest, 74
Messaging
    acceptable use, 214–216
    commercial, advent, 9–10
    components, 201–202
    content scanning, 221
    creation, 5
    features, 201–202
    importance, 200–201
    mass-mail, 216–219
    problems
        hoaxes, 206–207
        junk mail, 207–211
        overview, 202–205
        return mail, 211–213
        Trojan horses, 206
        viruses
            description, 205
            good times, hoax, 207
            Love Bug, 202–205
            scanning, 220–221
        worms, 205–206
    restrictions, 225
    retention, 223–224
    SMTP configuration settings, 226–230
Metcalfe, Robert, 5, 12–13
Mirrored sites, 269
Mockapetris, Paul, 8
Morris WORM, 9

National Physical Laboratory, 3–4
National Science Foundation, 11
Navajo Native American Language, 70
4-Net, 275–276
NetBus Detective 5.2, 274
Net-Commando 2000, 278
NetHound, 278
Networks
    control protocol, 5–6
    interface card, 15–16
    protocol, first, 5
    security, plans/policies, 55
    trusted, 45–49
NoBackDoors, 277
NPL. see National Physical Laboratory

Open systems interconnection model, 16–17
OstoSoft Internet Tools, 279

Packets
    filtering firewalls, 110–112
    sniffers, 79–80
    switching, development, history, 3–4
Palo Alto Research Center, 12
PARC. see Palo Alto Research Center
Partridge, Craig, 8
Passwords
    authentication and, 152
    authorization, 159–160
    basic authentication, 83–85
    crackable, preventing, 57
    management, 160
    use, guidelines, 57
PEM, 74
Performance indicators, 63
Perimeters, security, 49
PGP. see Pretty good privacy
Ping of death, 93
PKI. see Public key infrastructure
Plans and policies
    acceptable use, 59
    access control, 57
    change control, 60
    compliance, 60
    data classification, 56
    goals/objectives, 53
    implementation
        execution, 64–65
        goals/objectives, 62
        infrastructure, 63–64
        overview, 60
        pilots, 64
        scope, 62
        training, 64–65
    incident handling, 58–59
    network security, 55
    passwords, 57–58
    physical security, 55
    responsibilities, 53–55
    scope, 53
    training, 60
Point-to-point tunneling protocol, 95–96
Ports, 30–32
PortWatch, 279
Postel, Jon, 5, 8

PPTP. *see* Point-to-point tunneling protocol
Pretty good privacy, 74, 76
PrivacyMaker, 279
Process owners, 54
ProtectX, 278
Protocols. *see* specific protocols
Proxy-server firewall, 112–114
Pseudocode, 218
Public key infrastructure
  certificate
    authority, 178–183
    practice statement, 183–187
    revocation lists, 187–189
  closed systems, 178–179
  components, 171–172
  cryptography standards, 194–195
  key recovery, 189–190
  LDAP, 190–193
  open systems, 179–183
  service environments, applications, 170–171
  X.509
    attribute types and, 172
    certificate, 174–178
    concept of, 172
    infrastructure standards, 195–197
Public system, description, 179–180

Quality control, 243–244
Queen Victoria, 2

RAND Corporation, 3–4
RC2, 74
RC4, 74
Recovery. *see* Disaster recovery
Risk analysis
  aspects, 232–234
  assessment, 49–52
  competitive asset, 243–244
    costs
      appraisal, 246
      external, 246–252
      internal, 246
      prevention, 245
  control directory, 241–243
  definition, 232
  environmental risk table, 241–243
  formula, 232
  technology security, 237–241
  threats, 234–237

Roberts, Lawrence G., 3
Root certificates, 80, 186
Routing, 27–29
RSA Data Security, 74–75

SATAN, 276
ScanMail, 275
Scanning, 31–32
Secure hashing algorithm, 75
Secure/multipurpose Internet mail extensions, 74–75
Secure socket layer
  appliance
    extranet, 139–141
    network
      deployment, 135
      description, 134
      end-to-end/one way, 135
      key generation capacity, 135
      one-way/end-to-end, 135
      summary, 137–138
      transaction acceleration, 136–137
  basic function, 98–99
  description, 80
  development, 98
  enabling, 81–83
  encryption, 98–100
  handshake, 98–99
  legal issues, 101–102
  management, air gap, 144–144
  transactions, certificates, 102–106
Security
  managers, responsibilities, 54
  perimeters, 49
  zones, 49
Security analysis
  costs
    appraisal, 246
    external, 246–252
    internal, 246
    prevention, 245
  plans/policies
    acceptable use, 59
    access control, 57
    change control, 60
    compliance, 60
    data classification, 56
    goals/objectives, 53
    implementation, 60–65
    incident handling, 58–59

network security, 55
passwords, 57–58
physical security, 55
responsibilities, 53–55
scope, 53
training, 60
requirements, steps to, 42–45
risk assessment, 49–52
technology, 45–49
Service legal agreement, 256
SHA-1. *see* Secure hashing algorithm
Shakespeare, William, 70
Share finder, 279
Single sign-on programs, 164–166
SIZE, 226–227
Slater, Christian, 70
Smart cards, 154, 166–168
S/MIME. *see* Secure/multipurpose Internet mail
        extensions
SMTP configuration settings, 226–230
SPAM, 208
spam, 208–211
Spamming, 93
Spoofing attack domain name system (DSN) query, 93
SSL. *see* Secure Socket Layer
Stakeholders, 43
Stanford Linear Accelerator Center, 10
Surfing. *see* Scanning

TCP. *see* Transmission control protocol
TCP/IP. *see* Transmission control protocol/Internet
        protocol
Technology. *see* Information technology
Telegraph, 2–3
Telnet, 112–113, 210
Ticket-granting service exchange, 163
Tomlinson, Ray, 5
Tools, 273–281
Training policies, 60
Transmission control protocol
air gap architecture and, 147
development, 5
flooding, 93
function, 90
time sharing, 7
Transmission control protocol/Internet
        protocol
complexity, 90
components, 13–14

as defense standard, 7–8
development, 6–7, 90–91
ethernet in, 18–21, 24–25
function, 13–15
scope, 14–15
TCP/IP, 90–91, 94
Tribe flood network, 93
Triple DES, 74
Tripwire, 275
Trojan horses, 206
Trusted root database, 104–106
Turing, Alan, 70

Unix Security, 273

Vendors, 43
Virtual private networks
description, 95
requirements, 138–141
types
    IPSec, 96–97
    L2F, 96
    L2TP, 96
    PPTP, 95–96
Viruses
description, 205
good times, hoax, 207
Love Bug, 202–205
scanning, 220–221
VirusMD Personal Firewall, 280
VPNs. *see* Virtual private networks
VRFY, 226

Warm sites, 269–270
Web-based systems
air gap-based filtering proxies
    creation, 142
    description, 143
    external server, 143
    function, 143–144
    internal server
        authentication, 145
        benefits, 146–148
        inbound filtering, 145–146
        SSL management, 144–145
    security issues, 141–142
Web server, first, 10
Webtrends, 280
WinArp/Poink, 93

Windows NT intruder
  listing 1, 299–306
  listing 2, 306–307
  listing 3, 307–311
  procedures, 297–299
WINDOWS NUKE OOB attack on port
    139, 93
Windtalkers, 70
WorldSecure Mail, 278
Worms, 9, 205–206
Wozniak, Steve, 7

X.509
  attribute types and, 172
  certificate
    features, 174–177
    policies, 177–178
    revocation lists, 187–189
  concept of, 172

Zimmermann, Philip, 74
ZoneAlarm, 273
Zones, security, 49